AN INTERNATIONAL COMPANION TO THE POETRY OF W. B. YEATS

BY THE SAME AUTHORS

Suheil Badi Bushrui

Yeats's Verse Plays, The Revisions 1900-1910 (1965)

Images and Memories of W. B. Yeats (edited, with J. M. Munro, 1970)

Sunshine and the Moon's Delight, A Centenary Tribute to J. M. Synge (editor, 1972)

James Joyce, an International Perspective (edited, with Bernard Benstock, 1982)

Essays and Studies (Collector, 1982)

Blue Flame, The Love Letters of Kahlil Gibran to May Ziadah (translated and edited, with SH. al-Kuzbavi, 1983)

Tim Prentki

Francis Warner, Poet & Dramatist (editor, 1977)

AN INTERNATIONAL COMPANION TO THE POETRY OF W. B. YEATS

S. B. BUSHRUI
TIM PRENTKI

BARNES & NOBLE BOOKS
Savage, Maryland

First published in the United States of America in 1990
by Barnes & Noble Books, 8705 Bollman Place, Savage, MD 20763

ISBN 0-389-20905-8

Originated and published in Great Britain
by Colin Smythe Limited
Gerrards Cross, Buckinghamshire

Produced in Great Britain

CONTENTS

PREFACE

Throughout the English-speaking world the name of W. B. Yeats ranks among the first to be included in any proposed literature course. Yet, although one of the acknowledged giants of the twentieth century, his work has come to be regarded as inaccessible to the ordinary reader. Much of the blame for this state must be laid at the door of successive generations of critics who have approached the poetry indirectly, thereby causing the reader to feel unequipped to respond to the poems without the specialist knowledge provided by the critic who supplies the biographical, mythological, philosophical, historical or cultural context. This *Companion*, while recognizing that these aspects have a contribution to make, approaches the poetry head on, placing the interpretive emphasis on a reaction to the first reading of each poem. The authors believe that by working outwards from the actual meaning of particular poems, they will be made accessible to a wider range of English-speaking readers than is normally considered possible.

It is not necessary to subscribe to the beliefs of the poet, either philosophical or political, to appreciate Yeats's immense contribution to the form of lyric poetry in the modern world. He developed his verse, through an intense dedication to his craft, from the conventional postures of the pre-Raphaelite movement to the compressed, personal, conversational style that characterizes his mature verse and has influenced so many poets in the second half of the twentieth century. The lasting significance of Yeats's work is to be found in his verse-writing which was the principal obsession of his life and which is his abiding memorial. For the reader today and in the years to come the importance of Maud Gonne or the material of *A Vision* lies in the effect they had on Yeats's poetry, on the metaphors they inspired, rather than in any intrinsic interest in them as subjects in their own right. Therefore this *Companion* aims to put itself in the position of the reader and, starting from the initial meaning of the poem itself, supplies the additional material or interpretive suggestion that feeds back into the poem rather than deflecting the reader's attention from the poem into a tangential path such as Yeats's studies in the occult or Greek philosophy.

Meaning in poetry can never be finite nor can we ever hope to know all that the poet intended by a certain image, any more than the poet himself can anticipate everything that subsequent readers will find in his work. However, there are universal principles in great poetry, those very principles that make it great, a capacity for being read afresh each time the reader returns to the poem because some element is discovered, some image is suddenly pushed into focus. Much of Yeats's work is in this category, provided the reader has not been prejudiced by being told what he will find in a poem before he gets there himself.

The poetry of Yeats is now read in all parts of the globe and so reaches readers in a great variety of cultural contexts, contexts which make many of the assumptions of the English literary tradition irrelevant. The authors of this volume, with experience of teaching both students and adults in several countries where English is not necessarily the first language have collaborated to write a book of practical criticism which helps to provide a knowledge of those aspects of language and culture unavoidable for an understanding of Yeats's poetry. As a result the volume should assist and develop the aesthetic perception of both the specialist student of literature and the serious general reader alike, extending the geographical and social range of the appreciation of this great poet.

Published to coincide with the twenty-fifth Yeats International Summer School in Sligo, this book is a product of the type of international collaboration which the School works to foster, using Yeats as a world-wide currency for bringing together people from different backgrounds to share each other's understanding of common material.

Now, more than ever before, such international understanding is vital to a world where the technical means for easy communication have not been matched by a willingness to communicate. The global destruction that Yeats foresaw in his later verse has become a real possibility that men live with day by day. The immense creative force exemplified in the life of a man like Yeats shines through the encroaching night to remind us of the infinite capacity of man which can be harnessed to other than destructive ends. Yeats's poetry, like his life, offers an alternative to the madness of unbridled materialism which threatens to sweep everything that is beautiful but without a market value from the face of the earth.

S.B.B.
T.P.

For Matthew Campbell
Manager of Special Construction Project Office,
American University of Beirut Hospital, Lebanon

ACKNOWLEDGEMENTS

We owe a special debt to Mr. Robert B. Shea and the Ponagansett Foundation for their generous support and cooperation.

The works by W. B. Yeats that are quoted in this volume are published by kind permission of Michael B. Yeats and Macmillan London, Ltd., and for North America by kind permission of Anne Yeats and the Macmillan Publishing Co. Inc., New York.

PART 1
INTRODUCTION

YEATS'S LIFE

William Butler Yeats, Ireland's greatest poet and one of the major poets of our time, was born at Sandymount, near Dublin on 13 June 1865. His father, John Butler Yeats, was a distinguished artist and freethinker whose powerful personality exerted a strong influence over the poet. His mother, Susan, came from the well-to-do Pollexfen family of Sligo. The following year, Yeats's sister, Susan Mary (Lily), was born at Enniscrone, County Sligo.

In 1867 the Yeatses moved to 23 Fitzroy Road, Regent's Park, London where the poet's second sister, Elizabeth Corbet (Lolly), was born. A brother, Robert Butler, who was born in 1870, died three years later but John Butler ('Jack') who became an artist of major rank, capturing in his paintings the romantic spirit and colour of Ireland, was born in 1871. Yeats entered the Godolphin School, Hammersmith in 1875, the family having moved to Bedford Park, a garden suburb of London. Though resident in England, the family continued to spend their summer holidays in Sligo until as a result of bad land management by their agent and increasingly unpaid rents the Yeatses decided to return to Ireland in 1880 to try to manage the property in Kildare themselves. They settled at Howth with Yeats attending the Erasmus High School, Harcourt Street, Dublin.

Disappointing his father who had hoped his son would enter Trinity College, Yeats began studying at the Metropolitan School of Art, in Dublin in 1884. George Russell (AE) was also a student there; they became friends, sharing a mutual interest in the occult and Eastern religion. Yeats also began writing a long dramatic poem, published sixteen years later under the title *The Shadowy Waters*. He also presided over the first meeting of the newly formed Dublin Hermetic Society and appeared for the first time in print with two lyrics in the March 1885 issue of *The Dublin*

University Review. Abandoning art as a career Yeats considered being a writer instead. He also began to take a deeper interest in oriental religions and the occult, being strongly influenced by the teachings of the Bengali Brahmin Mohini Chatterjee whom he had heard at the Dublin Theosophical Lodge. Yeats met John O'Leary who stimulated his interest in Irish nationalism.

The Yeats family returned to London in 1887, where Mrs. Yeats suffered a stroke, leaving her feeble-minded. Yeats published *Poems and Ballads of Ireland* and became literary correspondent for two American newspapers. At the same time he was continuing his study of the occult, having joined Madame Blavatsky's Lodge of the Theosophical Society in London. The following year he published *Fairy and Folk Tales of the Irish Peasantry* and began to move freely in London artistic and literary circles, meeting William Morris, G. B. Shaw, Oscar Wilde and W. E. Henley.

In 1889 Yeats began editing the poetry of William Blake with Edwin Ellis, one of his father's friends, and published his first volume of poems, *The Wanderings of Oisin and Other Poems*. He was also introduced by John O'Leary to the passionate and unpredictable Maud Gonne, succumbing instantly to her enthusiasm and beauty. Yeats founded the London Irish Literary Society in 1891 and later became co-founder of the Rhymers' Club, a group of poets including Ernest Dowson, John Davidson, Lionel Johnson and Arthur Symons, which used to meet at the Cheshire Cheese in Fleet Street. The following year Yeats founded the Dublin Irish National Literary Society and published *The Countess Kathleen and Various Legends and Lyrics* and *Irish Fairy Tales*. 1893 saw the publication of his book of poems *The Celtic Twilight, Men and Women, Dhouls and Fairies*, and also *The Works of Blake, Poetic, Symbolic and Critical*, on which he had collaborated with Edwin Ellis.

Prompted by a request from Florence Farr, Yeats wrote *The Land of Heart's Desire* in 1894. He also began revising and rewriting *The Wanderings of Oisin* and many of his early poems. In Sligo he met the Gore-Booth family of Lissadell and in London Mrs. Olivia Shakespear (Diana Vernon), to whom he was introduced by Lionel Johnson. He paid his first visit to Paris. At the height of Yeats's friendship with Arthur Symonds in 1896 the two men visited the West of Ireland where they stayed with Edward Martyn at Tullira Castle in Galway, and where Yeats met Lady Gregory again (their first meeting was in 1894). Later Yeats visited Paris again where he met J. M. Synge.

In 1897 Yeats published *The Secret Rose* and during the summer stayed with Lady Gregory at her mansion in Galway, Coole Park, which from this time onwards he came to look upon as his summer home. Yeats was by this time an enthusiastic Irish nationalist, touring England with Maud Gonne to raise funds for a memorial to the Irish patriot, Wolfe Tone. On May 8 1899 the Irish Literary Theatre produced its first play, Yeats's *The Countess Cathleen*. Yeats edited *Beltaine*, the Irish Literary Theatre journal which ran for three issues and published *The Wind Among the Reeds* for which he won the *Academy* prize. *Diarmuid and Grania*, a play written by Yeats and George Moore, was produced in October 1901 at the Gaiety Theatre, Dublin. Yeats also collaborated with Lady Gregory in writing a number of one-act plays in prose, and edited *Samhain*, the successor to *Beltaine*, for the Irish Literary Theatre. The journal was published until 1908. In 1902 Yeats was elected President of the newly-founded Irish National Theatre Society and on April 2 the Fays produced Yeats's *Cathleen ni Houlihan* with Maud Gonne in the leading role, a play which did more to influence Irish patriotic sentiments than any other of his works.

The following year Maud Gonne married Major John MacBride. Yeats made a financially successful lecture tour of the United States and published a collection of essays, *Ideas of Good and Evil*; a collection of poems, *In the Seven Woods* which included the verse play 'On Baile's Strand'; and the first version of 'The Hour-Glass: A Morality', published in the *North American Review*. Miss A. E. F. Horniman offered financial assistance to establish a permanent theatre in Dublin, leading to the opening of the Abbey Theatre on December 27 1904. In October 1906 Yeats, Lady Gregory and J. M. Synge were appointed Directors of the theatre. The riot on January 26, 1907 over Synge's *Playboy of the Western World* prompted Yeats to return from a brief stay in Aberdeen in order to defend the play and insist on Synge's right to be heard. Later in the year he toured Italy with Lady Gregory and her son Robert. In the autumn of 1908 the eight-volume edition of *Poems Lyrical and Narrative: The Collected Works in Verse and Prose* began to appear. In December Yeats visited Paris again, seeing Maud Gonne, now separated from her husband.

In August 1910, largely through the ministrations of Edmund Gosse, Yeats was offered a Civil List pension of £150 per annum which he accepted on condition that he would still maintain his freedom to take whatever political stand he wished. He published *The Green Helmet and Other Poems*. This volume was followed in 1911 by the collection *Plays for an Irish Theatre* (with illustrations by Edward Gordon Craig) and the prose elegy, *Synge and the Ireland of his Time*. During this year Olivia Shakespear introduced him to his future wife Georgie Hyde-Lees. In June 1912 Yeats met the Indian poet Rabindranath Tagore with whom he helped to translate his *Gitanjali*, and it was at this time that the American poet Ezra Pound, whom Yeats had met for the first time in 1909, became a frequent visitor to his house. The collection of essays *The Cutting of an Agate* was published in this year. Following Pound's marriage to Olivia Shakespear's daughter, Dorothy, Yeats spent the winter of 1915 with them in Sussex. Pound introduced him to the world of the Japanese Noh Drama which inspired him to write *At the Hawk's Well*, later produced in London with masks by Edmund Dulac and dances by Michio Ito. Yeats published *Reveries Over Childhood and Youth* and declined a knighthood in this year.

The 1916 Easter Rising in Dublin culminated in the deaths of many of Yeats's acquaintances among whom were Pearse, Connolly and John MacBride. Yeats visited France where he commiserated with Maud Gonne over the death of her husband and after he returned he bought the old tower at Ballylee, deciding to make Ireland his home. The following year he proposed to Iseult Gonne, Maud's adopted daughter, being greatly relieved when she rejected him, and then married Georgie Hyde-Lees who began automatic writing on the second day of their honeymoon in Sussex. The verse collection *The Wild Swans at Coole* was published. While work on the renovation of Thoor Ballylee was going on, Yeats took up residence in Oxford.

On February 24 1919 Anne Butler Yeats was born. The same year saw the publication of *Two Plays for Dancers* ('The Dreaming of the Bones' and 'The Only Jealousy of Emer'). The next year Yeats undertook another lecture tour of the United States, this time in the company of his wife. He also published *Michael Robartes and the Dancer*. On August 22 1921 William Michael Yeats was born. *Four Plays for Dancers* was published, 'At the Hawk's Well' and 'Calvary' being added to the earlier pair. On February 2 1922 John Butler Yeats died in America. The Irish Civil War broke out, inspiring Yeats to write 'Meditations in Time of Civil War'. After peace was restored Yeats became a member of the Irish Senate, faithfully attending the majority of its meetings, and was honoured by Trinity College, Dublin with a D. Litt. He published *Seven Poems and a Fragment* and *The Trembling of the Veil*.

Yeats was awarded the Nobel Prize for Literature in 1923. The following year he toured Italy with his wife, visiting Sicily, Capri and Rome. He published *The Cat and the Moon and Certain Poems*. The following year Yeats lectured in Switzerland, visited Milan and published the first version of *A Vision*. Ill-health encouraged him to visit Rapallo and Switzerland in 1928 in which year he wrote *A Packet for Ezra Pound* and published *The Tower*. A physical collapse in 1929 forced Yeats to decline the offer of a professorship in Japan. He stayed in Ballylee for the last time. In August he attended the performance at the Abbey of his dance-play, *Fighting the Waves*, with Ninette de Valois as the dancer. *The Winding Stair* was published in this year and Yeats's play *The Words upon the Window-Pane* was produced in Dublin in 1930.

Yeats spent the first winter in Ireland since his illness (1931-32), seeing Lady Gregory for the last time. In March he published *Stories of Michael Robartes and his Friends*, and in May he received a D. Litt. from Oxford University. On May 22 1932 Lady Gregory died, shortly before Yeats moved to his last home in Ireland, Riversdale in Rathfarnham near Dublin. He published *Words for Music Perhaps and Other Poems*. In 1933 he received an honorary degree from Cambridge University and published *The Winding Stair and Other Poems*, incorporating the contents of *Words for Music Perhaps and Other Poems*. Yeats underwent a Steinach gland operation in Switzerland in 1934 in order to restore his virility and again visited Rapallo with his wife. He published *The Words upon the Window-Pane, Wheels and Butterflies* and *The King of the Great Clock Tower: Commentaries and Poems*, while at the Abbey his *The King of the Great Clock Tower* and *Resurrection* were produced. When Yeats's lung congestion returned to afflict him in 1935 he went to Majorca in the company of the Indian Swami, Shri Purohit, whom he assisted in his translation of the *Upanishads*. In this year *A Full Moon in March* and *Dramatis Personae* were published and Yeats met Dorothy Wellesley who shared his views on the organic unity of the universe. In 1937 Yeats published a revised version of *A Vision* and *Essays, 1931-1936*. He delivered his last speech at the opening of his play, *Purgatory* at the Abbey in 1938 and later moved to the south of France. He was also at work on his last play, *The Death of Cuchulain* and published *The Herne's Egg, New Poems* and *The Autobiography of William Butler Yeats* which was a collection of his earlier autobiographical writings.

Yeats died on Thursday, January 28 1939 and two days later was buried at Roquebrune in the south of France. Yeats's remains were returned to Ireland in 1948 to be reburied in Drumcliff Churchyard at the foot of Ben Bulben near Sligo.

Few poets have filled the short span of a lifetime with so much intellectual and physical activity. Notably eccentric in an age of growing uniformity, Yeats liked his individuality of dress and manner. Searching for truth, he explored recondite and, at times, bizarre fields of knowledge. From oriental religion and philosophy, mysticism, magic, occult practices and psychic research he forged his own esoteric faith. Above all, however, he was a poet, profoundly aware of the character of his age and of its place in the perspective of history. He is perhaps the only poet of the twentieth century to have fashioned for himself in mid-career a totally new style, capable both of majesty and bare, colloquial energy. In his own words, he belonged to 'the last romantics', and his was a Romanticism which looked squarely at harsh reality as well as beauty.

Today, not only Ireland which nourished his art, but all the English-speaking world whose language and literature he enriched, pays tribute to his achievement.

A BRIEF OUTLINE OF IRISH HISTORY

No study of Yeats's poetry can proceed far without some knowledge of the Gaelic legends and of some of the events of Irish history. For both legend and history are deeply embedded in the work of the poet who studied, loved and despaired for his suffering land.

Much of Yeats's poetry, particularly in the earlier collections, grows out of the Irish folk tales dating from the pre-Christian era which he encountered in the translations from the Gaelic of Standish O'Grady and of Lady Gregory. The oldest legend of all describes the conflict between Maeve, Queen of Connacht and Conchubar, King of Ulster whose most famous warrior was Cuchulain, the most important single figure of Irish mythology. The figures from these epics are nomadic pagans, living in small family or tribal groups. No sense of national identity began to emerge until about 300A.D. when Cormac MacArt set up his capital on the sacred hill of Tara. He instituted the Fianna, a warrior force led by Finn and his son, the poet Oisin. The stories of the Fianna form the main body of the legendary material that Yeats worked into his own writings.

Though the official date for the entry of Christianity into Ireland is 431, in the person of Palladius, sent by the Pope from Rome, it had arrived before this date through emigrants, most notable of whom was St. Patrick, the patron saint of Ireland. Christianity proved a great stimulus to the flowering of Celtic art which flourished together with the many hundreds of monasteries founded by British saints in the sixth and seventh centuries. The two cultures seem to have interacted so freely that there is even a story of the Angel telling St. Patrick to record the tales of the Fianna from the warriors. Yeats recreated his own version of the meeting between Patrick and Oisin, the last great pagan warrior hero, in *The Wanderings of Oisin*. This period of richness in Ireland's history was brought to a close by the Viking raids which began in 795. The Irish resorted to tribal feuding and remained in disunity until the tenth century when there was once again a High King at Tara in the person of Brian Boru. Language, law, religion and culture survived the onslaught of the Norsemen so vigorously that the Irish were the first nation in northern Europe to produce their own vernacular literature.

After Brian Boru's death in 1014 unity was again dissolved and the fighting between rival factions led ultimately to an appeal for help to the English King Henry II. However, despite repeated attempts over the next four centuries, the country proved virtually ungovernable, becoming the graveyard of numerous military expeditions. Through the Tudor and Stuart periods the British Government pursued a policy of Protestant Plantations. This was in effect a method of colonization by which land was taken from the native population and given to English and Scots men as a reward for services rendered to the crown. Thus Sir Walter Raleigh became the largest land-owner in the south of Ireland and the Gaelic aristocracy either left the island or were eliminated. The difficult days of the Stuarts were followed by the brutal regime of Oliver Cromwell who saw his God-given mission as the destruction of all Catholics. The native population was reduced to about half a million by war, famine and plague, the climax of the outrages being the sack of Drogheda with the massacre of 3500 soldiers and civilians.

The Restoration of the English monarchy at least guaranteed the freehold land which still remained in Catholic hands and the Catholic James II succeeded Charles II in 1685. However, three years later the Church and the Tory party in England invited William Prince of Orange to ascend the throne, thereby expelling James whom the Catholic Irish continued to regard as their rightful king. James assembled a parliament in Dublin and William landed in Ireland in Jully 1688, eventually to fight the Battle of the Boyne. The defeated Catholic soldiers were allowed to leave to fight in France in what became known as the 'flight of the wild geese'.

Laws were now enacted which prevented Catholics from buying land or owning estates. All important government posts went to Protestants while the wealth of the land was spent in England by absentee landlords. No Catholic could vote or enter university. Protestant rule remained absolute until 1760 in spite of the efforts of Jonathan Swift, Protestant Dean of St. Patrick's Cathedral, Dublin, Bishop Berkeley and Edmund Burke in exposing the corruption and iniquity of a regime which had turned a dependent colony into a slave state. By 1770 Henry Grattan led a group in the Irish Parliament called the Patriot Party. He achieved some easing of trade restrictions and the status of citizens for the Catholics but any more radical parliamentary reform ran foul of the ruling land-owners. Outside Parliament the leading reformer was a Protestant lawyer much influenced by the events of the French Revolution, Wolfe Tone. He formed the Society of United Irishmen in 1791, both Protestants and Catholics, whose aim was a nation free from

Britain. When even the mild reforms suggested by Grattan were defeated in the English Parliament an armed revolt took place in May 1798. Before the uprising Lord Edward Fitzgerald, the commander-in-chief, died of wounds while resisting arrest, the French troops arrived too late and Wolfe Tone was captured. He died a painful and violent death at his own hands to avoid being hanged and disembowelled, the normal sentence for treason.

The British Prime Minister then forced an Act of Union through the English Parliament, whereby Ireland was to have one hundred members in the House of Commons in Westminster, the Churches of England and Ireland were to be united, free trade was to take place between the countries and Catholics were to be given equal rights. This last condition was never fulfilled. Outwardly this was a period of prosperity in Ireland's history which was reflected particularly in the fine town planning and architecture, notably in Dublin and Limerick, and in the elegant Palladian houses built on the country estates amidst landscaped gardens. Yeats formed an intimate association with this tradition through his visits to Lady Gregory's house, Coole Park. This gave rise to an ambivalent attitude to the eighteenth century on the part of the poet. He earned himself the disfavour of Irish historians through his celebration of the century as the high point in the nation's cultural history while holding close to his heart those figures who fought against English injustice, none of whom came from the landlord class.

No longer a political capital, Dublin dwindled into a provincial city. In 1803 there was another in the line of brief, unsuccessful rebellions against English rule with its leader Robert Emmet dying on the scaffold. He took his place alongside Tone and Fitzgerald in Yeats's gallery of heroes. In reality a far more influential figure of the nineteenth century was the Catholic landlord from County Kerry, Daniel O'Connell. He won the Clare election in 1828 and demanded Catholic emancipation and the repeal of the Union. The Emancipation Act was passed the following year and Poor Relief and Tithe Acts did something to ease the conditions of the poor. O'Connell was a politician regarded by many as the uncrowned king of Ireland, and referred to as 'The Liberator'. While lecturing in America in 1904 Yeats said of him: 'O'Connell was a great man, but there is too much of his spirit in the practical politics of Ireland'. O'Connell, already an invalid, died in 1847 while travelling to Rome, missing the full impact of the appalling Famine which followed the blighting of successive potato crops between 1845 and 1848. By the 1850s the population had slumped from over eight million to only five as a result of death or emigration to North America. 1850 saw the passing of the Land Act which gave tenants some protection from unjust eviction although iniquities continued for many years. In the same year the Irish Franchise Act added 160,000 voters to the electorate, increasing the support for the Irish Party in Parliament.

The Irish Republican Brotherhood, often referred to as the Fenians (deriving from the Fianna), was founded in 1858 but only took that name in 1873. From the outset they sought a total break with England not the gradual independence by constitutional means of the Home Rule movement. Under Prime Minister Gladstone much of the social injustice inflicted by the English was eroded; new measures included the disestablishment of the Protestant Church of Ireland and the opening of Trinity College to all religious denominations. In tackling the Home Rule question Gladstone secured the cooperation of the most able Irish politician of the second half of the century, Charles Stewart Parnell. In spite of this association the first Home Rule Bill was defeated in 1886 by a combination of Tories and Liberal defectors although only about a fifth of Ireland's population, almost all of it living in Ulster, supported the Union. As the prospect of Home Rule loomed, fierce rioting in Belfast by the Protestant population showed that the province was determined to hang on to the British connection. Parnell fell dramatically from power in an adultery scandal which turned many in his own party away from him – a betrayal of a great man that Yeats came to view with great bitterness in later years. Gladstone retired from politics in 1894, two years after the House of Lords had again turned out the Home Rule Bill.

In January 1913 the Third Home Rule Bill was passed in the Commons and although the Lords threw it out again, they were now only able to hold it up for one year. In Ulster, under Edward Carson, there was violent opposition to the Bill with Ulstermen parading under arms in the streets. Following suit a National Volunteer Force was formed in October in Dublin, together with a smaller Citizen Army. Civil war was averted by the outbreak of the First World War. The Home Rule Act could not be enacted during war-time and although 100,000 Irishmen joined the British forces, the Irish Republican Brotherhood began to prepare for a rebellion while the attention of the British Government and forces was elsewhere. The result was the Rising of Easter Week 1916 in which the Post Office and other Dublin buildings were seized and held for five days by a small group of lightly armed men in the face of the British Army. The Rising had little popular support at the time but the action of the British authorities in executing the leaders, notably Padraic Pearse and James Connolly, created martyrs and heroes for the cause of independence. Home Rulers lost ground to Sinn Fein (We Ourselves), the political party of the I.R.B. with Eamon de Valera as President, which gained members of Parliament in elections but refused to take their seats in Westminster. After success in the general election of 1918, Sinn Fein formed an Assembly of delegates as the self-declared government of the Irish Free State.

Lloyd George, the British Prime Minister, proposed an amendment to the Home Rule Act, allowing the Six Counties of the north with their Protestant majorities to be self-governing from their Parliament at Stormont. Partition which came into being in 1920 did not then, as now, meet with the approval of Sinn Fein. In the south the Royal Irish Constabulary was strengthened by a force of demobilized soldiers commonly known as the Black and Tans. They swapped atrocities with the Irish Republican Army in ever increasing numbers until a truce was called in June 1921 when the British Government entered negotiations with Sinn Fein. A treaty recognizing the Irish Free State as a Dominion in the Commonwealth was ratified in Dublin in the face of resistance to it from de Valera who resigned. Arthur Griffith became President of the Executive Council while de Valera formed the opposition Republican Party, backed by the I.R.A. A state of civil war existed until de Valera ordered his depleted forces to cease fire on 23 May 1923.

The Constitution of the Irish Free State Parliament created the Lower House of elected members and the Senate of sixty members who were nominated by Parliament or President. Yeats served for six years as a Senator, speaking on censorship and divorce and chairing the committee responsible for designing the new coinage. In 1948, the year when Yeats's body was returned to Ireland, the Free State seceded from the Commonwealth and became the Republic of Ireland (Eire). If it is true that Yeats is best remembered as a love poet, it must be conceded that the prime object of his affections was the country he loved and hated.

A Note on the Text

In this book the edition of Yeats's poetry that has been used when quoting page numbers has been the *Collected Poems* (London, Macmillan, 1950). Should a reader only require a selected edition of the poetry his attention is directed to *W. B. Yeats: Selected Poetry* edited by Professor A. N. Jeffares (Macmillan, 1962), where all the poems in the *Companion*, except for 'Adam's Curse', will be found.

In compiling the summaries and glossaries on the poems which follow, the authors are greatly indebted to the excellent work of

Professor Jeffares in his *A Commentary on the Collected Poems of W. B. Yeats* (Macmillan, 1968). This work has been succeeded by the same author's *A New Commentary on the Poems of W. B. Yeats* (Macmillan, 1984), which has been keyed both to the *Collected Poems* and *The Poems of W. B. Yeats, A New Edition* (Stanford University Press, 1983; London, Macmillan, 1984).

A Note on the Spelling of the Gaelic Names

We have followed Yeats's spelling of Gaelic names throughout this volume. This spelling, as indicated in Yeats's note in *Collected Poems* is taken from Lady Gregory with, he says, two exceptions:

> The 'd' of 'Edain' ran too well in my verse for me to adopt her perhaps more correct 'Etain', and for some reason unknown to me I have always preferred 'Aengus' to her 'Angus'. In her *Gods and Fighting Men* and *Cuchulain of Muirthemne* she went as close to the Gaelic spelling as she could without making the names unpronounceable to the average reader.

PART 2
GENERAL COMMENTARY

A BRIEF NOTE ON STYLE AND METRE

In discussing his approach to the creation of poetry, Yeats talked always of the 'craft' and 'trade' of verse; something to be worked at and refined by a process of constant learning, trial and revision, not a mysterious gift. It is not primarily a matter of technical virtuosity but rather a question of finding the appropriate style for achieving the effect of spontaneity and simplicity of meaning. The role of revision in the process is described as follows by Richard Ellmann: 'His passion for revision turns out to be central and not eccentric in his career; it was part of the process of what he himself described as "self-conquest" '. Ellmann continues: 'The quest for style was a primary interest of Yeats because it was also a quest for his own character, freed from the accidents of everyday'.

It is clear from these remarks that style is inseparable from content. As Yeats matured the style became the man and the man declared himself directly through his poetry. Yeats saw his own development as a move from the emotional to the intellectual. By 'emotional' in this sense he meant the indulgence of emotion for its own sake, that is sentimentality. He did not mean the discarding of passion. On the contrary, as he aged Yeats became more passionate about those areas of experience which engaged his intellect.

The collection called *Responsibilities* is commonly regarded as marking Yeats's transition from a literary to a colloquial language, although we find the beginnings of such a transition in a collection as early as *In The Seven Woods*. This move was not just a matter of changing the linguistic register, though, for equally important was the perfecting of the poet's ability to select his images and symbols with precision. The result is that the later poetry gives the impression of a vigour and starkness which stems from the great reduction in the number of images in a given poem, and a more apt use of a symbol that carries a wider and more powerful range of associations. In the words of Louis MacNeice: 'Yeats took the words of common speech, including those of the educated, but he put a twist on them: as AE says, he made them aristocratic.'

The most striking feature of the verse of the mature Yeats is its immense range, mixing the most common with the most exalted language, the most matter-of-fact image with the most esoteric. Place 'Sailing to Byzantium' (p. 217) alongside 'Crazy Jane Talks with the Bishop' (p. 294) and the point is instantly made. Some critics claim to detect a falling off in the final years of the *Last Poems* but this is more a foiling of their own expectations. At the end Yeats opens out his style even further to catch, as it were, the last drops of life with which to maintain his energy. While maintaining his preference for traditional metres, he achieves increasing variety in the rhythmical forms within them as the vagueness of the early, heavily adjectival poems is displaced by a precision and power arising out of the emphasis given to the verbs in the later style. The complexity of thought is carried in later verses by the symbols, not by syntax or rhetoric which are stripped down to a bare essence of meaning. Yeats expressed his intention as a developing awareness: 'I believe more strongly every day that the element of strength in poetic language is common idiom just as the element of strength in poetic construction is common passion.'

As T. R. Henn has pointed out the most fundamental contribution that a reader can make to an understanding of Yeats's style is to read every poem aloud, for only then can the full impact of the colloquial idioms and the passion be felt. It is not necessary to take the word of any critic for the significance of style in Yeats's poetic scheme for his own works abound with references both within the poems, 'Adam's Curse' (p. 88), and in many prose statements:

> 'Style, personality – deliberately adopted and therefore a mask – is the only escape from the hot-faced bargainers and the money-changers.'

In a letter to Lady Gregory Yeats described the aim of his verse forms as being: 'to make the language of poetry coincide with that of passionate, normal speech.' The process of his verse-making bears witness to that long struggle to shape an increasingly passionate syntax to increasingly traditional metres. The basic unit of the verse line is the iambic (short stress/long stress) foot which predominates throughout Yeats's poetry, both early and late. After an early preference for tetrameters (four feet lines) the typical line from *In The Seven Woods* onwards is the pentameter (five feet). From then on there is an increasing use of monosyllabic and counterpointed feet, which allow the stress pattern of the verse to reflect more accurately the natural stress required by the sense.

In his search for appropriate stanza forms Yeats tried to apply a variety, reaching further back in the later verse to patterns which he associated with the earliest folk traditions. The most notable aspect of this search is the remarkable use to which he puts the old ballad device of the refrain in some of the *Last Poems*.

His normal practice was to compose a prose draft first, followed by rough verse drafts, before attempting a fair copy. Then would come publication of the poem in a magazine, after which several more revisions frequently occurred before the poem would be committed to a volume of verse. As this process suggests Yeats was a craftsman of enormous persistence and endurance, confirmed by a remark of his own to Lady Gregory: 'I, since I was seventeen, have never begun a story or poem or essay of any kind that I have not finished'.

The greatest single stylistic change occurs between *The Wind Among The Reeds* and *In The Seven Woods* with the introduction of the shorter eight-syllable line and a resultant compression leading to the stripping away of the often languid epithets of the pre-Raphaelite style. The rhythm becomes increasingly the servant not the master of the meaning, with a more colloquial diction and metre allowing the stress to fall on significant words. While the verse-line still controls the rhythmic structure of the poem, much of the poetry from *The Wild Swans At Coole* onwards is marked by the tension which Yeats builds in between the natural unit of speech and the verse-line.

A typical poem of the early period, 'To the Rose upon the Rood of Time' is written in heroic couplets, all of which are rhymed and all of which are end-stopped. All the lines are regular iambic pentameters and there is the usual cluster of compound epithets ('wood-nurtured', 'quiet-eyed', 'silver-sandalled') and the archaism 'chaunt'. The whole movement of the poem is away from this world towards an ideal one, reached through the lulling, trance-like hypnosis of the metric form.

'The Fascination of What's Difficult' shows the radical changes taking place in a poem marking the transition from early to mature style. Now the rhyme-scheme is less obtrusive though vitally important and Yeats is prepared to try the half-rhymes 'difficult' and 'colt' and 'blood' and 'cloud'. The major breaks in the syntax now occur in the middle of lines four and eight in keeping with the demands of sense. The basic unit is still the iambic pentameter but the standard short/long pattern is interrupted to allow the stress to fall naturally ('strain, sweat and jolt'). The sounds are much harsher and the vocabulary is taken from the real world, reversing the movement of the earlier poem into the ideal.

By the time of the *Last Poems* Yeats has that confidence in his chosen form which enables him to stretch its capabilities to the full, as the last verse of 'The Circus Animals' Desertion' shows. The iambic pentameter is now only used to give weight and finality to the last three lines after Yeats has exploited the possibilities in the earlier lines by including extra feet to add to the impression of the images crowding into and cluttering his mind restlessly, before the measured stress gives a feeling of slowing-down to the last lines. He is prepared to let 'can' rhyme with 'gone' and 'street' with 'slut', for the choice of word is now paramount. Stress and rhythm are now being created not simply adopted by the poet, so that the forms in reading seem unique and personal, although they are in fact carefully worked around traditional models. This is the measure of Yeats's technical genius.

SYMBOLISM

For Yeats the symbol is not an occasional device with which to embellish his poetry but a way of thought and a means of arriving at imaginative truth in his work. Though charts can be drawn to show how one symbol relates to another and what associations each one seemed to carry for the poet, such an approach gives rise to the impression that the symbols are somehow extra to the poems in which they are used. Yeats's symbols are not confined to one phase of his work but are prominent from early to late. Some symbols, indeed, are more in evidence in one particular period but they are usually found elsewhere as well. The rose, for example, dominates the collection of the same name where it becomes the central symbol for the expression of his work on occult studies in the poetry.

There are three main features to all Yeats's symbols. Firstly, they enable him to combine a directness of style or verbal simplicity with a meaning that would be too complex to express by any other means that avoided syntactical difficulty. Secondly, they enable the poet to invoke a wide range of traditional references which increase the frame of reference of the poem without loss of focus. Thirdly, and most important of all for a poet of Yeats's temperament, they supply the means by which he was able to fuse the movements of his intellect with those of his imagination into a concrete image.

Yeats's use of symbols underwent considerable change in the course of his poetry. In the earlier collections symbols are drawn mainly from Irish legend and occult religions with many poems built around the symbols. Later on, however, Yeats works symbols more fully into the fabric of the verse, drawing upon his personal experience to intensify the significance which the symbols carry for him. Thus the symbols of the later collections become inseparable from the poet and the poetry. They are no longer borrowed but taken over.

The Dancer

An examination of a few of Yeats's more consistent symbols can provide an illustration of his method and show how intimately these symbols are associated with the poet's own experience. A symbol which gains in significance as it occurs in a growing variety of contexts is that of the dancer. Its own qualities suggest a movement of rhythm combined with passion within the discipline of a certain style to produce an image of perfect poise. From this active harmony comes the idea of a symbolic reconcilement of the body with the mind or, in different contexts, emotion with thought and reality with dream. The notion of poise achieved through a balance of contrary tensions allows the dancer to become for Yeats an image for the perfect condition of art.

In several poems the figure of the dancer is linked with specific people in whom Yeats detected those qualities he associated with the symbol. For instance Iseult Gonne, Maud Gonne's adopted daughter, is the person addressed in 'To a Child Dancing in the Wind'.

Elsewhere the figure is Florence Farr, a distinguished actress who possessed in Yeats's words, 'an incomparable sense of rhythm and a beautiful voice'.

Loie Fuller is referred to by name as the dancer who inspired the image of the poem 'Nineteen Hundred and Nineteen' (p. 120). She was an American dancer at the Folies Bergères in Paris who became famous among the French poets and artists of the 1890s for her unconventional dancing, and especially for her Fire Dance. She stirred the imagination of both Mallarmé and Toulouse Lautrec, the first writing a long study of her, and the second capturing a famous dance in one of his paintings. Valued by some simply for her exotic naturalism, others found in her dancing the very quintessence of Art, suggesting simultaneously the antinomies of human experience: body and spirit, subjectivity and objectivity, dynamism and repose. It was this latter aspect of Loie Fuller's dancing which appealed to the French Symbolists and to Yeats.

The developing symbol of the dancer reflects in itself some of the major changes in Yeats's poetry and thought. In early poems the dancer is normally associated with either the state of fairyland or the state of blessedness beyond this life. In other words it is part of the movement away from reality into dream that is a feature of the poems of the Celtic Twilight. However, by the time we get to 'The Double Vision of Michael Robartes' (p. 86) the dancer is firmly associated with earthly love. From this moment on in the poems the dancer represents the perfection of life and art fused in the single image. For the later poems the image stands for the state of 'unity of being' where all the elements become inseparable in the harmonised soul. This expression of harmony, of the artist at one with his life is the point of the rhetorical question which closes 'Among School Children' (p. 127):

> O body swayed to music, O brightening glance,
> How can we know the dancer from the dance?

The Swan

Another symbol which acquires increasing significance as it moves through the body of the poetry is the swan. To the traditional associations of physical beauty and grace and the roots in both Celtic and Greek mythology are added several spiritual connotations in later poems. In many poems the swan refers directly to Maud Gonne who dominates much of Yeats's early work through the symbol of the swan and who is never far removed from the later poetry.

In 'The Wild Swans at Coole' they are simply emblems of beauty, dignity and fidelity but since these are qualities which the poet finds in increasingly short supply in the modern world there is already a sense in which they are suggestive of a civilisation at odds with our own:

> Unwearied still, lover by lover,
> They paddle in the cold
> Companionable streams or climb the air;
> Their hearts have not grown old;
> Passion or conquest, wander where they will,
> Attend upon them still.

The attribute of fidelity is drawn from the Celtic legend of two lovers Baile and Ailinn who died on being falsely informed of each other's death but were changed into swans linked together forever by a golden chain. The full power of the symbol in Yeats's poetry only appears, however, when the associations lent to the symbol by the Greek legend of Leda's rape by Zeus in the shape of a swan are added to the earlier Irish ones, 'Leda and the Swan' (p. 241). Besides begetting Helen and Clytemnestra (representing for Yeats the qualities of love and strife), Zeus chose this moment to be the annunciation of that spirit or essence of subjectivity which was destined to be the dominant force of Greek civilisation. This divine quality, associated through the legend with the swan, is thus best epitomised by Helen who was already one of the guises for Maud Gonne. Besides lending force to the references which occur in subsequent poems such as 'Among School Children' (p. 242) this added significance gives, as it were, retrospective force to a poem like 'No Second Troy' (p. 101) where the combination of great beauty and power of destruction traditionally associated with Helen becomes entirely appropriate for Yeats's view of Maud Gonne's devotion to the nationalist cause:

> Why, what could she have done, being what she is?
> Was there another Troy for her to burn?

In sacred literature the swan is normally taken to symbolize the human soul or spirit. When this knowledge is combined with Yeats's own interpretation of the Greek myth, the place of the swan in his later work from *A Vision* onwards is clarified. In a note to his play *Calvary* Yeats himself develops the significance of the symbol:

> Certain birds, especially as I see things, such lonely birds as the heron, hawk, eagle and swan, are the natural symbols of subjectivity, especially when floating upon the wind alone or alighting upon some pool or river, while the beasts that run upon the ground, especially those that run in packs, are the natural symbols of objective man. Objective men, however personally alone, are never alone in their thought, which is always developed in agreement or in conflict with the thought of others and always seeks the welfare of some cause or institution, while subjective men are the more lonely the more they are true to type, seeking always that which is unique or personal.

Thus it can be seen that those symbols which are most completely woven into the fabric of Yeats's work reveal an inexhaustible supply of meaning and association, reaching into every aspect of the poet's life and thought. The fully digested symbol never has a merely local or one-off significance as Yeats's own approach to the use of symbols reveals:

> Day after day I have sat in my chair turning a symbol over in my mind, exploring all its details, defining and again defining its elements, testing my conventions and those of others by its unity, attempting to substitute particulars for an abstraction like that of algebra.

The Tower

The most pervasive symbol of them all and consequently the one most difficult to detach from the contexts in which it appears, is that of the tower. It combines habitually personal references with traditional ones so that ultimately the tower comes to represent the whole work of the poet, his achievement, that which he will leave behind. So deeply embedded was the image of the tower in his consciousness, that he sought out an actual tower in which he could work to the utmost of his creative power. Thoor Ballylee, in the Barony of Kiltartan in County Galway, was bought by Yeats for £35 in 1917, becoming the summer residence of Yeats and his family from 1918 to the late 'twenties. Originally a Norman tower known as Islandmore Castle or Ballylee Castle, it was given its new name by Yeats to escape, as he put it, 'from the too magnificent word "castle",' feeling that 'Thoor' (Irish for tower) amended the softness of Ballylee. When Yeats bought the tower it was in ruins, and much reconstruction was needed to make it habitable. The dominant feature was the 'winding stair' which gave access to each floor from entrance to battlement. The great windows of the tower opened on the millstream rushing below and on 'old rugged elms, old thorns innumerable,' throwing green shadows on the water. Yeats found the tower 'full of history and romance' and acquired it 'as a permanent symbol of (his) work visible to the passer-by.' The tower had many romantic associations: in its vicinity and in one of the surrounding cottages lived Mary Hynes, whose beauty was celebrated by the blind Gaelic bard Raftery ('Coole Park and Ballylee' p. 275), who called her in one of his ballads 'the shining flower of Ballylee'; it was the seat of the aristocratic de Burgo family that ruled Galway; and it linked itself to all those towers mentioned in the poetry of Spenser, Milton, Shelley and Byron.

This archetypal symbol of the solitary intellect brooding upon the chaos of the world below was seen by Yeats to be the simplest and most concrete declaration of his position in the world. The tower came to embody for him the essence of his work, both poetical and political as is revealed in his 'Meditations in Time of Civil War' (p. 225). The winding stair of Babylon was the route by which man ascended to greatness as well as the motion of the gyre, Yeats's symbol for the means by which man perceives reality. As well as being the seat of intellectual wisdom it is also the source of creative energy and traditional symbol for sexual potency in the male. These traditional references combine with the historical associations relating to feudal times to embody Yeats's attitude to the aristocratic and heroic past of Ireland. In writing to Thomas Sturge Moore, the English poet, man of letters and wood engraver, who was his close friend for over two decades, and whose criticisms of 'Sailing to Byzantium' probably helped in the shaping of 'Byzantium' (p. 280), Yeats stressed the need to work symbols back to their place in the life of a living man: 'As you know, all my art theories depend upon just this – rooting my mythology in the earth.' The basis of Yeats's symbolic method is just this fusion of traditional, esoteric and common associations that the tower represents. A symbolism that is merely literary cannot connect with the reality of human experience. As Yeats expressed it at the climax of 'The Circus Animals' Desertion' (p. 391):

> I must lie down where all the ladders start,
> In the foul rag-and-bone shop of the heart.

The Gyre

This is the most complex of Yeats's symbols, closely related to the scheme of *A Vision*. At its most straightforward it is used to signify a single revolving cone by which time in the universe is measured, as in 'Sailing to Byzantium' (p. 104). Elsewhere Yeats complicates the symbol by using the image of a pair of interpenetrating cones representing forces acting on the soul in contrary movements. By itself the gyre or cone represents the pattern by which the material and spiritual universe is linked, the material being the base of the cone and the spiritual the apex or point. The interlocking gyres represent those forces that are always in conflict such as life and death, nature and supernature. However, this conflict exists within a framework of unity, symbolised by the sphere, the shape which represents ultimate 'unity of being'. This sense of conflict within unity is conveyed by the symbol of the sphere in 'Among School Children' (p. 127):

> . . ., and it seemd that our two natures blent
> Into a sphere from youthful sympathy,
> Or else, to alter Plato's parable,
> Into the yolk and white of the one shell.

Other Major Symbols

The following is a list of some of the other major symbols of Yeats. It must be remembered, however, that the precise reference carried by the symbol is only provided by the context in which it is used, so that those references given below should be treated as only the most general guides.

SYMBOL	ORIGIN	REFERENCES
Troy	Homer/Virgil	Destruction, Leda, Helen, Maud Gonne, the change of the historical cycle
Falcon/Hawk	Egyptian/Irish folklore	Subjective man, immortality, spirit, the soul's guardian
Heron/Curlew	Sligo countryside	Solitary, contemplative man
Hare	Myth	Magic properties, the soul's metamorphosis
Cat	Folklore/Egypt	Moon, witchcraft, female principle
Dolphin	Myth	Fidelity, sex, joy in life
Phidias	Greek sculptor	Perfection of Greek civilisation, creator of perfect human form
Michelangelo	Italian sculptor and painter	High point of the last thousand years, creator of perfect human form
Tree	Biblical Tree of Life, Sephirotic Tree of Hermetic religion	Conflicting aspects of mortal life, ultimate unity of existence
Rose	Hermetic religion, Dante	Perfection of immortal beauty, Maud Gonne

MAGIC, MYTH AND LEGEND

Madame Blavatsky

In 1878 Helena Blavatsky, the Russian-born spiritualist, founded the London branch of the Theosophical Society. Theosophy (from *theos*: god, and *sophia*: wisdom) begun in India, is the study of the divine by means of mystical revelations from Indian Mahatmas and Tibetan gurus. The aim of the society was the creation of a universal brotherhood, open to any race or religion, to undertake the study of the sacred books and to investigate some of the psychic phenomena which Madame Blavatsky had observed in India. Yeats read the book in which she set out these ideas, *Isis Unveiled* (1877). The emphasis on man's role as a spiritual being put theosophy in a close relationship with the 'middle way' of Buddhism, the Cabbalah and the mystic tradition of the Hindu Upanishads. In 1885 Yeats helped to found the Dublin Hermetic Society as a result of which he met the Brahmin, Mohini Chatterjee, whose doctrine of reincarnation, later reinforced by his study of the Neoplatonists, was still vividly recalled by the poet many years later:

> I have been a king,
> I have been a slave,
> Nor is there anything,
> Fool, rascal, knave,
> That I have not been.

MacGregor Mathers

Yeats joined the Blavatsky Lodge in 1887 and as a result of contacts there was initiated into another occult society, the Hermetic Order of the Golden Dawn, whose leader was MacGregor Mathers.

There were ten initiation rites into the Order of the Golden Dawn, through which the initiate climbed the Sephirotic Tree of Life in a series of deaths and rebirths of the spirit to reach, at the top, union with God. Mathers had two purposes for the order: the recreation of ancient magical rites and achieving visions through meditation on certain occult symbols. Yeats describes his method in *The Trembling of the Veil*:

He gave me a cardboard symbol and I closed my eyes. Sight came slowly, there was not that sudden miracle as if darkness had been cut with a knife, for that miracle is mostly a woman's privilege, but there rose before me mental images that I could not control: a desert and a black Titan raising himself up by his two hands from the middle of a heap of ancient ruins. Mathers explained that I had seen a being of the order of Salamanders because he had shown me their symbol, but it was not necessary even to show the symbol, it would have been sufficient that he imagined it.

A poem such as 'The Two Trees' (p. 54) deals with this same set of symbols. It is in the early poetry that their presence is felt most obviously, for later on the occult symbols are submerged or combined with others to broaden their associative range. Yeats criticized the Blavatsky Lodge and left after three years but he progressed to the highest level in the Order of the Golden Dawn, becoming Adeptus Exemptus in 1916. He encountered much criticism from friends such as John O'Leary and George Russell, who thought he was wasting his time but he was encouraged by the hours spent with his uncle, George Pollexfen. He too was fascinated by magic and astrology and Yeats spent much time with him and his housekeeper, Mary Battle, while on his holidays in Sligo. But as George grew older, he gradually withdrew into a secluded world of melancholia and hypochondria and the poet saw less of him. Yeats was greatly saddened to see the man for whom he had an enormous affection abandoning an active life for an escapist world of astrological dreams.

Religion

Yeats clearly felt the need to make his own religion because the world and his father's influence had deprived him of any of the orthodox ones:

I was unlike others of my generation in one thing only. I am very religious, and deprived by Huxley and Tyndall, whom I detested, of the simple-minded religion of my childhood, I had made a new religion, almost an infallible church of poetic tradition, of a fardel of stories, and of personages, and of emotions, inseparable from their first expression, passed on from generation to generation by poets and painters with some help from philosophers and theologians. I wished for a world, where I could discover this tradition perpetually . . . I had even created a dogma: 'Because these imaginary people are created out of the deepest instinct of man, to be his measure and his norm, whatever I can imagine those mouths speaking may be the nearest I can go to truth.'

His mind was already tuned in to the wavelength of the communicators of *A Vision* even this early in his career. Indeed, the interest in the occult proved life-long, forming part of Yeats's quest for a pattern of symbolic thought through which to comprehend the universe. His early experiences encountered through the study of magic were stored up and modified by time, to be recalled when some political or personal event thrust them into his conscious mind in a new context which reasserted their significance. Only by studying the world of the spirit would the world of matter be comprehended, and the occult was the means by which these two worlds could be brought into contact. The aim was also to achieve a fuller understanding of human experience in this life because, for Yeats, that experience was the centre for all other thought, the mind of man being the still centre of the turning world.

Lionel Johnson, poet, critic and member of the Rhymers' Club, to whom Yeats dedicated *The Rose*, directed Yeats to read Plato, and Madame Blavatsky recommended the Neoplatonist philosophers. Here Yeats found Plato's principle of the immortality of the soul confirming his own conviction. In the *Meno* Plato wrote:

> Since the soul is immortal and has been born many times and has seen the things of this world and of Hades and all things, there is nothing which it has not learned. So that it is no wonder that she should be able to recollect virtue and all other things, seeing that she has learned them previously.

Myth

The links that Yeats was thus able to make between his occult and his philosophical studies are made explicit by F. A. C. Wilson in *W. B. Yeats and Tradition*:

> The symbolic system of Neoplatonism was fixed and one might even say rigid: the sea, for example, symbolised always 'the waters of emotion and passion', or more simply life; man was consistently thought of as the beggar, dressed in the rags of mortality; the tomb, the forest and the cave were all symbols of the material world; after death, the soul, often accompanied by a mystic escort of dolphins, crossed the sea to heaven, the Isles of the Blessed. Yeats knew this system of symbolism from several sources: from Madame Blavatsky, in his formative years; then from Taylor's translation of the commentators on Plato, and especially from Porphyry's essay on 'The Cave of the Nymphs'; also from Plato himself, Plotinus . . . and the other Platonic philosophers he had read. He took it over into his verse in the confidence that it would prevent his own symbolism from being arbitrary or unintelligible; it was traditional, for it had persisted throughout the middle ages, where it influenced among others, Dante, and, later, Spenser; and, as the symbolism of a religious

system which he himself was largely able to accept, it is clear that he thought of it as profound. In using it, again, he had precedent in the work of two English poets he particularly admired: Blake . . . and . . . Shelley.

The poem which most fully demonstrates this strand of Yeats's mythology and which indicates how deeply it was embedded in his poetic consciousness by the time he had achieved the summit of his artistic success is 'Byzantium' (p. 153), a poem that is wrought from

> Those images that yet
> Fresh images beget,
> That dolphin-torn, that gong-tormented sea.

Magic

The explicit references to magic as such diminish in number after reaching their climax in the 1901 essay 'Magic' from *Ideas of Good and Evil* (1903). Hereafter the knowledge and the images gleaned from his occult studies are no less important to Yeats, but they are now fused with other aspects of his work until they emerge, recast in their new form, in *A Vision*. The statement of his position in that essay gave him the platform from which to develop and transform his occult studies into the stuff of poetry:

> I believe in the practice and philosophy of what we have agreed to call magic, in what I must call the evocation of spirits, though I do not know what they are, in the power of creating magical illusions, in the visions of truth in the depths of the mind when the eyes are closed; and I believe in three doctrines, which have, as I think, been handed down from early times, and been the foundations of nearly all magical practices. These doctrines are:
>
> 1) That the borders of our mind are ever shifting, and that many minds can flow into one another, as it were, and create or reveal a single mind, a single energy.
>
> 2) That the borders of our memories are as shifting, and that our memories are a part of one great memory, the memory of Nature herself.
>
> 3) That this great mind and great memory can be evoked by symbols.
>
> I often think I would put this belief in magic from me if I could, for I have come to see or to imagine, in men and women, in houses, in handicrafts, in nearly all sights and sounds, a certain evil, a certain ugliness, that comes from the slow perishing through the centuries of a quality of mind that made this belief and its evidences common over the world.

Yeats was conscious of the esoteric aspects of this area of his work, and sought channels by which it might be linked to the lives of the common people, the Irish peasants through whom, he felt, that ancient, pagan link with the hidden, supernatural world might be preserved in the face of 'the filthy modern tide.' This desire to recreate the heroic and essentially pre-Christian past in the Ireland of his own day is reflected in a comment from *Autobiographies*:

> . . . I have noticed that clairvoyance, pre-vision, and allied gifts, rare among the educated classes, are common among peasants. Among those peasants, there is much of Asia, where Hegel has said every civilization begins. Yet we must hold to what we have, that the next civilization may be born, not from a virgin's womb, nor a tomb without a body, but our own rich experience.

Legend

This theory of a common fund of myth through which ordinary people could maintain contact with the supernatural world suggested to Yeats that consciousness of the past could unify a fragmented people in the modern age. As far as the unification of the Irish people was concerned, Yeats considered it vital to make the people conscious of their cultural heritage through a common fund of folk-lore, classical Irish legend, and mystic symbolism. While it may be readily supposed that mystic symbolism was never likely to develop into a popular movement, Yeats never succeeded in combining the folk-lore with the legend either. The difficulty lay with the content and style of the legends themselves. Those ancient tales that Lady Gregory researched with Yeats and culled from the neighbouring districts had, in fact, little common ground with the world of the peasants. They were the stories of an aristocratic past, enshrining the values of an heroic age and celebrating its love of life in a way which exerted an immense appeal over someone of Yeats's essentially aristocratic outlook, but which were unlikely to find much favour with the mass of the populace in a democratic age. Yeats expressed his hopes for the revival of these legends in his preface to Lady Gregory's 1904 edition of *Gods and Fighting Men*:

> Surely these old stories, whether of Finn or Cuchulain, helped to sing the old Irish and the old Norman-Irish aristocracy to their end. They heard their hereditary poets and story-tellers, and they took to horse and died fighting against Elizabeth or against Cromwell; and when an English-speaking aristocracy had their place, it listened to no poetry indeed, but it felt about it in the popular mind an exacting and ancient tribunal, and began a play that had for spectators men and women that loved the high wasteful virtues.

Cuchulain

Whether or not this picture existed only in the fancy of the poet, there was one figure who escaped the confines of a dead history and that was Cuchulain, who became for the poet the image or embodiment of all those heroic virtues he wished to be able to claim for himself. Cuchulain, the 'Hound of Culain', is the greatest champion of Ulster and hero of the Red Branch cycle of tales. Legend fixes the date of his death around 2 A.D., and says that he was slain at the age of twenty-seven. Of all the mythological themes that interested Yeats, Cuchulain had the most enduring influence on him. He was many things for Yeats: a national symbol; the hero *par excellence*; a representative of the heroic and aristocratic values that he believed in; but above all he was the chief representative of the heroic age which Yeats hoped Ireland would recreate. Yeats identified himself with Cuchulain who became his most enduring 'Mask'. Two of Yeats's final works were the poem 'Cuchulain Comforted' and the play *The Death of Cuchulain*, emphasizing how closely the figure of Cuchulain was bound up with Yeats's attitudes to nationalism, heroism, mysticism and, finally, to himself. The most powerful evocation of the hero comes in the climactic final verse of 'The Statues' where the vivid memory of the Easter Rising as a modern example of ancient heroism inspires the poet to an affirmation of faith in the nobility of his race corresponding to their place in his scheme of history. So much of the power stems from the multiple associations in the image of Cuchulain:

> When Pearse summoned Cuchulain to his side,
> What stalked through the Post Office? What intellect,
> What calculation, number, measurement, replied?
> We Irish, born into that ancient sect
> But thrown upon this filthy modern tide
> And by its formless spawning fury wrecked,
> Climb to our proper dark, that we may trace
> The lineaments of a plummet-measured face.

It is typical of Yeats's view of life and approach to poetic technique that the apotheosis of his work on the ancient legends should arise in the context of his own immediate experience. Whether in pursuit of mystic revelation, philosophy or folk history, the poet sought constantly the knowledge they brought him, not as an end in itself, but as a means of affirming the centrality of the experience in this life of the unique individual through the medium of his verse.

NATIONALISM AND POLITICS

Yeats's nationalism began and ended with the countryside around his native Sligo. As a boy he was given to wandering its quiet ways listening to the voices of the other world in the wind. Growing up in Sligo and London he experienced directly the contrast between an older rural pattern of life still in touch with its ancient legends and a modern industrial society in pursuit of material goals. Yeats felt England to be an example of a society corrupted by this vulgar materialism and therefore progress for his native Ireland could only be achieved through independence from British rule.

However, though his political stance could be described as broadly nationalistic, it contained ambiguities, many of which derive from his birth in the land-owning Protestant class in a Catholic country. Historically, Ireland possessed a different middle-class to the English type, in that its place was taken by the professions – doctors, lawyers and so on – from which most of Ireland's writers came. On either side were the peasants in their cottages and landlords in their 'big houses'. Traditionally the fight for a free Ireland was also a fight to remove the Protestant oppressor, although many of the leading figures in the struggle for independence had, paradoxically, been from the Protestant section of society. Perhaps an awareness of his position as a representative of a minority in the population was responsible for some of the aloofness in his temperament which is reflected in his dealings with politicians and political movements. He had avoided the fragmented committee structures and the compromises and deals of the various nationalist groupings which devalued that for which they were fighting; though he would make use of them when he felt he could manipulate them for his own ends.

Yeats's great admiration for Charles Stewart Parnell stems from a view of him as existing above the squabbles and intrigues of lesser men. He saw in him that pride of personality and coldness which he associated with the ancient heroes of the Irish legends. Yeats believed that Parnell was the greatest Irish statesman, and he never forgave Ireland for not standing behind him at the time of his greatest need. That this feeling stayed with him and fuelled his contempt for those politicians who betrayed Parnell is clear from the late poem 'Parnell's Funeral' (p. 174):

> All that was said in Ireland is a lie
> Bred out of the contagion of the throng
> Saving the rhyme rats hear before they die.

As necessary as political freedom for Yeats was the establishment of a literary and artistic revival which in a free Ireland could seriously affect the course of history by restoring the old traditions of visionary thought and heroic action. This was where Yeats saw that he could make his best contribution by putting the Irish in touch with their own past and reviving the values of that past in its contemporary art forms. This was the motive behind his energetic endeavours in setting up the various literary societies that he organised around the turn of the century. The man who provided him with the initial inspiration to undertake this task was John O'Leary who represented for Yeats the old, heroic spirit of pre-Christian Ireland.

With the death of O'Leary on St. Patrick's Day 1907 Yeats felt that an era was over, that a vital link with a richer past had been severed. This emotion is expressed powerfully in 'September 1913' (p. 55):

> Romantic Ireland's dead and gone,
> It's with O'Leary in the grave.

Though the genius of Yeats tends to cloud a view of the lesser writers around him, in the same way that many see only Shakespeare in the English renaissance, he was in fact part of a movement which had already begun at the time that he joined it. Standish James O'Grady is usually regarded as the father of the Irish Literary Revival. He was a historian whose work had a great influence on Yeats. O'Grady's *History of Ireland: Heroic Period* (1878) and his *History of Ireland: Cuchulain and His Contemporaries* (1880) provided modern Irish literature in English with its epic romances, reminding Yeats and other Irish writers of their past heritage and introducing them to the great figures of Irish mythology: Maeve, Fergus, Deirdre and Cuchulain.

There are two strands to Yeats's nationalism; one overtly political, sharing the common goal of a break with England, a feeling strengthened by the impact of Maud Gonne on him which finds expression in the speech made for the Wolfe Tone centenary in 1890:

We hated at first the ideals and ambitions of England, the materialisms of England, because they were hers, but we have come to hate them with a nobler hatred. We hate them now because they are evil. We have suffered too long from them, not to understand, that hurry to become rich, that delight in mere bigness, that insolence to the weak are evil and vulgar things . . . We are building up a nation which shall be moved by noble purposes and to noble deeds.

and the other, much more enduring strand which took as its aim the reawakening of the consciousness of a nation. This aim Yeats expressed six years later on a lecture tour of the U.S.A.:

We wish to preserve an ancient ideal of life. Wherever its customs prevail, there you will find the folk song, the folk tale, the proverb and the charming manners that come from ancient culture. In England you will find a few thousands of perfectly cultivated people, but you will find the mass of the people singing songs of the music hall . . . In Ireland alone among the nations that I know you will find, away on the western seaboard, under broken roofs, a race of gentlemen keep alive the ideals of a great time when men sang the heroic life with drawn swords in their hands.

In reworking the old myths for his narrative and lyric poems Yeats saw himself not gratifying some personal whim but engaging himself on the necessary and urgent task of taking his country's cultural heritage out of mothballs. He believed in the possibility of a cultural unity being created out of common myths from which the nation could draw sustenance at a time of great crisis:

Have not all nations had their first unity from a mythology that marries them to rock and hill? We had in Ireland imaginative stories, which the uneducated classes knew and even sang, and might we not make those stories current among the educated classes, rediscovering for the work's sake what I have called 'the applied arts of literature', the association of literature, that is, with music, speech and dance; and at last, it might be, so deepen the political passion of the nation that all, artist and poet, craftsman and day-labourer would accept a common design?

Dramatic proof that the Irish Literary Revival had penetrated to the world of political action was furnished by Padraic Pearse's invocation of Cuchulain in the Post Office during the 1916 uprising.

One crucial element absent from the cultural past of Ireland was the drama. To compensate for this Yeats focussed his energies, especially in the first decade of this century, on creating an independent Irish theatre. The result was the Abbey Theatre, which flourishes to this day. The successful birth of the theatre bears witness to Yeats's abilities of organization, cooperation and to his willingness to suffer the meetings and routine work necessary to launch the project. They are not qualities normally associated with a solitary, lyric poet but they represented an important aspect of his personality. Yeats was greatly helped by the quality of the people who worked with him but it was he who united them in a common purpose. Lady Gregory was the most important single influence on Yeats's approach to the theatre project and she worked tirelessly in all capacities to get the theatre open. It was out of meetings between her, Yeats and Edward Martyn that the Irish Literary Theatre was created, from which grew the Abbey. It was Yeats who attracted Annie Horniman to the project for she had earlier helped to finance the production of Yeats's *The Land of Heart's Desire* in London and had designed *The King's Threshold*. It was largely due to her generosity that funds were made available for launching the Abbey Theatre in 1904.

The poems of this period, that is *The Green Helmet and Other Poems* and *Responsibilities* collections, are predominantly bitter in tone, expressing the poet's frustration at the inability of his people to behave truly in the spirit of their ancient traditions. The controversy of the proposed gallery for Hugh Lane's pictures in Dublin furnished him with yet more evidence of the loss of the attitude of nobility in the world around him:

> That things it were a pride to give
> Are what the blind and ignorant town
> Imagines best to make it thrive. (p. 119)

Given Yeats's view of the contemporary political scene the events of Easter Week 1916 came as a profound shock and turning point in his life. The Rising took place on Easter Monday 1916, and lasted for five days until April 29, but by May 12 the leaders of the Rising, several of whom were Yeats's fellow workers in the literary movement, were condemned to death and executed. When Yeats first received the news his feelings were ambivalent, but there is no doubt that the event shocked him deeply, and his comments in his letters to Lady Gregory and John Quinn in 1916 reveal the degree to which the Rising had touched him: 'I had no idea that any public event could so deeply move me – and I am very despondent about the future'; 'We have lost the ablest and most fine natured of our young men. A world seems to have been swept away'. The sacrifice of the martyrs struck a deeply responsive note in him, which appealed to his notion of the heroic ideal. The leaders were henceforth admitted into Yeats's pantheon of the immortals of Irish history alongside Wolfe Tone, Emmet, Parnell and Cuchulain. He expressed it thus in 'Easter 1916' (p. 93):

I write it out in a verse –
MacDonagh and MacBride
And Connolly and Pearse
Now and in time to be,
Wherever green is worn,
Are changed, changed utterly:
A terrible beauty is born.

Many events during the Troubles of the subsequent years in the struggle for freedom sickened Yeats and convinced him that the end of the millenium with its accompanying destruction was at hand. Several such events are recorded in his 'Meditations in Time of Civil War' (p. 112) and particularly distressing was the assassination of his close friend and Minister of Justice in the Irish Free State, Kevin O'Higgins. Yeats described him as the 'one strong intellect in Irish public life'. Nevertheless Yeats worked throughout these difficult years as a Senator. His appointment came as a result of his literary eminence and the honour he had brought his country, rather than of his political activity. Nevertheless Yeats took his responsibilities seriously and soon achieved a reputation as an eloquent speaker. In the Senate he leaned towards the more conservative elements, notably the Southern Unionists and was appointed to advise the government on matters concerning education, literature and the arts. He gave his own justification years before for the loss of time that might have been devoted exclusively to his own interests: 'A good Nationalist is, I suppose, one who is ready to give up a great deal that he may preserve to his country whatever part of her possessions he is best fitted to guard . . .'

In the last decade of his life after he retired from the Senate Yeats withdrew from any active interest in politics. Much has been made of his supposed interest in The Blueshirts (who supported European Fascist ideas) under General O'Duffy. As soon as Yeats knew anything about the aim of the movement he withdrew what little interest he had shown.

In the last analysis Yeats's is the nationalism that is simply the celebration of all that is best in the history of the race; an affirmation of his unbroken link with the land itself, symbolised by his return to it. The message of 'Under Ben Bulben' is not, ultimately, a political one:

Cast your mind on other days
That we in coming days may be
Still the indomitable Irishry.

THE POET'S VISION

On October 21, 1917 Yeats married Georgie Hyde-Lees. Four days later she tried automatic writing as a way of distracting the poet from the melancholy that had settled over him. What she wrote took up ideas of which she knew nothing but which related closely to the life-long preoccupations of Yeats. When he considered devoting all his energies to the exposition of these communications, they told him: 'we have come to give you metaphors for poetry'.

The communications occurred almost daily for over three years and the result was the first edition of *A Vision* in 1925. Yeats was not satisfied by the work, and there were still more communications to be processed, so he published a revised edition in 1937. In its final form it is the exposition of a system of thought about the soul in and beyond life and the meaning of history, worked out in geometrical symbolism based on the esoteric doctrines in which both Yeats and his wife had made themselves experts over a number of years. The essence of the work is the notion of two movements of the human soul, one towards perfect self-realization and the other towards perfect self-abnegation. All moments of existence can be seen in these terms be they a single action, a life, a series of incarnations, a cycle of civilizations or the universe itself. The Greek philosopher Empedocles called these impulses Strife and Love; one separating, the other fusing. Nothing can exist except by the interaction of these two forces. Yeats expounds the process through the incarnations of a single soul. These incarnations are taken to correspond to the phases of the moon, one night of the lunar month representing one incarnation. When a soul achieves total self-realization it is in a state of perfect poise called 'Unity of Being'. All that happens during this incarnation corresponds to the ideal that is desired by the soul – or as it is expressed in his poem 'Solomon and the Witch' (p. 199), 'Chance being at one with Choice at last'. This is the fifteenth phase or full of the moon. But there is no incarnation at this phase in the living world because there is no conflict. It is a form of superhuman beauty occasionally encountered by visionaries in special places as in Michael Robartes's vision on the Rock of Cashel in 'The Double Vision of Michael Robartes' (p. 192):

> Although I saw it all in the mind's eye
> There can be nothing solider till I die;
> I saw by the moon's light
> Now at its fifteenth night.

Out of this phase the move begins towards objective reality. At the opposite pole there is no body either because the soul has no will and takes in everything from outside without conflict. This incarnation, the moon's darkness, is also beyond the world:

> On the grey rock of Cashel the mind's eye
> Has called up the cold spirits that are born
> When the old moon is vanished from the sky
> And the new still hides her horn.

Between these two all human life is moving. Lives are shaped by the soul's four 'Faculties': 'Will', 'Mask', 'Creative Mind' and 'Body of Fate'. Will is the energy that sets up the drive to self-realization. It sets before itself an image of its opposite and strives to become that. This image is called the Mask. Creative Mind is a kind of memory of ideas, the power of thought learnt in past lives. Its purpose is to understand the exterior circumstances that affect the soul. These circumstances are called the Body of Fate. Man perceives it as external but really it is formed from the memories of the events of the soul's past lives. Thus there are two processes at work in the soul: the Will is attempting to become the Mask and the Creative Mind is trying to understand the Body of Fate. These two work to confuse each other. Up to the fifteenth phase Will is the dominant force. After that phase Creative Mind replaces it. Yeats sees them as two gyres whirling in opposite directions. Plotted two-dimensionally as a wheel it can be seen that half the phases, Eight to Twenty-two belong to the brightness of the moon; these are the 'antithetical' phases: 'In an antithetical phase, the being seeks by the help of the Creative Mind to deliver the Mask from the Body of Fate'. The dark side from Twenty-two to Eight is called 'primary': 'In a primary phase the being seeks by the help of the Body of Fate to deliver the Creative Mind from the Mask.'

The system does not supply any one ideal by which all mankind can be measured. Reality is a phaseless sphere but the mind of man can only grasp it as a series of opposed pairs. The soul is more than the sum of its incarnations.

With more communications came the second and third books of *A Vision*, *The Completed Symbol* and *The Soul in Judgment*. These two consider what is behind life. *The Completed Symbol* tries to fit the gyres of life into the wider scheme of the after-life. The soul of man in eternity is called his Daimon. In this scheme the Faculties are voluntarily acquired powers of the incarnate Daimon operating between birth and death. Four 'Principles' are inherent in the nature of the Daimon – 'Spirit' and 'Celestial Body', or mind and its object, and 'Husk' and 'Passionate Body', or sense and its object. The four Principles also have a whirling gyre but its circle is wider than that of the Faculties because it includes the time between death and birth as well as this life.

As in most symbolic thought, the moon is the light of the changing, transitory world, in Yeats's terms, the light of subjective perception and the sun is the light of the supersensory world, the light of the fundamental laws of the universe. The gyre of the Principles is a solar day in which life between birth and death is night, or a solar year with life as its winter season. This gyre is measured by the signs of the Zodiac. All experience in life emanates from the Faculties. After death the spirit reworks the knowledge which the Faculties brought it during its life. This is the process which is described in *The Soul in Judgment*.

First comes a vision of the impulses and images from the life just completed. This is an experience comparable with that recorded elsewhere as seeing the whole of a past life in an instant at the moment of death. In Ireland the spirit of the departed is commonly said to remain close to the body for some time, hence the tradition of the wake held for the spirit before it departs its earthly abode.

The second phase is the meditation over the whole experience of life which is a much slower process. This requires the spirit to live over and over in order of intensity the events of its mortal life that moved it most deeply. Then these events are lived and relived in the order of their happening until they are fully understood and assimilated into the spirit. At the end of Yeats's play *Purgatory* the Old Man understands the futility of his attempt to interfere with this process as it affects the spirit of his mother. Only some sort of divine intervention can release her from her dream:

> Her mind cannot hold up that dream.
> Twice a murderer and all for nothing,
> And she must animate that dead night
> Not once but many times!
>   Oh God,
> Release my mother's soul from its dream!
> Mankind can do no more. Appease
> The misery of the living and the remorse of the dead.

All emotion that was uncompleted in the mortal life has to be exhausted by living out those emotions through an enacted fantasy of the soul or 'dream' as Yeats refers to it in *Purgatory*. In the terms of the system, Spirit makes Passionate Body intelligible before Husk and Passionate Body fade away.

The third phase is the understanding of good and evil which is achieved by the soul reversing the moral positions of its mortal life. Where it inflicted suffering it must now suffer itself in the same measure and where it was the slave it must now be master. Unlike the first and second phases this is not a state of dream. The fourth phase is the condition of blessedness, passed in a trance of equilibrium where the soul is at one with the Universal Soul.

The fifth phase initiates the movement towards rebirth. The soul shapes a new Husk and Passionate Body and waits for the appropriate conditions for rebirth to occur in the universe. The sixth phase is that of foreknowledge where the soul foresees the life it will have after rebirth and accepts it before birth takes place. During its sleep in the womb, the soul accepts the justice of the future that awaits it.

The soul is committed to the cycle of its lives without the possibility of stopping or changing. However, the system is rescued from that historical determinism which was the ground of Yeats's aversion to Marxism by an escape clause known as the Thirteenth Cone. This is the moment when we are released from the twelve circumscribed revolutions of the gyre, finding ourselves at one with the phaseless sphere, reality which sets us free. This process should not, however, be thought of as an escape from experience but rather the full acceptance of it. The fundamental view supporting the system is one which affirms the value of the experience of life and therefore seeks to understand it more fully and more deeply. The failure to take on the experience proper to that phase delays the soul's advance through the cycle of lives but normally the time between death and birth is three generations and the soul's full cycle of lives takes about two thousand years. This figure is needed to correlate men's lives with the cycle of history, with which the rest of the book deals.

The ancient astronomers made all their calculations from the Great Year – the moment when all the constellations were said to return to their original positions. At this moment history would begin again. Yeats worked out that the Great Year would come round every twenty-six thousand years, neatly correlating with the twenty-six incarnations of the soul. Each millenium is like a wheel with its own full moon, the period of its greatest cultural achievement, and its own dark moon, the descent into chaos and anarchy. A civilization sweeps through its phases in two thousand years. Referring back to the historical periods for which there are records, the Greek civilization was seen to be in an antithetical phase and the Christian in a primary one. Greek civilization manifested its beginnings in about 1000 B.C. and was announced, for each civilization has its annunciation, by the divine swan's rape of Leda. From her eggs came two sets of twins, Castor and Pollux and Helen and Clytemnestra, the Love and Strife of Empedocles. This is the reference in the opening verse of 'The Gyres' (p. 337):

> Irrational streams of blood are staining earth;
> Empedocles has thrown all things about;
> Hector is dead and there's a light in Troy;
> We that look on but laugh in tragic joy.

According to Yeats the third egg was hung in a Spartan temple and will hatch something from the remote past that will determine the essence of the future when the moment for the annunciation of the next millenium is at hand. The dove descended on the Virgin Mary mid-way through the period of the Greek civilization which died about 1050 A.D. in the Dark Ages of western Europe. About 2000 A.D. will be the mid-point between the death of the antithetical cycle and its rebirth. Whatever the new cycle will be it will be as Christianity was to the Greek world; the focus of all that is opposite to the dominant values of our era. It is this view of history which underpins the terrifying climax of 'The Second Coming' (p. 210):

> The darkness drops again; but now I know
> That twenty centuries of stony sleep
> Were vexed to nightmare by a rocking cradle,
> And what rough beast, its hour come round at last,
> Slouches towards Bethlehem to be born?

The 'rough beast' will possess an antithetical personality restoring pride in the works of the individual and seeking the supernatural through the forms of nature and not a transcendent God. However, Yeats himself warns us against the complacency of prediction:

> Something of what I have said it must be, the myth declares, for it must reverse our own era and rescue past eras in itself; what else it must be no man can say, for always at the critical moment, the Thirteenth Cone, the sphere, the unique intervenes.

It is not useful to debate the truth or significance of *A Vision* for anyone but Yeats. The consequences for his poetry were considerable, not just in the subject matter released into the poems but also in the style in which that matter is expressed. The system gave a logical coherence to what had previously been ideas and images scattered in a more random way through the poems. It is not so much that *A Vision* supplied new thoughts as that it supplied a new structure for old thoughts. It is a mythological work not an historical or philosophical analysis, a different creation myth told in a whisper for the ears of one man alone. Its fundamental movement is the reverse of the mystics, taking Yeats back into the life from which the richness of the later poetry is drawn. In a letter to Edmund Dulac in 1937 Yeats wrote of *A Vision*:

> I do not know what my book will be to others – nothing perhaps. To me it means a last act of defence against the chaos of the world and I hope for ten years to write out of my renewed security.

There are several critical works available to the student of *A Vision*. The authors strongly recommend A. G. Stock's two chapters on *A Vision* in *W. B. Yeats: His Poetry and Thought*, the most succinct and coherent introduction to the subject. The above section and the first part of the following one is a summary of her work.

HISTORY AND CIVILIZATION

Dove or Swan, the fifth book of *A Vision*, deals with history in cycles of one thousand years. History for Yeats is a combination of his understanding of art, thought and religion. The first cycle known to us is that of the ancient Greek civilization. Yeats saw this as starting with the tribes of Greece who broke up the empire to live in a condition of intellectual anarchy. By Homer's day the idea of civil order had been born which in turn gave way to a later feeling for solitude, a manifestation of the subjective tradition, seen among the pre-Socratic philosophers and in the art of Phidias. Periclean Athens was, of course, the full moon phase of the era with the domination of art and culture. Yeats called the Greek civilization 'subjective' in the sense that it sought to realize its greatness and beauty within human life, not through a transcendence of it. The gods are present within this world which is itself a mirror of divinity. The high point of this era was reached in the realization of the divine within the individual, not through a self-effacing unity with the transcendent One. On the other hand Greek secular intellect was classified by Yeats as 'primary'. He regarded Plato as preparing for the Christian rejection of the world by conceiving of governing absolutes existing beyond the world of nature. The ancients, by contrast saw men as fragments of the divine but Christ gathered all divinity into his own person, so that God became everything and man nothing. Christianity was the Nemesis of this civilization, turning its beliefs about and making weaknesses of its strengths. Sexual love, that process which involves the seeking of the opposite and delight in the consequent possession, became evil. The position of love was usurped by sacrifice and service. In its early phases Christianity was transcendental, coming closest to that state of Unity of Being in the visionary art of Byzantium in the time of Justinian. Of all ages, Yeats saw in it the most perfect expression of the unseen, the supernatural, made visible through the forms of art. Yeats saw the end of this era most clearly exemplified in the Dark Ages of western Europe where there was a controlling religious unity through the domination of the Catholic Church but where the secular intellect had been virtually extinguished.

Then Yeats traces the main phases of the last one thousand

years in increasing detail as the evidence grows. Moving out of the darkness of the fragmented mind, he noted the emergence in the Romance and Gothic periods of an impulse to celebrate delight in life. As a result of this impulse although having to operate within the prevailing movement towards objectivity, the solitary personality begins to be expressed again, Dante furnishing the first major example. Art and poetry now expresses curiosity and interest in the living world about it instead of gazing exclusively towards heaven. For this era the Renaissance is the phase of Unity of Being, coming nearest to that moment of complete poise in the Italian painters of the fifteenth century.

After this high point the objective spirit starts to appear in art and literature, philosophy and science. The forces of creativity come, in this phase, from the external world with an ever increasing emphasis on empiricism. Personality fights back in the face of overwhelming odds in the Romantic Revival of the eighteenth century, that period most dear to Yeats as far as his view of Ireland was concerned, for the reassertion of the ancient values through the culture of the 'big house'.

The essence of this culture Yeats discovered in the person of Augusta Gregory and her home Coole Park. Lady Gregory achieved some prominence as a dramatist, her collction *Seven Short Plays* (1909) containing those by which she is best-known, and for her work with Yeats on founding the Irish National Theatre. However, she is best remembered for the help and encouragement she gave to promising young Irish writers, most notably Yeats, throwing open her hospitable, well-ordered country house at Coole Park, and offering them sympathy, hospitality and informed criticism of their work. Yeats acknowledged his debt to her in many places, an example being his poem 'Friends' (p. 139):

> And one because her hand
> Had strength that could unbind
> What none can understand,
> What none can have and thrive,
> Youth's dreamy load, till she
> So changed me that I live
> Labouring in ecstasy.

Like the period of the Romantic Revival struggling to assert itself in spite of the larger movement of history, so Yeats saw the small group of friends centred on Coole Park forming an isolated enclave, a small flame gradually, inevitably being absorbed into the great darkness of the disintegration of the millenium. With the death of Lady Gregory that flame guttered close to the point of extinction. It is this feeling which informs the climax of 'Coole Park and Ballylee, 1931' (p. 275):

> We were the last romantics – chose for theme
> Traditional sanctity and loveliness;
> Whatever's written in what poets name
> The book of the people; whatever most can bless
> The mind of man or elevate a rhyme;
> But all is changed, that high horse riderless,
> Though mounted in that saddle Homer rode
> Where the swan drifts upon a darkening flood.

Her death seemed all the more final following the loss of her only son, Robert, in the First World War. Robert Gregory created set-designs for some of Yeats's plays, won Yeats's respect and admiration, and became his friend. He symbolised for Yeats, among other things, the heroic character that has achieved Unity of Being, the Renaissance man. This view prevails in Yeats's elegy 'In Memory of Major Robert Gregory' (p. 148):

> Soldier, scholar, horseman, he,
> As 'twere all life's epitome.
> What made us dream that he could comb grey hair?

A poem very different in tone, 'An Irish Airman Foresees his Death' (p. 152), reveals Robert Gregory as a Mask of the poet, demonstrating again Yeats's capacity for shaping events that touched him closely into the model of his thought. The stress on balance in the poem shows the force with which Yeats identified Robert Gregory as a man in that rare condition of unity and that for such men, who have seen all before they begin on their lives, the experience of death is acceptable, even in the right, heroic circumstances, desirable:

> A lonely impulse of delight
> Drove to this tumult in the clouds;
> I balanced all, brought all to mind,
> The years to come seemed waste of breath,
> A waste of breath the years behind
> In balance with this life, this death.

The relationship between the house and its inhabitants is reciprocal. They have each made the other. The house makes clear to those who live there the values of a different age and the people in turn give something to the house so that the best of the present age may be held in trust for the next. Now, however, the millenium approaches and all will be swept away, both people and place alike. Though there is comfort in the knowledge that men will build again, as far as the poet is concerned the memories, such as those revealed in *Autobiographies*, made Coole Park unique:

> A glimpse of a long vista of trees, over an undergrowth of clipped laurels, seen for a moment as the outside car approached her house on my first visit, is a vivid memory. Coole House, though it has lost the great park full of ancient trees, is still set in the midst of a thick wood, which spreads out behind the house in two directions, in one along the edges of a lake which, as there is no escape for its water except a narrow subterranean passage, doubles or trebles its size in winter. In later years I was to know the edges of the lake better than any spot on earth, to know it in all the changes of the seasons, to find there always some new beauty. Wondering at myself, I remember that when I first saw that house I was so full of the mediaevalism of William Morris that I did not like the gold frames, some deep and full of ornament, round the pictures in the drawing-room; years were to pass before I came to understand the earlier nineteenth and later eighteenth century, and to love that house more than all other houses.

So bound up with Yeats's vision of modern history was Coole Park that he could envisage with the vividness of actuality the destruction of the property even before it happened. He knew that its time had gone and with the passing of Lady Gregory, the content was buried, leaving only the shell of its former glories.

By the mid-nineteenth century Yeats considered that western civilization had almost reached the phase of the complete surrender of the will that is found at the moon's dark:

> I think of recent mathematical research; even the ignorant can compare it with that of Newton – so plainly of the Nineteenth Phase – with its objective world intelligible to intellect; I can recognise that the limit itself has become a new dimension, that the ever-hidden thing which makes us fold our hands has begun to press down upon multitudes. Having bruised their hands upon that limit, men, for the first time since the seventeenth century, see the world as an object of contemplation, not as something to be remade, and some few, meeting the limit in their special study, even doubt if there is any common experience, doubt the possibility of science.

Ultimately, for Yeats, history could not be planned but only made by people being true to what they are, by living in phase. An aristocratic age crumbles when its spirit hardens into hierarchical forms like the feudal system trying to live on its privileges while neglecting its responsibilities. This is the thought of the first part of the 'Meditations in Time of Civil War' (p. 225):

> O what if levelled lawns and gravelled ways
> Where slippered Contemplation finds his ease
> And Childhood a delight for every sense,
> But take our greatness with our violence?

On the other hand a democratic age ends by losing its awareness of God. It exalts equality for equality's sake in the cause of administrative efficiency. This was anathema to Yeats, for whom the personality of the individual was all important. His view with its supernaturalism and delight in life is essentially pagan, reaching back to the ancient Irish legends.

The terrible destruction and casual violence which he records in 'Meditations in Time of Civil War' are worked into the pattern of history expressed in the horror and bitterness of 'Nineteen Hundred and Nineteen' (p. 232). The vision of the collapse of a civilization into its dark chaos calls forth comparisons between Greek and Irish civilizations as the regret for the lost art of Athens

> And gone are Phidias' famous ivories
> And all the golden grasshoppers and bees

makes way for the ferocity of his reflections on the present state of his own land:

> We pieced our thoughts into philosophy,
> And planned to bring the world under a rule,
> Who are but weasels fighting in a hole.

Into the brutalities of the Troubles, Yeats reads two thousand years of human endeavour vanishing into the dark. The experience does not alter his philosophy, for he records without sentiment:

> But is there any comfort to be found?
> Man is in love and loves what vanishes,
> What more is there to say?

In 'Meditations in Time of Civil War' he acquiesces reluctantly in the demise of the great house culture and all it had been to him. He retreats, actually and symbolically, into the bare, simple tower of Ballylee as a refuge and contrast to all the prophesied destruction which is raging in actuality around him. The position of many of the *Last Poems* is already being taken up; not indifference, for he was still very much engaged in the affairs of the world, but that dispassionate quality which saw beyond the immediate devastation. Even in 'The Second Coming' (p. 210) where the image of the 'rough beast' almost overwhelms other considerations, there is a strong sense of the place of the age in the spectrum of eternity. Even as Christianity appeared terrifying and incomprehensible to the Greek civilization, so what is to come which cannot be predetermined, will appear to us as frightening in its aspect as must the Sphinx to those who preceded the great Egyptian age:

> A shape with lion body and the head of a man,
> A gaze blank and pitiless as the sun.

At the end there is nothing for it but to accept the great scheme and to remain true to that delight in life which has been the guiding principle almost from the first. Yeats looks into the dark, into the chaos, into Plato's cave and from beyond the world of nature comes the injunction which forms the key note of *Last Poems*, announced in 'The Gyres' (p. 337):

> What matter? Out of cavern comes a voice,
> And all it knows is that one word 'Rejoice'.

Looking back it comes as a shock to realize that this was the message so often trying to reach us in the earlier volumes.

PEOPLE

Sir Roger Casement (1864-1916)

In 1913 he retired from a distinguished life in the diplomatic service and became a member of *Sinn Fein*. When war broke out he was in Germany, seeking support for a rising. He spent the first year of the war trying to organise an Irish Brigade from prisoners of war. He returned to Ireland in 1916 in a German submarine to call off the rising. He was arrested on landing and took responsibility for the Rising which had begun already, thus allowing Ireland a public hearing through his own trial. After being convicted of treason against Britain, he was hanged in London. He was Knighted in 1911 for his work in exposing the atrocities in the Belgian Congo, and the Putamayo region of the Amazon.

James Connolly (1870-1916)

He was an Irish labour leader and one of the leaders of the Rising. In 1896 he founded the Irish Socialist Republican Party, and two years later launched *The Workers' Republic*, a militant Labour weekly. He organised and led the Citizen Army which was later transformed into the larger Volunteer force. In the Rising he was commandant of the force that occupied the General Post Office in Dublin. He was badly wounded in the fighting and after the surrender he was tried by court martial and sentenced to death. He was taken out on a stretcher, tied to a chair, and shot by firing squad.

Florence Farr (1860-1917)

She produced Yeats's *The Land of Heart's Desire* (written at her request) in 1894 and acted in *The Countess Cathleen* in 1899. In 1905 she arranged the performance of *The Shadowy Waters* at a Theosophical convention. She became an intimate friend of Yeats, and most probably was the one woman Yeats had loved before Maud Gonne entered his life. A mystic, an occultist and a feminist, she had a dynamic and unusual personality. Later she decided to abandon European civilization for the Orient, where she went in search of a spiritual life, taking up a teaching post at a Buddhist institute, Rasmanathan College, in Ceylon, where she died of cancer.

Oliver St. John Gogarty (1878-1957)

Gogarty, who was once likened to a Renaissance prince reigning over Dublin, was poet, surgeon, playwright, politician, aviator, Senator, classical scholar, and above all a wit. Joyce immortalized him as Buck Mulligan in *Ulysses*, and Yeats, with whom he enjoyed a lifetime of friendship, spoke of him as the most accomplished man in Dublin. Yeats first met Gogarty in 1901 and founded his version of *Oedipus Rex* on a verse translation especially prepared by Gogarty. They met often in later years and attended Senate meetings together. Gogarty was a prolific writer, his best works being *An Offering of Swans*, with a preface by Yeats, and *As I was Walking Down Sackville Street*, a record of the Dublin of his time.

Iseult Gonne (1894-1954)

She was Maud Gonne's illegitimate daughter. In 1917, after proposing to Maud for the last time and being rejected, Yeats in a desperate mood proposed to Iseult who also refused him. She had a warm affection for Yeats, but looked at him more as an uncle than a suitor. Iseult fascinated the poet, reminding him of her mother's dazzling beauty. In 1920 Iseult married the Irish novelist and poet Francis Stuart, whose autobiography *Things to Live For* tells the story of her life.

Maud Gonne (1866-1953)

She was the daughter of an English colonel. After a career as a governess and actress, she consecrated all her efforts to the cause of Irish Nationalism, her political outlook being both militant and violent. Yeats first met her in 1889, when she visited his father's home in Bedford Park. Yeats was overwhelmed by her beauty and immediately fell in love with her. He courted her with a steady devotion for thirteen years without success, expressing his hopeless love for her in numerous poems. She appears there under many guises: she is the Rose in the early poetry; the beautiful Deirdre, for whom Usna's sons died; and the classical Helen, who burnt the 'topless towers'. It is certain that her influence on Yeats was great and she was destined to change his whole attitude to life. Early in Yeats's poetry she is represented as a woman betrayed by a generous spirit, and it is with this tragic personality that she enters his system and mythology in *A Vision*. Despite Yeats's repeated proposals of marriage, she married Major John MacBride in 1903, but two years later the marriage broke up and the couple separated. After MacBride's death in 1916, Yeats renewed his proposal but was again refused. Nevertheless they remained close friends until the poet's death. In her autobiography *A Servant of the Queen*, Maud gives her version of her relationship with Yeats.

Eva (1870-1926) and Constance (1868-1927) Gore-Booth

Eva left Lissadell in 1897 to do social work in Manchester, becoming a powerful force behind the organization of women workers and the women's suffrage movement. Constance, once said to be the finest horsewoman in Ireland, left Lissadell for Paris in 1898. She studied painting there and married Count Casimir de Markiewicz, a Polish nobleman. The couple settled in Dublin where dissatisfaction with the social life turned Constance to revolutionary politics. She founded the Fianna Scouts; joined the Citizen Army in 1914; and in the Easter Rising acted as deputy-commander of the contingent which held Stephens' Green. After her surrender she was tried and condemned to death, but later reprieved on account of her sex. She was imprisoned in England, but on her release she returned to Ireland, where she became Minister of Labour in the Cabinet of the First Dail in 1919. She continued to play an active role in Irish politics until her last years, when she became a social worker in the Dublin slums.

Lady Gregory (1852-1932)

She was born (Isabella) Augusta Persse into a Protestant landed family in County Galway. She was introduced to the Irish myths and taught some Gaelic by the family nurse. When she was twenty-eight she married Sir William Gregory, the ex-Governor of Ceylon, who was sixty-three and the owner of Coole Park. When he died twelve years later, she devoted herself to making her home a sanctuary for writers and artists. Yeats collaborated with her on a number of literary projects and his experience of being received in her home shaped his attitude to the great house culture of the eighteenth century which he subsequently worked into his view of civilization. Lady Gregory's painful and brave struggle against cancer is recorded by Yeats in 'Coole Park and Ballylee, 1931' (p. 275).

Robert Gregory (1881-1918)

He was the only son of Lady Gregory, educated at Harrow School and Oxford. An interest in painting took him for a course of study at the Slade School of Art in London, where he married a fellow student in 1907. After a period in Paris he returned to spend most of his time at Coole Park. In October 1914 he exhibited his painting in London, and in 1915 he joined the army. In January

1916 he transferred to the Royal Flying Corps and later was awarded the 'Légion d'Honneur' and the Military Cross. On January 23, 1918 he was killed in action over the North Italian Front.

Georgie Hyde-Lees (1894-1968)

She married Yeats at the Harrow Road registry office in London on October 20, 1917. Ezra Pound was best man. There were two children, Michael and Anne. Mrs. Yeats became her husband's secretary, typing most of his work and sharing his interests in psychic research and spiritualism. During their honeymoon, Mrs. Yeats attempted automatic writing, and this became the basis of her husband's system of mystical philosophy as expounded in *A Vision*, on which much of his later poetry depends. After her husband's death, Mrs. Yeats preserved all his papers and made them available to scholars. She arranged her collection of Yeats MSS., and donated them to the National Library of Ireland.

John MacBride (1865-1916)

Major MacBride was well-known in Ireland as the leader of the pro-Boer Irish Brigade in South Africa. His two year marriage to Maud Gonne ended in separation. He played a leading part in the Rising, commanding the Jacob's factory garrison with Thomas MacDonagh. He was tried by court martial and shot.

Thomas MacDonagh (1878-1916)

He was a poet, critic and close friend of Patrick Pearse. He worked at St. Edna's with him and was therefore deeply committed to Ireland's cultural heritage.

MacGregor Mathers (1855-1918)

In 1889 Samuel Liddell Mathers translated *The Key of Solomon*, a book which besides containing much basic information concerning Cabbalistic lore, also included tables of geometrical patterns and stylized emblems which might be used for the evocation of spirits, together with instructions for their proper use. The book made a deep impression on Yeats, and the extent of Yeats's indebtedness to it may be measured by comparing his own designs in *A Vision* with those in *The Key of Solomon*. Another of Mathers' translations, *Kabbalah Unveiled* (1887), also influenced Yeats, providing inspiration for much of his major occult symbolism. Yeats first met Mathers at the British Museum, and it was he who was responsible for initiating Yeats into the Order of the

Golden Dawn. Shortly afterwards there was a threat of a great schism in the order as a result of Mathers' conduct. He was finally expelled from the order with a few others and created a new order, the Stella Matutina. Yeats took an active part in all this, and the episode is recorded in *Autobiographies* where considerable space is devoted to Mathers, who is described as 'a born teacher and organiser', but also as one who suffered from 'notable faults of temper and of mind.' He married the beautiful sister of Henri Bergson, the French philosopher, and in 1890 was appointed Curator of the Horniman Museum at Forest Hill, a post he lost after a quarrel. In 1891 he left England for France, where he lived in Paris until his death.

John O'Leary (1830-1907)

Born in Tipperary, he became a leading member of the Fenian organization while still a medical student at Trinity College, Dublin. He was arrested in 1865, chiefly on account of his anti-British articles in *The Irish People*, and after being tried and condemned for treason, he was sentenced to twenty years hard labour, which was remitted after he had spent five years in prison. He settled in Paris from 1870-1885, returning to Ireland as soon as it was possible for him to do so. He became President of the Young Ireland Society and of the Irish Republican Brotherhood. Yeats joined both organizations and took part in their debates. The first meeting between Yeats and O'Leary took place in 1886 at the Dublin Contemporary Club. It was from O'Leary that Yeats learnt his early lessons in nationalism, and to him he owed his newly found identity as an Irish poet writing for Ireland. Both agreed that what Ireland needed most was a great national literature of the first order, and it was towards fulfilling this purpose that Yeats directed all his efforts.

Charles Stewart Parnell (1846-1891)

He was leader of the Irish Parliamentary Party and a great advocate of Home Rule. At a time when all hopes for the cause of Irish independence were lost, Parnell seemed to be the one man who could succeed. Through his great gifts of eloquence and his even greater gifts of organization, the Irish Parliamentary Party was progressing rapidly towards Home Rule, but Parnell's chairmanship was terminated by a majority vote of his party on account of his affair with Mrs. Kitty O'Shea, whose husband filed divorce proceedings against his wife, citing Parnell as co-respondent. Divorce was granted on November 17, 1890 and Parnell was deposed nine days later, as a result of his followers in Parliament withholding their support. He died in October 1891, and although Yeats met the mail boat that brought his body back to Ireland, he did not attend the funeral because he shrank from vast crowds.

Patrick Pearse (1879-1916)

He was a poet and founder of St. Edna's School, Dublin. He had been attracted by the Gaelic movement at an early age, and thus founded his bilingual school to inculcate the idea of an independent, Gaelic Ireland. He played a dominant role in planning the Rising and he was elected President of the Provisional Government. Like MacDonagh, he was tried by court martial and shot.

George Pollexfen (1840-1910)

Yeats's maternal uncle was one of his father's early friends. In his youth he was a great horseman, but was also fascinated by magic and astrology, interests which lasted longer than his horsemanship. Yeats spent much time with him and with his housekeeper, the Mary Battle of *Autobiographies*, (see p. 36).

Ezra Pound (1885-1972)

An American poet and critic, he edited *Poetry* and *The Little Review*, two influential literary magazines, and composed a series of *Cantos*, a rambling, obscure piece of writing, supposedly modelled after the *Divine Comedy* of Dante. Pound will probably be remembered less for his own work than for his influence on other writers, notably T. S. Eliot and W. B. Yeats, both of whom readily acknowledged their debt to him. Before the First World War he became a leader of the Imagist Movement, a group of poets who favoured precise, 'hard, dry' images and rhythms close to everyday speech. In 1913 he became secretary to Yeats, whose poetry at this time began revealing traces of Imagist doctrine. Pound was also responsible for introducing Yeats to the world of the Japanese Noh play, a genre which influenced Yeats's dramatic writing after 1915.

Olivia Shakespear (1867-1938)

She was a beautiful and sensitive novelist, unhappily married to a barrister much older than herself. Yeats called her 'Diana Vernon' in manuscript notes of *Autobiographies* in order to hide her real identity. Yeats first met her through her cousin, Lionel Johnson, in 1894. The liaison began in 1895 and lasted for about a year while Yeats was still in love with Maud Gonne. At one time Yeats and Olivia Shakespear planned to elope, but Maud Gonne was never far enough from Yeats's mind. However, for a short time Yeats found solace in the arms of this talented woman. Although the love affair did not last, the friendship between them endured for over forty years, until her death. Yeats wrote a number of poems to her.

Shri Purohit Swami

Yeats met Shri Purohit Swami in London and went with him to Majorca in 1935 to work with him on a translation of the *Upanishads*. Yeats wrote introductions to two of the Swami's books and in the autobiography *An Indian Monk* wrote that it was 'something I have waited for since I was seventeen years old . . . bored by an Irish Protestant point of view that suggested by its blank abstraction chloride of lime'. Shri Purohit is the last major figure in Yeats's tradition of Indian thought that began with Mohini Chatterji and was carried on through Rabindranath Tagore. Yeats found in this branch of Indian thought that emphasis on the life of the soul which he found to be so lacking in western civilization. In 1937 *The Ten Principal Upanishads* was published by Faber, translated by Shri Purohit Swami and W. B. Yeats and with an introduction by W. B. Yeats.

John Millington Synge (1871-1909)

The outstanding example of a talent fostered by Yeats and the Abbey Theatre was the poet and dramatist Synge. Yeats met him in Paris in 1896 and encouraged him to go to the Aran Islands off the coast of Galway, suggesting that he turn his attention to writing drama which would reflect the lives of the islanders. This Synge did with considerable success, notably in *Riders to the Sea*. The production of his *The Playboy of the Western World* at the Abbey in 1907 provoked riots and furious controversy over its unflattering presentation of the Irish. Yeats was upset at his countrymen for their behaviour over the production and his dislike of the mass of the population and its political leaders increased still further.

Rabindranath Tagore (1861-1941)

One of India's most famous poets, he was born into a distinguished and aristocratic Bengali family, long associated with Indian nationalism. Yeats first met Tagore in 1912, helping him with the translation of his *Gitanjali*. Yeats expressed his admiration for Tagore enthusiastically in his introduction to this work, and in a preface written for Tagore's play *The Post Office*, produced by Yeats at the Abbey Theatre in 1913. Although Yeats was disappointed with some of Tagore's later work, the contact with him strengthened Yeats's early interests in the Orient, and further stimulated his studies into Eastern thought, religion and philosophy.

Dorothy Wellesley (1889-1956) (Lady Gerald Wellesley, later Duchess of Wellington)

She was a minor English poet, who was introduced to Yeats, who praised her work for its elemental imagery, masculine rhythm and precision of style. Yeats derived a great deal of friendship and literary opinion from his close relationship with Lady Dorothy, finding her, after the death of Lady Gregory, a representative of the traditional aristocratic culture he admired. Her house at Penns in Sussex represented for him what Coole Park had been once. She published the correspondence between W. B. Yeats and herself in *Letters on Poetry from W. B. Yeats to Dorothy Wellesley*, which is an excellent account of Yeats's thoughts about poetry and his own work during the last four years of his life.

John Butler Yeats (1839-1922)

The poet's father was critic, philosopher, painter and brilliant conversationalist. In 1857 he entered Trinity College, Dublin where he was expected to take orders but rejected a career in the Church, reading classics, metaphysics and logic instead. Despite a desire to be a painter he began to study law. In 1863 he married Susan Pollexfen, settling at Sandymount, Dublin. He was called to the bar in 1866 but gave it up a year later to study art in London, where he worked with Samuel Butler. Between 1872 and 1902 the family moved several times between England and Ireland. In 1908 he went to America for a brief visit, was welcomed by John Quinn (1870-1924), an American lawyer of Irish emigrant parentage, a close friend of both Yeats and his son, and stayed until his death. William was the only member of the family to visit him. His father exercised a strong influence on Yeats, helping him to develop an interest in drama, an acute appreciation for literature, and an independent outlook. See William M. Murphy's biography *Prodigal Father* (Cornell University Press, 1978) for the definitive 'life'.

Jack B. Yeats (1871-1957)

Artist and author, he was the youngest of John Butler Yeats's children. After passing most of his childhood in Sligo, he studied art at Westminster School and by 1900 had established himself as a cartoonist and illustrator. From 1887 to 1910 he worked mainly in pen and ink and water colour, but his reputation rests on his later oil paintings done between 1930 and 1955. His writings have received less attention, but he was a writer of novels, stories, memoirs and dramas. Despite rumours of strains in their relationship, Yeats wrote of his brother Jack in *On the Boiler* with enthusiasm and warmth when considering his prose work *A Charmed Life*, and at least one of his paintings, 'Memory Harbour', left an everlasting impression on Yeats.

PLACES

Sligo

The landscape of Yeats's childhood and youth and of his early poetry was the green alluvial plain of Sligo and the country immediately surrounding it, where Ben Bulben (the Peak of Gulba) and Knocknarea (the Hill of the Storms) dominate the scene. This area of the west coast of Ireland seemed to have remained untouched by the forces which were robbing Europe of its countryside and, according to Yeats, was a place 'where you can wander without aim, and where you can never know from one day's adventure what may meet you with tomorrow's sun.' The whole area was rich in historical and legendary associations: it was the arena of great battles fought between the men of Ulster and the men of Connacht, and the names of Ailill, Maeve, Cuchulain, Finn, Oisin, Diarmuid and Grainne, and even St. Patrick were associated with the footpaths Yeats trod. The landscape and people of Sligo proved to be a life-long inspiration to the poet, and it was there that he asked to be buried. Nine years after his death, his body was interred in Drumcliff churchyard, not far from 'a little two-storeyed house,' once the home of John Yeats, the poet's great-grandfather, one time Rector of Drumcliff. See T. R. Henn's essay 'The Place of Shells' in his *Last Essays* (Colin Smythe, 1976).

Lissadell

The home of the Gore-Booth family, it was built in 1832 and stands ten miles from Sligo and five from Drumcliff. A late Georgian mansion of dark grey granite, it is surrounded by tall trees that stretch to the sands of Lissadell Bay. The southern aspect of the house looks out over the bay onto a magnificent scene from Rosses Point to Knocknarea. Yeats visited Lissadell sometime in 1894, and met the two daughters of the house, Constance and Eva. Like Coole Park, Lissadell became part of Yeats's mythology, representing the fast-disappearing aristocratic traditions and way of life. The picture Yeats remembered of the two girls in their days of youth formed part of that world he saw diminishing in grandeur and importance, and when they died, he wrote an elegy for that lost way of life, 'In Memory of Eva Gore-Booth and Constance

Markiewicz' (p. 263).

Coole Park

This was the home of the Gregory family for two hundred years until 1932. Set in an open park, it gave an impression of homeliness rather than the more formidable defensive qualities of the typical great house. The sturdy facade was broken by a semicircular Palladian window above a square porch. Victorian bay windows overlooked the lake on the west side. In the eighteenth century Richard Gregory collected a fine library to which Lady Gregory added after the death of her husband. In 1898 when Yeats first went to Coole, he was in poor health and without a home. Lady Gregory acted as a nurse to him as well as supplying the conditions in which Yeats could work. He wrote later, 'I found at last what I have been seeking always, a life of order, and of labour, where all outward things were the image of an inward life.' From this time on Yeats's poetry is full of images drawn from the landscape of Coole which gave their names to two of the collections, *In The Seven Woods* and *The Wild Swans At Coole*. Coole became the embodiment for Yeats of the eighteenth century tradition of aristocratic living, which combined the virtues of nobility with those of intellect. Yeats paid this tribute to Coole Park in a talk he gave for the B.B.C. in 1937:

> From my twenty-seventh year until a few years ago all my public activities were associated with a famous country house in County Galway. In that house my dear friend, that woman of genius, Lady Gregory, gathered from time to time all men of talent, all profound men, in the intellectual life of modern Ireland.

Thoor Ballylee

Thoor Ballylee, in the Barony of Kiltartan in County Galway, was bought by Yeats for £35 in 1917, becoming the home of Yeats and his family from 1918 for the following ten years. Originally a Norman tower known as Islandmore Castle or Ballylee Castle, it was given its new name by Yeats to escape 'from the too magnificent word "castle",' the softer 'Thoor' being Gaelic for tower. When Yeats bought the tower it was in ruins, and considerable reconstruction was needed to make it habitable. The tower with its seventy three stairs from entrance to battlement consisted of the ground-floor, which was the Dining Room, and three other floors. The first was the Living Room; the second the Bedroom; and the third the Strangers' Room, off which opened the tiny, dark 'Secret Room'. The great windows of the tower opened on the millstream rushing below. Yeats found the tower 'full of history and romance' and acquired it 'as a permanent symbol of [his] work visible to the passer-by.' In 1965 the restoration was completed with funds from the Irish Tourist Board.

Dublin

Yeats lived in several different parts of Dublin in the course of his life. He was born at 'Georgeville', No. 2 Sandymount Avenue, a six-roomed, semi-detached house in a quiet residential suburb on the edge of the city. Nearby Sandymount Castle was owned by the poet's great-uncle, Robert Corbet. It was another eighteenth century 'great house' with imitation Gothic additions to which the Yeats family went often. The largest church ever built in Ireland is Dublin's St. Patrick's Cathedral on the site of a pre-Norman church, associated by legend with the Saint. Many of the great servants of Ireland lie inside it including Jonathan Swift, Dean of the Cathedral Chapter from 1713-1745, who was much loved and admired by Yeats. After Yeats's death the Dean of the Cathedral wrote to Mrs. Yeats suggesting that the poet be buried in the Cathedral. She declined because Yeats had already signified that he wished to be buried in Sligo. Another building that dominates the imagination of the Dublin people is the General Post Office with its classical columns at the front in Sackville Street (now renamed O'Connell Street). It was all but destroyed in the Rising when it was the headquarters of insurgents. Now only the front remains and inside is a statue commemorating the Rising, *The Death of Cuchulain*. Between 1922 and 1928 the Yeats family lived at 82 Merrion Square, the finest Georgian square in Dublin. It was built during the time of Grattan's Parliament at the end of the eighteenth century, the period much admired by Yeats. The house contained several large rooms including a double drawing-room where Yeats held literary evenings. For several years the centre of Yeats's activity in Dublin was the Abbey Theatre, which opened on Tuesday, December 27, 1904. One entrance opened onto Abbey Street, while the main one was in Marlborough Street. Entering through the double glass doors into the small lobby, the play-goer would be confronted by the portraits which hung around its walls of such as Lady Gregory and Miss Horniman. The intimate theatre managed to seat about five hundred people in close contact with the stage. The present day New Abbey Theatre is built on the site of the original and has a main auditorium and a studio theatre.

PART 3
SUMMARIES & COMMENTARIES

CROSSWAYS (1889)

The title 'Crossways' was chosen because Yeats 'tried many pathways' in this collection. Concerning the date of the poems he wrote in 1925 that

> Many of the poems in *Crossways*, certainly those upon Indian subjects or upon shepherds and fauns, must have been written before I was twenty, for from the moment I began *The Wanderings of Oisin*, which I did at that age, I believe, my subject matter became Irish.

Despite the extensive revisions to which the collection was subject, the essentially Pre-Raphaelite flavour remains. The treatment of pastoral and classical themes is romantic in the tradition of Shelley and Keats. When the subject matter becomes first Indian and then Irish the style remains the dreamy, epithet-laden one of the poet who imagines his art as an escape from the world. Isolation is the essential prerequisite for the poet's contemplation of his own emotional state, which is always more vivid than the misty background of the dream world in which the internal drama is played out.

At this time in his career Yeats was involved with the fashionable poets of London literary circles, notably Johnson and Dowson, who modelled their poetic style on that of the previous generation of poets and prose writers, Rossetti, Swinburne, Ruskin and Pater. The style was ornate, dreamy and concerned with art in preference to life. Yeats's own father was a Pre-Raphaelite painter in this school and passed the influence on to his son. Yeats mixes in his more personal influences such as Blake, Shelley, Spenser and the speculations derived from his theosophical studies, but the style of the collection is still essentially a borrowed one.

The poems in this section were first brought together as a collection under this title in *Poems* (1895), though most had been published in Yeats's early books or in periodicals before this date.

THE SONG OF THE HAPPY SHEPHERD

First Line: 'The woods of Arcady are dead,'

Collection: 'Crossways' (1889)

Original Titles: An Epilogue To 'The Island of Statues' and 'The Seeker', 'Song of the Last Arcadian'

First Published: *The Dublin University Review,*, October 1885

Summary:
The age of the ancients is long passed and the modern world feeds on facts not dreams. The glorious deeds of a mythical past are now only preserved in the power of the word. The search for action and truth in the external world is futile, since they exist only in the dreams and heart of the solitary man. It is better to tell your story to a sea shell which will transform it into song. The shepherd must leave to sing of the old days to the spirit of a faun. He goes, exhorting the reader to dream.

The first stanza opens with a lament for the passing of the Arcadian world and its attendant 'joy'. That world lived by 'dreaming' while the present one survives on 'grey Truth'. However, the world still looks back to those days which can now only be reached, through all the changes that Time has flashed past us, by words. What has become of the old warrior kings who mocked words by the actions of their noble lives? They live only through the stories written of them which are forced on unwilling school children. The world itself may only be a word, heard for an instant in the eternity of the dream.

Stanza two urges the reader not to look for truth among the 'deeds' of the world around him but to search for it in his 'own heart'. Nothing can be learnt from the astronomers for their star-gazing has killed any imaginative grasp of 'human truth'. Instead go to the shore and tell your tale to a shell which will act upon it like a poet, changing it to song with the melodies of the sea, until the song itself fades away into the eternal 'for words alone are certain good'.

In stanza three the shepherd tells us he must be gone to serenade the grave of a young deer 'before the dawn'. The deer enjoyed a happy existence and the shepherd dreams that its ghost is cheered by hearing of the olden times of 'earth's dreamy youth'. The earth no longer dreams so 'thou', the spirit of the faun and the reader, must dream instead to find the truth.

Glossary:

1 'Arcady'	The ideal rural paradise of the ancient world.
9 'Chronos'	The Greek god of Time. Father of Zeus, Poseidon, Hera and other gods and goddesses.
12 'Word be-mockers'	The warring kings are men of action not words.
12 'Rood'	The cross of Christ.
23 'Sooth'	Poetic word for 'truth'.
29 'Optic glass'	Telescope.
32 'Bane'	Poetic word for ruin or cause of sorrow.
33 'Cloven'	Split in two.
41 'ruth'	Pity.
56 'poppies'	The juice of the poppy possesses narcotic qualities.

Commentary:
The poem reflects Yeats's early devotion to Spenser and Keats. The romantic treatment of a pastoral theme has not yet been replaced by the Irish material. He sings of 'Arcady' not Eire, but the 'warring kings' are already waiting at the edge of the poem. The frequent use of consciously poetic words such as 'bane' and 'sooth' and the deliberate archaisms like 'be-mockers' shows that the poet's style is not yet fully formed. The long vowels of the heavy but abundant epithets which clog the pace of the poem are a legacy of the Pre-Raphaelites, contributing such words as 'dreary', 'dusty', 'pearly' and 'dreamy'.

However, the poem contains an important statement of the poet's image of himself. He recognises the need to place himself outside the world of common things if he is to find his vocation as a poet. It is a solitary role requiring great introspection. His own created world, the world achieved by dreaming must be made more real than the world itself. The shepherd is happy because he has found a means of recreating his experience. He states with confidence his basic credo that 'words alone are certain good'. He finds his own rather than borrowed words for the climax of the first stanza.

THE SAD SHEPHERD

First Line: 'There was a man whom Sorrow named his friend'

Collection: 'Crossways' (1889)

Original Title: Miserrimus

First Published: *The Dublin University Review*, October 1886

Summary:
A shepherd in a sorrowful state tries to tell his story to the stars, then to the sea, and finally the dewdrops. None of them will listen. So he picks up a shell on the shore in the hope that he will draw comfort from hearing his own words echoed back to him. But when he sings the shell only returns an 'inarticulate moan'.

The poet tells of a man whose only companion is 'Sorrow'. This shepherd walks with his friend along the 'sands' in the wind to experience the presence of sorrow more intensely. He asks the 'stars' to 'comfort' him but they are too involved in their own mirth and song. He calls on the 'dim sea' to be an audience to his tale but she stays lost in her own 'dreams'. Fleeing the shore he pours out 'his story' to the 'dewdrops' he finds in a 'gentle valley' but they do not hear his words because they are listening for 'the sound of their own dropping'. The sorrowing man then returns to the 'shore' and, finding 'a shell', thinks that if he tells his story to the shell it will return his own words into his 'hollow, pearly heart' and the comfort of the words may lift his 'ancient burden' from him. So he sings to the lip of the shell but it too is sad and transforms his song to a noise he cannot understand and forgets about him in comforting herself.

Glossary

4	'where windy surges wend'	Where gusts of wind blow.
9	'Dim sea'	The sea is the Neo-Platonic symbol for the process of daily life.
15	'Naught'	Nothing.
25	'nigh the pearly rim'	Close to the lip of the pearl-coloured shell.
26	'lone'	Uninhabited, lonely.
28	'wildering'	Bewildering.

Commentary:
This pastoral lyric is written to accompany *The Song Of The Happy*

Shepherd. This shepherd is sad because, unlike his counterpart in the earlier poem, he finds no means of recreating his life in art. Thus 'the song' is missing from the title even as it is missing from the poem. The shepherd, the standard personification for the poet in pastoral lyrics, seeks out a desolate place which should be appropriate for inspiring his verses even as melancholy seems an appropriate state of mind. Again the rhythms are heavy and sonorous and the phrases ('pale thrones', 'pearly rim') Pre-Raphaelite. Yet though language and image are still derivative, the will to be a poet is strong.

THE INDIAN UPON GOD

First Line: 'I passed along the water's edge below the humid trees,'

Collection: 'Crossways' (1889)

Original Title: From the Book of Kauri the Indian — Section V. On the Nature of God

First Published: *The Dublin University Review*, October 1886

Summary:
The Indian sets the mood for the poem by describing the peaceful condition of his spirit in a landscape which is itself a reflection of his inner harmony. He then hears the various creatures which comprise the scene speak to him. The moorfowl, the roebuck and the peacock each tell him that their notion of God is a perfect specimen of themselves.

Glossary:

1 'humid' damp.
2 'rushes' marsh plants.
3 'moorfowl' water-birds.
6 'bill' beak.
9 'lotus' kind of water-lily; one of the sacred symbols of Hinduism and Buddhism.
11 'tinkling' sound like a small bell.
13 'roebuck' type of deer.
14 'Stamper' one who makes a downward beat with the foot.
17 'peacock' male bird with brilliant plumage.
20 'languid' drooping for lack of vitality.
20 'myriad' vast number.

Commentary:
This is one of three poems in the collection which shows the influence Hindu thought had on Yeats after he heard the Brahmin Mohini Chatterjee talk in Dublin in 1886. The language of the poem with its heavy, slow-moving adjectives reinforces the poet's tendency to overwork epithets in this period of his writing. The idealised landscape serves to isolate him further from the experiences of the living world. But while the style of the poem is one which he later abandoned, much of the thought was to remain with Yeats to become influential in shaping the evolution of his art. The vision of God for each of the creatures mentioned is entirely subjective, pointing to the denial of a materialist, objective view of the world and asserting the primacy of the individual soul in the search for eternal absolutes pursued not in death but through life lived at its fullest. The poem thus indicates how early in his career the poet was starting to formulate the central concepts of his philosophy even though the expression of these concepts is derivative and self-consciously poetic.

DOWN BY THE SALLEY GARDENS

First Line: 'Down by the salley gardens my love and I did meet;'

Collection: 'Crossways' (1889)

Original Title: An old song resung

First Published: *Poems* (1895)

Summary:
This two-stanza poem which became popularised as a folk song expresses the moral that love and life should both be 'taken easy' if they are to be without trial and tribulation. The poet learns a lesson from what is natural in life ('the leaves on the tree', 'a field by the river', and 'the grass on the weirs') and from the loved one of the poem with her 'snow-white feet' and 'snow-white hand' who is a spirit of nature. It is a modified version of a folk song.

Glossary:
1 'salley' Willow.
7 'weirs' Dams across the river.

Commentary:
In a note to the edition of 1899 Yeats called the poem 'an extension of three lines of a folk song sung to me by an old woman of Ballisodare'.

THE BALLAD OF MOLL MAGEE

First Line: 'Come round me, little childer;'

Collection: 'Crossways' (1889)

Original Title:

First Published: *The Wanderings of Oisin and Other Poems* (1889)

Summary:
Moll Magee tells her story to an audience of children from whom she asks pity. Her husband was a fisherman and she worked all day in the sheds by the shore, salting the herrings. Exhausted from her work, she returned to attend to her new-born baby. She fell asleep on top of the baby and killed her. As a consequence her husband gave her some money and sent her away. When the money had gone she found a friend to tell her story to. The friend says her husband will come for her. But Moll grieves all the time for the child, comforting herself with the belief that she is in heaven seeing God looking down on poor people like herself. Having heard the story, she hopes the children will no longer throw stones at her.

Glossary:

1 'childer'	children.
3 'mutter'	talking quietly to herself.
6 'say'	sea.
12 'pebbly'	road made of pebble stones.
13 'weakly'	weak.
16 'morn'	morning.
24 'Kinsale'	fishing port in Co. Cork.
32 'boreen'	Irish word for lane.
34 'byre'	cow shed.
40 'sup'	soup.
42 'agin'	again.
48 'keenin'	wailing a song of grief.
49 'she'	the dead child.

Commentary:
This ballad is from the group of poems which mark Yeats's turning to Irish material for the substance of his verse. In taking a story from Irish peasant life Yeats suggests, even this early, his intention of becoming the cultural historian of the Irish nation. The attempt at simplicity is weakened by the self-conscious poeticisms and the borrowed style which extends to the standard sentimental view of God as guardian of the poor. Nevertheless the ballad form helps to strip much of the dream-laden language so that the narrative can advance unhindered.

THE ROSE
(1893)

The Rose poems were gathered under this title according to the poet because in them 'he has found, he believes, the only pathway whereon he can hope to see with his own eyes the Eternal Rose of Beauty and of Peace'. This group of poems deals with three main areas; personal, occult and Irish. The first area centres on his frustrated love for Maud Gonne, the single person whose shadow falls longest across the early collections. The second area arises out of Yeats's knowledge of the Rosicrucian and cabalistic doctrine that he acquired in the Order of the Golden Dawn and which provided him with both the rose and the tree symbolism. The third area, following on from *The Wanderings of Oisin*, is served by the ancient fables of pre-Christian Ireland, specifically the saga concerning the heroes of Ulster, Cuchulain, Fergus and King Conchubar.

The collection shows important advances on the previous one. Yeats is beginning to incorporate his own most deeply felt experience into the body of his lyrics even though the manner of that incorporation is still self-consciously poetic. The feelings aroused in him by Maud Gonne are the main source of the raw material for the best of his earlier poetic work. Though literary poses are being struck, an element of the real feeling informs the verses.

Another element destined to feed into the poetry for the rest of Yeats's work is that of the Irish legends. He was by now seeing himself as the poet of the Irish nation, responsible for restoring their noble traditions to the Irish people. The focus for this movement is the figure of Cuchulain who is introduced in this collection and who was destined to become the Mask of the poet himself. At the end of his life Yeats was still putting the stories of Cuchulain into the forms of his art.

The collection shows Yeats starting to use symbolism as a structural device not only within the same poem but also to unify the whole collection. The use of the rose for this purpose anticipates a similar practice with, for example, the wild swans and the winding stair, and, most notably, the tower. Here the rose is essentially a symbol borrowed from occult and literary sources, whereas most of the later ones will be personal symbols made universal through their contexts.

The poems in this section were first brought together under this heading in *Poems* (1895), but Yeats added 'Who Goes with Fergus' and 'To Some I have Talked with by the Fire' when they were printed in *Collected Poems*.

TO THE ROSE UPON THE ROOD OF TIME

First Line: 'Red Rose, proud Rose, sad Rose of all my days!'

Collection: 'The Rose' (1893)

Original Title:

First Published: *The Countless Kathleen and Various Legends and Lyrics* (1892)

Summary:
The poet asks the Rose, symbol of perfect beauty, to be near to inspire him while he recounts the old tales such as Cuchulain's fight with the sea, Fergus and the Druid and the sadness of the Rose herself. Her presence will enable the poet to find an element of the immortal in all that is mortal. In the second stanza he again asks for the Rose to approach but not too close in case she should so overwhelm his imagination that she would cut him off entirely from the life of the earth that surrounds the poet in the present. In the last couplet he summons her again for she must be close by if he is to sing of times past and things long dead.

Glossary:

Title: To The Rose Upon The Rood Of Time	In Rosicrucian symbolism a conjunction of the feminine rose and the cross forms a mystic marriage of immortal perfection.
3 'Cuchulain'	The legendary champion of Ulster and Ireland's greatest warrior. He became for Yeats the chief representative of the heroic age which the poet hoped Ireland would recreate.
4 'The Druid'	The Druids were priests of a pre-Christian religion with magical powers.
5 'Fergus'	Fergus MacRoy, King of Ulster, who sought wisdom from the Druid.
7 'silver-sandalled'	The stars are pictured wearing sandals of a silver colour to dance in.

10 'boughs'	Branches of a tree.
21 'chaunt'	Chant.
23 'Eire'	The ancient kingdom of all Ireland; originally a name of the Tuatha de Danaan or tribes of the goddess Dana.

Commentary:
This two-stanza lyric poem in heroic couplets invokes the spirit of the 'red Rose' which is to inspire Yeats in the writing of *The Rose* collection. The poem acts as an introduction for this collection, announcing the major themes of 'old Eire and the ancient ways' and the occult mysticism of the 'high and lonely melody'. As in other early poems the verses are over-loaded with vague adjectives while the regularity of the end-stopped lines adds to the rather ponderous movement. This effect is lessened by the alliterations and internal rhythms, anticipating later aspects of Yeats's technique. The poem reflects Yeats's reading during this period: inevitably the ethereal quality drawn from the Pre-Raphaelites but more specifically the influences of Shelley who gave to the Rose an aspect of its symbolism – Intellectual Beauty – and Blake whom Yeats was editing at this time. ('The weak worm' for instance is Blake's symbol for mortal, common things.)

The strength of the poem is derived from the tension revealed by its title between immortality and mortality. The Rose is identified as 'Eternal Beauty' but it can only be perceived in such things as an actual rose which must die. Thus while the poet wishes to experience the influence of the Rose, he does not wish to be overwhelmed totally by its power and so lose contact with this world. He would rather forgo his art at the intersection of the two worlds where a man may sense the presence of the immortals without becoming blind to 'common things'. The conflict between the solitary, dreaming poet and the artist who was to fight his battles in this world is already signalled in this poem.

FERGUS AND THE DRUID

First Line: *Fergus*. 'This whole day have I followed in the rocks,'

Collection: 'The Rose' (1893)

Original Title:

First Published: *The National Observer,* 21 May 1892

Summary:
Fergus has been following the Druid who has used his magical powers to take on the shape of the raven and the weasel until he has finally appeared to Fergus in the shape of a man. Fergus tells the Druid how he bequeathed his kingdom to Conchubar when it had become a burden to him. But he has not been able to shake off his kingly feelings as easily as the crown itself and so has come to the Druid for the unearthly wisdom which can liberate him. The Druid shows Fergus his frail appearance and tells him he cannot fight, has not been loved by woman, nor been a help to man. Fergus nevertheless describes a king as one who labours and dies for the dreams of others. Then the Druid gives Fergus a bag of dreams which, when opened, will attach themselves to him. With this power Fergus can see his previous incarnations as a water-drop, a ray of light, a fir-tree, a labourer and a king. The knowledge, though, has not fulfilled him but left him empty. Now he understands the terrible price of the Druid's gift.

Glossary:

1 'lingered'	Remained.
10 'Conchubar'	Ancient King of Ulster whose war-chief was Cuchulain.
35 'quern'	A hand-mill for grinding corn.
40 'small slate-coloured thing!'	Early versions read: 'small slate-coloured bag of dreams'.

Commentary:
Part of the promise to tell the ancient tales of his country delivered in the previous poem, is fulfilled here through the device of a conversation between King Fergus and a Druid, indicating Yeats's growing interest in dramatic composition. The King and the Druid represent the opposite poles of active and passive, waking and dreaming, in the world and out of the world. They are another

version of that tension between the mortal and the immortal described in 'To A Rose Upon The Rood Of Time'. The Druid inhabits any shape he chooses but belongs to none whereas Fergus, whatever he tries to help him forget his existence, is trapped in the prison of his kingship: 'And still I feel the crown upon my head'. The Druid's 'dreaming wisdom' has been achieved at the expense of participation in life. While he knows all, he has felt nothing. Fergus in taking the 'little bag of dreams' exchanges feeling for knowledge but the ability to see all his former incarnations has revealed the pointlessness of all human activity so that now he has 'grown nothing'. The poem reflects the poet's experience of contrary impulses: the one towards an aloof, ascetic contemplation which will bring knowledge without understanding, and the other towards the experiencing of all emotions ending in the futility of death.

CUCHULAIN'S FIGHT WITH THE SEA

First Line: 'A man came slowly from the setting sun,'

Collection: 'The Rose' (1893)

Original Title: The Death of Cuchullin

First Published: *United Ireland*, 11 June 1892

Summary:
A man comes to Emer where she is weaving and dyeing and tells her that the object of his watch is approaching. Emer asks why he is so afraid of this event and the man replies that the approaching man is bringing his young mistress with him. Emer goes with the watchman who is her son and tells him his life as a herdsman does not fit his status. She tells him that the man who is coming must die and though her son is in awe of the man's power in battle he asks her where this adversary can be found.

Emer tells him to approach the camp of the noble warriors of Ulster and to announce his name only 'at sword-point' and to wait for the man who has sworn to the same oath. Among the knights in camp is Cuchulain whose exploits are being celebrated in song. He tells someone to discover the identity of the man who waits in the wood. The messenger informs Cuchulain that the stranger will only give his name upon compulsion and challenges the man who has sworn the same oath. Cuchulain himself is this man and he goes out to fight. Cuchulain asks the man if he wishes to die that he dares to fight with him and says that the man's face reminds him of a woman he once loved. Cuchulain deals the man a fatal blow and hears him name himself Cuchulain's son before he dies.

Glossary:

Title: 'Cuchulain'	See gloss to 'To A Rose Upon The Rood Of Time' line 3.
2 'Emer'	Wife of Cuchulain.
2 'raddling raiment in her dun,'	Dyeing clothes in red ochre in her fortress.
6 'web'	The cloth which she has woven.
11 'cars'	Chariots.
13 'blench'	Flinch.
16 'one'	Eithne Inguba, Cuchulain's mistress.
16 'sweet-throated'	With a melodious voice.
17 'You dare me to my face'	You are bold enough to say such things directly to me.
21 'herd'	Herdsman.
33 'The Red Branch Camp'	The camp of Ulster's noblest warriors belonging to the order of the Red Branch.
36 'lineage'	Line from which a man is descended.
45 'Conchubar'	King of Ulster and Cuchulain's lord.
46 'brazen strings'	Strings the colour of brass.
48 'amid'	In the middle of.
64 'sped'	Prospered.
76 'Druids'	Priests with magical powers.
79 'raving'	In a rage of madness.
80 'chaunt'	Chant.
86 'the invulnerable tide'	The sea which cannot be harmed by blows.

Commentary:

This poem forms part of a large body of work on Cuchulain which Yeats created throughout his writing life. The only other poem to deal specifically with Cuchulain is the late one, 'Cuchulain Comforted', for the bulk of the material comes in the five plays which make up the Cuchulain cycle: *At The Hawk's Well, The Green Helmet, On Baile's Stand, The Only Jealousy Of Emer* and *The Death of Cuchulain*. The events covered in 'Cuchulain's Fight With The Sea' are recreated in the earliest of these plays, *On Baile's Strand* (1904). It is clear from the poem itself that the events of

Cuchulain's life were conceived by the poet in dramatic form since the narrative immediately gives way to dialogue as the poem proceeds by confrontations between pairs of characters. The theme, with its inversion of the Oedipus myth, reaches back to the oldest dramatic archetypes as well as the deepest recesses of the poet's sub-conscious fears of childlessness and Oedipal guilts.

Actually, Cuchulain was many things for Yeats: a national symbol; the image of the brave and noble man, the man of action he longed to become; a symbol for his struggle for his country's intellectual freedom; an embodiment of his heroic-aristocratic philosophy. He was a human redeemer – but, above all, the chief representative of the heroic age which Yeats hoped Ireland would recreate and relive.

THE ROSE OF THE WORLD

First Line: 'Who dreamed that beauty passes like a dream?'

Collection: 'The Rose' (1893)

Original Title: *Rosa Mundi*

First Published: *National Observer*, 2 January 1892

Summary:
The first line questions the idea, often held by poets, that beauty does not last. As illustration the poet points to two ideal figures of beauty, Helen and Deirdre, for whom men were prepared to die. The idea of the permanence of beauty is developed in the second verse where the eternal 'lonely face' of beauty is contrasted with the impermanence of mortal men and the material world itself. The third verse extends the idea further, commanding God's angels to show respect for this vision of eternal beauty which predates their own existence as well as that of all mortal men. God in fact made the world itself for this immortal rose.

Glossary:

3 'betide'	happen.
4 'Troy'	Troy was burnt in the war between the Greeks and the Trojans.
5 'Usna's children'	most famous of whom was Deirdre whose beauty provoked death and destruction among the old folk heroes of Ireland.

7 'waver'	falter.
8 'race'	fast-flowing channel of water.
9 'foam of the sky'	clouds.
11 'archangels'	highest ranks of angels.
13 'lingered'	stayed.

Commentary:
While the language of this poem is typical of Yeats's insubstantial, dream-laden style of this period, its structure is that of a closely worked lyric which develops a single idea with exquisite logic. From the opening challenge to the conventional position, the poet proceeds to his proof by means of his all-embracing symbol for things eternal, the rose. Here, as elsewhere, the presence of the immortal in a mortal world is confirmed for him by Maud Gonne who in turn represents Helen of Troy and, on this occasion, Deirdre as well. The poem indicates the depth of the influence of Platonism on Yeats's thinking during this period with this confident statement that essence or pure form precedes existence. Much of the tightness of the poem's concept stems from the combination of the rhyme scheme (abbab) with the metrical pattern (55553) which serves to slow down and stress the shortened final line of each verse. The elusive symbol of the rose again stands for the embodiment of eternal elements located in this life.

THE LAKE ISLE OF INNISFREE

First Line: 'I will arise and go now, and go to Innisfree,'

Collection: 'The Rose' (1893)

Original Title:

First Published: *National Observer*, 13 December 1890

Summary:
A poetic dream of an idyllic existence to which the poet 'will arise and go now'. The natural setting of Innisfree – plants and vegetables, materials, insects, and climate, as well as the glade and the water – contrasts sharply with 'the roadway' and 'the pavements grey', on which the poet stands as he muses.

Glossary:

2 'wattles'	Twigs interlaced to make a wall.
4 'glade'	Space between trees.
8 'linnet'	Small song-bird.
10 'lapping'	Sound made by the ripples on the lake against the bank.
12 'core'	Innermost part.

Commentary:
Yeats called this poem: 'my first lyric with anything in its rhythm of my own music'. It expresses his desire to escape from London into the rural landscape of his childhood in County Sligo. While he later expressed displeasure at the Biblical opening of the poem and the inversion of the second line, there is a simplicity of style emerging from the misty poeticism of the Celtic Twilight and a personal rhythm felt in a line such as:

> 'I hear lake water lapping with low sounds by the shore'.

THE SORROW OF LOVE

First Line: 'The brawling of a sparrow in the eaves,'

Collection: 'The Rose' (1893)

Original Title:

First Published: *The Countess Kathleen and Various Legends and Lyrics* (1892)

Summary:
The first stanza presents the reader with a scene of natural order and harmony which keeps all pictures and sounds of men out of the poet's mind. Then the image of a girl appears to him bringing with her the terrible destruction of ancient civilization. Her effect on the scene is to change harmony to discord. The same elements which made up the opening picture of order without humanity now form themselves into a lament to accompany the appearance of human form into the scene.

Glossary:

1 'The brawling of a sparrow in the eaves'	The noisy quarreling of a sparrow under the roof.

4 'blotted out'	completely hidden.
5 'A girl'	Helen of Troy, Yeats's usual symbol for Maud Gonne.
7 'Odysseus'	He sailed with the Greek fleet to recover Helen. His twenty year adventures returning from Troy to Ithaca are told in Homer's *Odyssey*.
8 'Priam'	Last king of Troy; father of Hector, Paris and Cassandra.
9 'clamorous'	The eaves are full of the discordant noise of the sparrows.

Commentary:
This is one of a group of poems in the volume written for Maud Gonne and was subject later to very careful revision. It is built on the contrast between the first and last verse – two scenes apparently identical but represented in contrasting moods. The reason for this contrast is supplied by the central verse which introduces the agent of disorder, the girl who embodies a destructive passion. In the person of Helen of Troy, one of Yeats's most important symbols, the paradox of perfect beauty as the source of destruction for human ambition is explored for the first of many times in Yeats's poetry. At the level of Helen, the girl prefigures the later civilization poems, but as Maud Gonne she represents those forces of passion which draw the poet away from the isolated, lonely world of his earliest poems. This poem draws much of its power from the pun on 'arose' (a rose) which sets up the conflict between the ideal abstraction of perfect beauty which the rose symbolizes throughout this collection and the actual girl responsible for so much ugliness and death in the real world. The 'sorrow' may be love's destructive and unrequited parts but in turning the poet's attention to 'man's image and his cry', love is serving the cause of art in pushing Yeats down the path which was to make him a great poet of the human condition.

THE TWO TREES

First Line: 'Beloved, gaze in thine own heart,'

Collection: 'The Rose' (1893)

Original Title:

First Published: *The Countess Kathleen and Various Legends and Lyrics* (1892)

Summary:

In the first verse the poet asks his loved one to perceive the Tree of Life which is growing in her heart. It is a fertile, leafy and fruit-laden tree which creates both beauty and harmony in the individual soul and in the universe.

Verse two invokes the spectre of another Tree, the Tree of Knowledge with its images of the fallen world. This is a winter tree, broken and sterile. The picture which dry thought conjures up is not of the soul's immortality but the body's decay. Like the tree in a dead season, the body must be destroyed and abstract thought, associated with evil spirits ('demons') and 'the raven', the bird of death, will speed up the progress of the body towards its night.

Glossary:

2 'The holy tree'	The Sephirotic tree of the Cabbala and the tree of knowledge. In Cabbalistic tradition the Tree of Life is an apple tree growing from earth to the apex of heaven with the sun and moon for its fruit. The souls of the dead and angels perch in its branches and beasts and fallen angels live in its shade. Blake suggested the opposition of the Tree of Knowledge to the Tree of Life to Yeats.
6 'dowered'	Endowed with.
15 'gyring'	Revolving.
15 'spiring'	Turning in a spiral movement.
16 'ignorant'	Innocent of destructive thoughts.
18 'the winged sandals dart'	The youthful soul is imagined making the light, swift movements of a dancer.
22 'The demons'	Perhaps referring to abstract thought.
22 'subtle guile'	Cunning tricks.
25 'fatal image'	The Tree of Knowledge not of Life.
29 'barrenness'	Inability to create life.
31 'The glass of outer weariness'	The image of the body's fatigue and decay.
34 'The ravens of unresting thought'	Intellectual activity without the soul's inspiration, bringing on death.
38 'ragged wings'	They are ragged because their plumage is ruffled by the wind and because they are old.

Commentary:

Although the immediate context of the poem is the frustration felt by the poet at Maud Gonne's devotion to a life of politics rather than of love, the image of the trees moves the lyric onto a universal plane. In essence there is no choice to be made for 'the two trees' are one, each the reverse image of the other. The soul in this life cannot escape confinement in the body which is a prey to the demons of time and 'the ravens of unresting thought'. The form of the poem reflects its content with each verse, both of twenty lines, providing the reverse image of the other with the body's form being conceived as the mirror's reflection of the substantial soul. Each feature of the soul's beauty finds its counterpart in the ugliness of the body.

TO IRELAND IN THE COMING TIMES

First Line: 'Know, that I would accounted be'

Collection: 'The Rose' (1893)

Original Title: Apologia Addressed to Ireland in the Coming Days

First Published: *The Countess Kathleen and Various Legends and Lyrics* (1892)

Summary:
The poet asks to be considered a member of the group of poets who make their subject-matter out of Irish history. He should not be thought any the less patriotic for being concerned with the search for perfect Beauty and Truth, since it is these eternal qualities which have kindled the flame of Irish nationalism. In the second verse the poet asserts that his claim is in fact stronger than that of the popular, nationalist poets since he is trying to infuse the ancient mythology with a new life which transcends nationality and makes a universal mark. The poets who lack a sense of an eternal perspective, 'measure', see their political invective, 'rant', consumed by the elements while this poet pursues a goal of absolute Truth. The poet must write according to his personal vision, his 'dream', for though his own life is only a brief instant in Time which may disappear without trace in God's eternal presence, his words can nevertheless supply a record for those to come of how he allied himself to this search for eternal values in the framework of mortal life.

Glossary:
4 'rann' Verse of a poem in Irish.

6 'the red-rose-bordered hem' — The edge of the gown covering the symbolic figure of Truth and Beauty.

8 'the angelic clan' — Band of God's angels.

10 'to rant' — To shout angrily.

13 'Time bade all his candles flare' — Time ordered his candles to burn at full brigntness to illuminate the search for this perfect Truth.

18 'Davis' — Thomas Davis (1814-45) founded *The Nation*, and was leader of the Young Ireland party as well as a writer of popular poems and prose.

18 'Mangan' — James Mangan (1803-49), romantic Irish poet and essayist.

18 'Ferguson' — Sir Samuel Ferguson (1810-86), Irish lawyer, poet and antiquary who translated Gaelic legends.

19 'ponders well' — Thinks deeply upon.

36 'winking' — Opening and closing.

39 'benighted' — Covered by the night.

42 'truth's consuming ecstasy' — A feeling of heightened passion in the presence of truth that devours all mortal elements.

44 'God goes by with white footfall' — God passes through eternity with an ageless tread.

Commentary:

Yeats defends himself in this poem against the charge of mysticism levelled at him by such as John O'Leary and Maud Gonne, who felt he should be concerned with more obviously Irish themes than the medieval and occult symbolism associated with the rose. The poet maintains that it is through his search for the universal elements of Truth and Beauty, as represented by the person of Maud Gonne, that he can renew the ancient glories of pre-Christian Ireland. He lays great stress on the concept of 'measure' which is associated with the symbol of the rose and contrasted with the temporary elements of mortal life that lack this quality. Though the poem is addressed to Ireland the 'you' of the third verse is also Maud Gonne, the principal object of his 'dream' of perfection. The poem is an early example of Yeats's decision to locate his poetry in the mortal world while still hoping to find an embodiment of the eternal, spirit world within it.

THE WIND AMONG THE REEDS (1899)

The collection shows some of the influence of the poet's discussions in the Rhymers' Club, in particular the effects of the French Symbolists to whom he was introduced by Arthur Symons. 'The Song of Wandering Aengus' (p. 66) with its direct approach and changed emphasis from the adjective to the noun furnishes the best example of this technique. Elsewhere the pre-Raphaelites, notably Rossetti and Pater, still predominate, reflected in the languid tone and epithet-burdened rhythms of a self-conscious poeticism. In conflict with this form is a new source of energy in the poems deriving from the effects of the experience of love on his work. The volume attempts to plot the poet's unrequited passion for Maud Gonne through the medium of Irish mythology and occult symbols. In addition, the complicating factor of his passionate affair with Olivia Shakespear gives rise to a sensuousness which although held in check beneath the idealized surface of most of the poems, points the way to later developments.

The first versions of the collection showed Yeats the emerging dramatist adopting different voices for different poems reflecting opposing aspects of the poet's personality to which he assigned names and characters. The three voices were those of Aedh who offers all he has to that which he loves; Michael Robartes collecting his possessions to himself; and Hanrahan too changeable by nature to acquire any wealth in this world. The device served to liberate the poet from any constraint in addressing his most personal lyric to Maud or Olivia. The dominant image running through the volume is that of hair which gathers an increasingly sensuous context of meaning to it as it moves through the poems carrying much of the weight of the poet's sexual longing. The major symbol is the wind as announced in the title of the collection. It stands for vague hopes and desires and is the natural link with the other world being the element in which the immortals' presence can be felt as shown in the opening poem of the group *'The Hosting of the Sidhe'* (p. 61). In selecting the order of the poems Yeats organised the volume to give the overall impression of an affair that has gone wrong and is starting to fade in the less physical poems towards the end of the collection. Throughout the impulse is essentially lyrical with as yet no evidence of the dramatic language of the poet's new style.

THE HOSTING OF THE SIDHE

First Line: 'The host is riding from Knocknarea'

Collection: 'The Wind Among The Reeds' (1899)

Original Title: The Faery Host

First Published: *The National Observer,* 7 October 1893

Summary:
The poet describes the progress of the spirits through the Irish countryside of his early years. The seductive Niamh calls to mortals to enchant them, as she did Oisin, into immortality. However, her words also warn that anyone caught in the spell will no longer be satisfied with the mortal life. The poet answers by asking where in life there is a vision to compare with what Niamh offers.

Glossary:

Title: 'The Sidhe'	Gods of ancient Ireland and the Gaelic word for 'wind'.
1 'The host'	The faery troop.
1 'Knocknarea'	The mountain in Sligo where Maeve, Queen of the western Sidhe is said to be buried.
2 'Clooth-na-Bare'	'Old woman of Bare' who tried to drown her faery life in Lough Ia in Sligo.
3 'Caoilte'	Companion of Fiann and of Oisin. Swiftest runner of the Fianna.
4 'Niamh'	The beautiful faery queen who takes Oisin to the Land of the Young for 300 years.
8 'agleam'	Shining with excitement.
13 ''twixt'	Between.

Commentary:
The movement of the wind across the landscape was taken by the Irish peasants as a sign of the presence of the faeries or 'Sidhe'. Yeats tries here to recreate the sound of the whispering, rushing wind in the evocative, incantatory movement of his lyric. This essentially oral, musical verse still contains the typical tension of a pulling in two directions; the lure of the immortal world is

seductive but, as Oisin discovered, cannot ultimately satisfy all the passions of a mortal while once a man has glimpsed 'our rushing band' he will never be content with the things of this life.

THE SONG OF WANDERING AENGUS

First Line: 'I went out to the hazel wood,'

Collection: 'The Wind Among The Reeds' (1899)

Original Title: A Mad Song

First Published: *The Sketch*, 4 August 1897

Summary:
The poem tells of Aengus, god of youth and poetry, going at night to catch a 'little silver trout' with a berry for bait. He puts the trout on the ground to light a fire to cook it and when he looks for it, it has turned into a girl who calls his name and runs away.

Aengus spends the rest of his life in pursuit of her and still affirms at the end that he will pick the fruits of immortality with her.

Glossary:

Title: 'Aengus'	The god of Youth, Beauty and Poetry who reigned in the Country of the Young.
3 'hazel wand'	The hazel was the Irish Tree of Life or Knowledge, associated with magical properties.
14 'apple blossom'	Yeats always associated this with Maud Gonne.
21 'dappled'	With patches of light and shade.
22 'pluck'	Pick.
23/24 'The silver apples of the moon,/The golden apples of the sun.	The solar and lunar principles when fused form the alchemical emblem of perfection.

Commentary:
This popular narrative bears further witness to the increasing directness of Yeats's style. Whether it is read, along with 'The Hosting Of The Sidhe', as a poem about a mortal poet who puts himself into contact with the faeries who often used the disguise of a fish, and thus becomes seduced by a vision of immortal beauty which haunts the rest of his days, or as a version of Yeats's

frustrated longing for Maud Gonne, the strength of the poem rests in its use of uncluttered images of light. From fire-light to the light of dawn when miracles usually occurred, the quest of Aengus is associated with varying intensities of light until it climaxes in the union of both sources of light:

> The silver apples of the moon,
> The golden apples of the sun.

This metaphor for happy love – which also applies to artistic perfection – equates the sun with the intellect and the moon with the imagination and apples with 'the Tree of Good and Evil'.

HE MOURNS FOR THE CHANGE THAT HAS COME UPON HIM AND HIS BELOVED, AND LONGS FOR THE END OF THE WORLD

First Line: 'Do you not hear me calling, white deer with no horns?'

Collection: 'The Wind Among The Reeds' (1899)

Original Title: The Desire Of Man and Woman

First Published: *The Dome,* June 1897

Summary:
The poet has been changed to 'a hound with one red ear' which must forever chase its beloved in the form of a 'white deer with no horns', experiencing contrary emotions. He was changed by one with magic powers and now he can only look forward to the release which will come with the end of the world.

Glossary:

1	'white deer with no horns'	The emblem for the female's desire for the desire of the male.
2	'a hound with one red ear'	The emblem for the male's desire.
6	'A man with a hazel wand'	Aengus, Master of Love.
10	'the Boar without bristles'	An ancient Celtic image for the darkness which will destroy the world.

Commentary:
This lyric born of sexual frustration at Yeats's inability to free himself from his desire for Maud Gonne never connects the symbolism with the emotion or the mythology with the experience which it is intended to illuminate. Nevertheless it affords an example of the way in which Yeats was now trying to use mythology to come to terms with his most personal feeling. He feels himself to be powerless before the will of immortal forces, personified as 'a man with a hazel wand', which compels him to love even when he is 'looking another way', presumably at Olivia Shakespear. The human being is an instrument of an independent passion as Yeats wrote in *The Symbolism of Poetry*:

> All souls, all colours, all forms, either because of their pre-ordained energies or because of long association, evoke indefinite and yet precise emotions, or, as I prefer to think, call down among us certain disembodied powers, whose footsteps over our hearts we call emotions.

HE BIDS HIS BELOVED BE AT PEACE

First Line: 'I hear the Shadowy Horses, their long manes a-shake,'

Collection: 'The Wind Among The Reeds' (1899)

Original Title: Two Love Poems. The Shadowy Horses. Michael Robartes bids his Beloved be at Peace.

First Published: *The Savoy*, January 1896

Summary:
The poet hears the noise of the horses which bring Death to him. They are associated with the North, the place of Sleep but are to be heard also in the East of Hope, the West of Dream and the South of Desire. They make their mark on the 'clay' of life. He asks his beloved to drive from him the sight and sound of the horses by the passionate intensity of her physical presence.

Glossary:

1 'Shadowy horses' — The horses of Mannannan, ruler of the country of the dead.

3 'The North' — The Fomoroh, gods of night, death and cold, were of the north and winter.

6 'roses of crimson fire'	The south is associated with passion. The red rose is the traditional emblem of love.
8 'The Horses of Disaster'	They are the bringers of death.
9 'Beloved'	The poem was written to 'Diana Vernon', Yeats's pseudonym for Olivia Shakespear.
12 'tumultuous feet'	The noise made by the horses' feet creates confusion.

Commentary:
The poem is notable for announcing the effect that Yeats's affair with Olivia Shakespear was to have on his poetry. He asks his love to hide 'the Shadowy Horses' from him by her physical presence and she was indeed to be instrumental in helping to disperse the mists of poetic vapours to let in external reality. The symbolism of the four quarters of heaven with its 'clinging creeping night' and 'pale dew' is already starting to look insipid when set against the beauty of his love's heart and her hair on his breast.

HE REPROVES THE CURLEW

First Line: 'O curlew, cry no more in the air,'

Collection: 'The Wind Among The Reeds' (1899)

Original Title: Windlestraws 1. O'Sullivan Rua to the Curlew

First Published: *The Savoy,* November 1896

Summary:
The poet asks the curlew to stop its mournful cry or at least to direct it to the ocean because its sound recalls the image of a past lover. The noises of the wind are sufficient to recall the pain of life without the addition of the curlew's song.

Glossary:

1 'curlew'	Long-beaked wading bird with a throbbing cry.
2 'water in the West'	Atlantic Ocean. West is also the region of dreams for Yeats.
6 'wind'	Symbol for a vague idealism carried through the voices of the spirit world.

Commentary:
This is one of a group of love lyrics which are written around the break-up of Yeats's affair with Olivia Shakespear over his continued love for Maud Gonne. While the language still evokes the languid softness of the early poems, the imagery shows a marked transition to a more sensual experience with the displacement of 'the rose' by 'hair' as the dominant image.

HE HEARS THE CRY OF THE SEDGE

First Line: 'I wander by the edge'

Collection: 'The Wind Among The Reeds' (1899)

Original Title: Aodh to Dectora. Three Songs 1

First Published: *The Dome,* May 1898

Summary:
The poet hears the sound of the wind in the reeds and weed at the side of the lake and the voice of the wind seems to be telling him that he will never achieve a physical union with the woman he loves until the entire universe is destroyed.

Glossary:

3	'sedge'	Waterside plants.
4	'axle'	On which the universe spins.
7	'the banners of East and West'	Day and night.
8	'the girdle of light is unbound'	The sun leaves the constellation.

Commentary:
Yeats's frustration over his unrequited love for Maud Gonne is gathering intensity throughout the collection and is suggested here in the cosmic violence of the image conveyed on the wind, that carrier of voices from the spirit world.

THE SECRET ROSE

First Line: 'Far-off, most secret, and inviolate Rose,'

Collection: 'The Wind Among The Reeds' (1899)

Original Title: O'Sullivan Rua to the Secret Rose

First Published: *The Savoy,* September 1896

Summary:
The poet asks the Rose of Perfection and Beauty to 'enfold' him and hold him in a state of ecstasy beyond the normal experience of daily living. He goes on to list those who have experienced the condition of the Secret Rose. The poet says that he, too, is to wait for the moment when he will be touched by its mystery.

The Rose has been sought in Christian religious passion and in the state induced by wine by those who have made their lives beyond the toil of earthly existence in ecstasy or trance. The Rose's leaves encompass the Three Wise Men and Conchubar who saw Christ being crucified in a trance induced by the Druids, and awakening from it, died in a fit of passion. They have held Cuchulain in his passion for the immortal Fand for whom he renounced the glory of the world and his wife Emer, and Caolte when he attacked the gods in their den and feasted for a hundred days and grieved in the grave-yards of his kinsmen. King Fergus felt her presence when he abdicated the crown and the cares of rule and took his poets and jesters off into the woods, and so did the man who sold all he had to search all over the world for a woman of such radiant beauty that men could thresh their corn in the middle of the night by the light from a stolen lock of her hair. The poet also awaits the moment when contrary emotions are reconciled in the Rose. When will the stars be blown out of the sky like the sparks from a blacksmith's forge? Is not the hour of the Rose, heralded by the wind, at hand again?

Glossary:

7 'great leaves'	This is the Rosicrucian emblem of the four-leaved rose.
9 'the king'	Conchubar, King of Ulster.
12 'him'	Cuchulain who fell in love with Fand, wife of Mannannan.
15 'Emer'	Wife of Cuchulain.
16 'liss'	Fort.

Line	Word	Meaning
16	'him'	Caolte.
18	'barrows'	Burial mounds.
19	'the proud dreaming king'	Fergus.
20	'bard'	Celtic poet.
22	'him who . . .'	In 'The Red Pony', a tale in Larminie's *West Irish Folk Tales*, a light draws him to a box containing a lock of hair. The young man then spends his life seeking the owner of the lock.
22	'tillage'	Cultivated land.
25	'A woman of so shining lovliness'	Maud Gonne.
28	'thy great wind'	The wind which heralds the end of the world.
30	'smithy'	Blacksmith's shop.

Commentary:
With this poem Yeats returns to the Rose as symbol for the perfection of immortality achieved in another world. It was the Rose which provided inspiration for the visionaries of the past in general and the figures from Irish mythology in particular. This ecstatic condition brought on by the Rose's influence is not the product only of love for religious passion and drink are also capable of putting the human mind within its orbit. The poet hopes that his experience of the Rose will result in the reconciliation of opposites.

THE TRAVAIL OF PASSION

First Line: 'When the flaming lute-thronged angelic door is wide;'

Collection: 'The Wind Among The Reeds' (1899)

Original Title: Two Love Poems. The Travail of Passion

First Published: *The Savoy*, January 1896

Summary:
The poet writes that at times of passionate intensity a person can endure everything. Like Christ during his crucifixion, the poet at the height of his sexual passion sees himself imparting an intimation of the immortal world ('dream') to his beloved.

Glossary:

Title 'Travail'	Laborious effort.
1 'the flaming lute-thronged angelic door'	The door to the world of the immortals, surrounded by bright light and angels playing lutes.
3 'scourge'	whip.
3 'the plaited thorns'	Christ's crown of thorns, plaited round his head.
5 'the vinegar-heavy sponge'	The sponge soaked in vinegar to increase the pain of the wound.
8 'Lilies of death-pale hope'	The lily symbolizes hope but is also white like a corpse in death.

Commentary:
Very unusually Yeats draws on Christian imagery taken from the story of the Crucifixion to build the poem around a pun on 'passion' which focusses the contrast between the New Testament images and the more typical pre-Raphaelite ones associated with Yeats's early work. The figure of the priest administering the eucharist is paralleled by the lover about to consummate his sexual passion, both states opening windows onto the immortal life of the spirit. The poem is addressed to 'Diana Vernon' and again highlights the increased sensuality of the poems concerning the relationship with Olivia Shakespear.

HE WISHES FOR THE CLOTHS OF HEAVEN

First Line: 'Had I the heavens' embroidered cloths,'

Collection: 'The Wind Among The Reeds' (1899)

Original Title: Aedh wishes for the Cloths of Heaven

First Published: *The Wind Among the Reeds* (1899)

Summary:
The poet declares that if he possessed the cloths of heaven made up of the perfect harmony of silver and gold and covering day, night and the time between, he would spread them beneath the feet of the one whom he is addressing. But since he is a poor man and has only his dreams, he has spread those instead. He asks his loved one to step lightly for she is walking on his dreams.

Glossary:

1 'the heavens' embroidered cloths'	The sky is pictured as three cloths covering the earth; one for day; one for night; and one for dusk and dawn.
2 'Enwrought with'	made up out of.

Commentary:
The Wind Among The Reeds collection contains much of the poetry of dreams and it is often the foot of Maud Gonne which treads a measure through the verses for Yeats's intense frustration over their relationship is the impulse behind many of the poems. The experience of having his dreams trodden on was to encourage the poet to make his futile dreams of a tougher material.

HE THINKS OF HIS PAST GREATNESS WHEN A PART OF THE CONSTELLATIONS OF HEAVEN

First Line: 'I have drunk ale from the Country of the Young'

Collection: 'The Wind Among The Reeds' (1899)

Original Title: Song of Mongan

First Published: *The Dome*, October 1898

Summary:
Having tasted the drink of the immortals Mongan weeps with the knowledge this has brought him. He thinks of an earlier incarnation as the Tree of Life, containing the opposites of the guiding Pole Star and the confusing constellation of the Plough. Then he was a rush set on the floor and then a man who set himself against intimations of the divine ('the wind'). He knew only that his love for a woman would not be consummated until after his death. It is a torment to hear the mating calls of other creatures.

Glossary:

1 'I'	Mongan, a wizard and king who remembered his past lives.
4 'The Pilot Star and the Crooked Plough	The Pole star and the Plough from their Gaelic names.

5 'times out of mind'	For a longer time than anyone can remember.
6 'rush'	Used as a floor covering.

Commentary:

The poet imagines himself in the person of Mongan, who, like Fergus in 'Fergus and the Druid', has bought the knowledge of his previous incarnations at the price of despair in knowing he will not enjoy the woman he loves on this side of the grave. Yeats once again interprets his own emotions through the medium of a mythology which he adapts for his own purposes.

IN THE SEVEN WOODS (1903)*

The content of this collection is dominated still by the relationship between Maud Gonne and the poet. As a consequence of her marriage in 1903 the poet presents himself as a rejected lover who has lost all hope. Given the situation the tone of many of the poems is perhaps surprising for it is not overwhelmingly gloomy. By 1908 when Yeats arranged the order of the poems for publication, Maud was already separated from her husband and Yeats was a trusted friend. The title poem of the volume establishes at once a somewhat detached, reflective tone which the poet uses with an irony revealing his own situation. The Seven Woods are those of Lady Gregory's estate and the influence both of Lady Gregory herself and of her house is felt throughout this period of Yeats's writing, inspiring him to transmute the complaints of the defeated lover into the immortal song of art.

However, the most significant development in the collection is the emergence of a new poetic style. The language is now more down-to-earth, the syntax less involved and the images used more sparingly and to more precise effect. Yeats's work in the theatre must take much of the credit for this change, particularly the discovery of that conversational, apparently casual approach to the lyric which was to prove a typical element in his finest work. The importance of art in reordering and qualifying the private life of the emotions is seen, characteristically for this period, in the metaphor of 'play' in 'Never Give all the Heart' (p. 87). The most important poem for showing the emergence of this new style is 'Adam's Curse' (p. 88). Here the transitional nature of the collection is revealed in the blend of the former lyrical dreaminess with the new sense of actuality deriving from the recollection of a real incident recorded in a conversationally vivid style.

* The collection was published in 1903 both in Ireland and the U.S.A., however *Collected Poems* and all other collections of Yeats's work published after 1920 for no apparent reason give the date 1904.

THE FOLLY OF BEING COMFORTED

First Line: 'One that is ever kind said yesterday:'

Collection: 'In The Seven Woods' (1903)

Original Title:

First Published: *The Speaker*, 11 January 1902

Summary:
In the first verse a friend of the poet tells him that the woman he loves is now showing signs of aging and because of this he will gradually find it easier to bear his loss if he only shows 'patience'. The heart of the poet speaks in reply to this, saying that these words are no source of comfort to him since the woman possesses the kind of beauty that develops into a special type of distinction as she gets older. Indeed, in many ways she is now more beautiful than she was when young.

Glossary:

1	'One that is ever kind'	Probably Lady Gregory.
2	'Your well-beloved's'	Maud Gonne's.

Commentary:
This poem is a good illustration of some of the developments which distinguish *In The Seven Woods* from the previous collections. The form of the poem shows the influence of writing for the theatre on Yeats's poetry at this time. There is a directness and sharpness of focus which is beginning to dispel the mists of the first phase and anticipates something of the tougher, sinewy quality first seen in 'Adam's Curse'. There are fewer adjectives now and every element contributes more directly to the sense of pain which culminates in the last couplet, where the reader is led to expect that a sight of the loved one's face will provide some consolation, until the last line tells us that the face would merely confirm all that the heart has been saying. As elsewhere, the poem contributes to the process by which Maud Gonne almost ceases to be a person for Yeats and becomes a symbol for the immortal qualities in mortal life.

NEVER GIVE ALL THE HEART

First Line: 'Never give all the heart, for love'

Collection: 'In The Seven Woods' (1903)

Original Title:

First Published: *In The Seven Woods* (1903)

Summary:
The poet urges the reader not to surrender his 'heart' entirely to a woman who is devoted ('passionate') to a cause other than love for she will take a man's love for granted, supposing it unchanging. The poet knows that what is beautiful 'is but a brief, dreamy, kind delight.' These women have given their hearts in the game of life rather than love, a game which the poet is prevented from playing 'well enough' by the handicap of his love. The man who has written these words knows the price of surrender: 'For he gave all his heart and lost'.

Glossary:
14 'lost' A reference to Maud Gonne's marriage.

Commentary:
This poem reflects the loss felt by Yeats at the news of Maud Gonne's marriage. There is now directness and simplicity in the language with the only metaphor of the poem, that of 'the play', reflecting Yeats's experiences with the Abbey Theatre with which he was now fully involved. To act the part of the lover is a matter of technique and the poet knows he has acted it badly for he has allowed his own feelings to inhibit his performance: 'deaf and dumb and blind with love'.

ADAM'S CURSE

First Line: 'We sat together at one summer's end,'

Collection: 'In The Seven Woods' (1903)

Original Title:

First Published: *Monthly Review*, December 1902

Summary:
The poet is holding a conversation about poetry with two women. The first stanza sets the scene for the conversation, announces its subject 'poetry' and gives the poet's central statement that a line of poetry must read like the labour of a moment even though it has taken 'hours' of picking and unpicking to produce. The poet continues to pursue the theme declaring that it is preferable to wash a kitchen floor on your knees 'or break stones' in the open air because poetry is 'harder' work than these even though 'the noisy set', the self-confident rising middle-classes whose opinions are listened to by others, call a poet idle. One of the women listening, Kathleen Pilcher, whom, the poet predicts, many will love in vain, replies that to be a woman is to know that beauty is also hard labour even though this knowledge is not learned at school. The poet takes up the theme again declaring that as a result of man's removal from Paradise, everything worthwhile must be worked at. There was a time when lovers considered that their subject had to be worked at and learned in the way that poetry is worked at although in the modern world it is taken for idleness. Conversation ceases and they fall to a contemplation of the twilight. The poet thinks of the moon worn by the action of time even as a shell is smoothed by the action of the tide. The poet, in the final stanza, has a thought fit only for Maud Gonne which he therefore cannot speak. He imagines himself loving her in the old way he has been describing and that their affair had 'seemed happy'. But even so time had acted on them, too, to give them the same melancholy aspect as the 'hollow' moon.

Glossary:

2	'That beautiful mild woman'	Maud Gonne's sister, Mrs. Kathleen Pilcher.
3	'And you and I'	Maud Gonne and Yeats.
6	'naught'	Nothing.
7	'marrow-bones'	Knees.
9	'pauper'	Beggar.

24 'compounded of high courtesy'	In the Middle Ages there was an elaborate ritual for pursuing a love affair.
29 'embers'	Piece of coal or wood in a dying fire.
39 'hollow'	Empty.

Commentary:

This poem belongs to that transitional phase in Yeats's poetic development when he was moving from the romantic mysticism of his youth to a harsher, more abrasive intellectual genre, based in a recognisably real world. The effects of this transition are highlighted in this poem; in particular, in the first stanza. The opening six lines set the mood for a reverie in that archetypal romantic tradition represented by Shelley or Victor Hugo. The reader is brought up short in the seventh line, however, by a jarring, anti-Romantic line: 'Better go down upon your marrow-bones / And scrub a kitchen pavement, . . .'. Whereas the first six lines derive their mood from the nineteenth century, the following eight lines anticipate the innovatory rhythms and diction of the modern age as represented by such poets as T. S. Eliot and W. H. Auden or, indeed, what came to be thought of as typical in the later poetry of Yeats.

In this abrupt transition in the first stanza, mirroring the poet's larger change of poetic style, the romantic spell cast by the opening lines is shattered; further, the poem is permanently marked by a sense of dislocation which cannot be put right in the remainder of the poem, even though it reverts to the style and mood of the opening lines. Closer scrutiny of the poem reveals that this 'dislocation' is reflected in the structure and technique of the poem as well. The verse measure is the iambic pentameter but there are constant breaks in the metrical pattern; in the line 'Like an old pauper, in all kinds of weather;' the metrical stress only coincides sporadically with the actual, spoken stress-pattern and the line has one syllable too many. The rhyme scheme is aa, bb, cc, etc., but Yeats allows himself considerable flexibility in the use of devices such as 'eye rhyme' ('strove'/'love'). The stansaic form is unorthodox being five stanzas of 14, 6, 7, 6 and 5 lines respectively.

This dislocation, heralded by the abrupt change of the first stanza, underlined by the mixing of classical poetic diction with the colloquial rhythms of Yeats's 'common syntax', and sustained throughout by the informal structure of the poem, reveals, powerfully and effectively, the central theme of the poem which is the poet's sense of *spiritual* dislocation: in a setting which provides all that might be thought needful for inspiring the sentiments of Romantic poetry — a summer evening, congenial company including a beautiful women — the poet's voice is sad and muted, unable to articulate the traditional response; far from giving free rein to his fancy, or letting his imagination soar, he merely records a brief conversation on the prosaic subject of work. The poet implicitly acknowledges that it is impossible for him, living at a time of national and global disorder with the world drifting irrevocably towards mass slaughter and destruction, ever to recapture the innocent spirit of the Romantics or to believe in the Arcady that they portrayed, with its rustic simplicity and moral certitudes. The poet is living, for better or for worse, in a world controlled by the 'bankers, schoolmasters and clergymen' of the first stanza, who have overturned the old aristocratic modes of life and thought, and replaced them with their own mercantile systems of value.

The fitful, enigmatic conversation, with its indecisive conclusion, faithfully records the doubt and uncertainty experienced by one who feels that the values he holds dear have become outmoded by what 'the martyrs call the world'. The immediate subject of the conversation is 'labour': the labour of a poet to perfect his poem, 'stitching and unstitching'; the labour of a woman simply to be beautiful; the labour of a courtly lover to express his love in fitting tones. Yet this type of labour is placed in sharp contrast with the labour of that 'noisy set of bankers, schoolmasters, and clergymen'; indeed, although in the poet's opinion his kind of labour is in some ways more strenuous than 'scrubbing pavements' or 'breaking stones', paradoxically, the men of the world abuse people like him for being 'idlers'. The conflict between these two classes of workers goes far beyond the mere question of the relative value of their areas of work, to touch on a fundamental problem, namely: what are those goals in life that are, in the final analysis, worth working for? The three classes of labour discussed in the conversation differ from those of the bankers and schoolmasters principally in this, that their motivation is nothing more than a strong feeling for beauty, a belief in the absolute value of beauty *per se,* and a conviction of the essential nobleness of a life dedicated to the cause of beauty. The real threat of the bankers is that the values for which they work have apparently won the field against the insubstantial aesthetic of the poets who find themselves, confronted by such formidable odds, in a crisis of self-doubt which creates a dislocation of the spirit.

This dichotomy of feeling, running throughout the poem, is caught up and restated in the final two stanzas: the poet describes the falling day in terms which recall the Pre-Raphaelite William Morris but the urge this creates in his heart to express his love to the woman 'in the old high way of love', is checked and subdued by his overwhelming feeling of weariness: '. . . it had all seemed happy, and yet we'd grown / As weary-hearted as that hollow moon.' The use of the image of the 'moon', a symbol of weariness, and the 'washing of time's waters' — running water being symbolic of the passage of time — here gives greatly increased poignancy to the sense of fatigue.

When Adam fell from grace by eating of the Tree of the Knowledge of Good and Evil, he was expelled from Paradise and condemned by God to toil and labour (to eat his bread 'by the sweat of his brow' — see Genesis, III: 19). This is the 'curse' of the title of the poem. Man had embarked on a life in which he could never again hope to recapture the state of sublime bliss he had known previously. Yeats feels himself to be in a similar predicament as a poet in the twentieth century who feels that the dictum of the Romantic poets which was once held unchallenged, has been lost for ever:

> 'Beauty is truth, truth beauty,' — that is all
> Ye know on earth, and all ye need to know.
> (Keats)

The poem is unique in providing the exact instance of the moment when the 'new manner' appears for the first time in Yeats's verse. The opening and the closing of the poem are written as poetry in the way that a contemporary critic would have understood the word. They echo the Romantic tradition of Shelley filtered by the Pre-Raphaelites. However, in between we are accorded a glimpse of the everyday images and conversational rhythms that are to set the pattern for the future development of his own and much of the verse forms of the twentieth century.

THE OLD MEN ADMIRING THEMSELVES IN THE WATER

First Line: 'I heard the old, old men say,'

Collection: 'In The Seven Woods' (1903)

Original Title:

First Published: *Pall Mall Magazine*, January 1903

Summary:
The poet records the words of the very old men who look down at the water and contemplate the decay of all earthly life and the passing away of all that is beautiful.

Commentary:
The ironic title betrays the tone of bitterness which pervades the poem. Again the conversational structure which was to prove such a vital feature of the development of Yeats's poetic craft is present, and the sparse poem is stripped of all images except for the immediate, concrete reality of the twisted thorn-trees and the claws, suggesting that the men have been gradually returning to their native landscape for years until they finally disappear into it altogether.

O DO NOT LOVE TOO LONG

First Line: 'Sweetheart, do not love too long:'

Collection: 'In The Seven Woods' (1903)

Original Title: Do Not Love Too Long

First Published: *In The Seven Woods* (1903)

Summary:
The poet warns his 'sweetheart' not to love 'too long' as he did, becoming as unfashionable as 'an old song'. His love and he were so close to each other when young that they even shared their thoughts. But his former beloved 'changed' in an instant. He repeats his advice lest his 'sweetheart' suffer the same fate.

Glossary:
8 'We were so much at one' The friendship with Maud Gonne.
9 'She changed' A reference to her marriage.

Commentary:
The simplicity typical of the personal lyrics in this collection is apparent in this brief lament. It is a quality which lends universality to the lines and prevents them from falling a prey to self-pity.

THE GREEN HELMET AND OTHER POEMS (1910)

This collection furnishes several examples of the strengthening of that conversational style begun in the previous volume. Yeats was working constantly at the business of the Abbey Theatre during these years and therefore having to deal with many matters of both routine and public nature very different from the imaginative world in which he had steeped himself as a young man. The process of revising all his work to date for the *Collected Works* caused him to write less new poetry but to consider deeply his role as an Irish poet. The consequences of his adoption of a public 'mask' are to be felt in all subsequent volumes.

Even in those poems which still treat of his feelings for Maud Gonne she has somehow been turned into public property through her apotheosis as Helen of Troy ('No Second Troy', p. 101) where it is her relationship to the Ireland of her own day which is as important as the poet's private feelings. While there are now fewer poems the scope of the subject matter is much wider as Yeats involves himself with contemporary political controversies as in 'Upon a House Shaken by the Land Agitation' (p. 106) where his feelings about Coole Park are set in the context of current political unrest. One of the finest lyrics of the collection, 'All Things Can Tempt Me' (p. 109) refers to this change of focus in his life and work and his intention of no longer creating verses out of the old heroic material. In Yeats's play *The Green Helmet*, the helmet belongs to the Red Man whose challenge is accepted by Cuchulain. As a result of which Cuchulain is rewarded with the helmet at the end of the play. Similarly, Yeats accepts the burden and the distinction of making himself the 'hero' for modern Ireland, loyally but impartially speaking out to her citizens through the medium of the artist.

NO SECOND TROY

First Line: 'Why should I blame her that she filled my days'

Collection: 'The Green Helmet And Other Poems' (1910)

Original Title: Raymond Lully and His Wife Pernella

First Published: *The Green Helmet and Other Poems*, (1910)

Summary:
The poet asks why he should blame his old love (Maud Gonne) for making him miserable and for trying to inspire men who lack the 'courage' to fulfil their 'desire' with a call to 'violent' action. He asks what other course could have given her peace of mind, since she is endowed with an aristocratic, passionate and heroic nature. What else could she have done in this unheroic age when there is no Troy to be consumed in the flames of her destructive beauty?

Glossary:

1	'her'	Maud Gonne.
2	'of late'	She withdrew from public life after the break-up of her marriage.
3	'most violent ways'	Acts of subversion, intimidation, murder and arson.
4	'the little streets'	The poor who are urged to rise up.
5	'Had they but courage equal to desire'	They do not have the heroism necessary to fulfil their dream.
8	'tightened bow'	To launch the arrow of desire. An image taken from Blake.
9	'not natural in an age like this'	Yeats felt she belonged to the classical age.
10	'high and solitary and most stern'	That is like a Greek statue.
12	'another Troy'	Maud Gonne is always associated with Helen.

Commentary:
This poem continues the new trend towards directness and simplicity in Yeats's lyrics. Again the dominant note is one of quiet dignity and poignance, replacing the earlier bitterness and self-pity. In the political activity which diverted Maud from

her proper course of love, she stood out beside the mediocre personalities of the other activists. Yeats finds that her qualities which echo those of the classical Greek civilization, 'high and solitary and most stern', àre inappropriate to the grey modern age. He locates the appropriate symbol for her, Helen of Troy, in that earlier age. Helen's beauty was also beyond description and her public activity resulted in catastrophe. Yeats began increasingly to feel that he was living in a transitional period between two civilizations, similar to the period of the Graeco-Trojan war. Henceforth the classical rather than the Irish mythology claims a prime share of Yeats's attention.

THE FASCINATION OF WHAT'S DIFFICULT

First Line: 'The fascination of what's difficult'

Collection: 'The Green Helmet And Other Poems' (1910)

Original Title:

First Published: *The Green Helmet and Other Poems*, (1910)

Summary:
The poet complains that his interest in complicated problems has caused the spoiling of unpremeditated pleasure and creativity. The poetic inspiration, rather than being a God-given lightness of touch, is instead drudging along under a heavy burden. So the poet blames his involvement with the theatre for the erosion of his muse and vows to release it from its shackles before another day is wasted.

Glossary:

2 'sap'	Vital spirits.
2 'rent'	Torn.
3 'spontaneous'	Instant, uncalculated.
4 'ails'	Afflicts.
4 'our colt'	Pegasus, the winged horse of the poetic muse.
6 'Olympus'	Greek mountain, regarded as the home of the gods.
8 'road-metal'	In *Art and Life* (1910) T. Sturge Moore wrote that 'Swift, as a rule, used his Pegasus for a cart-horse, since it was strong, and he sorely importuned by the press of men and notions in need of condign punishment: but even when plodding in the ruts, its motion betrays the mettle in which it here revels.'

10 'dolt' Idiot.

Commentary:
The poem characterizes the mood of the whole collection with its blend of exasperation and advance in poetic style — the style, in fact, being largely a product of the mood. There is a new note of harshness and realism reflected in both the vigorous, masculine rhythms with meaning running over beyond the ends of lines and sentences starting in mid-line. The vocabulary is also, like the thought, drawn from the daily life of men; most notably the verbs Yeats selects such as 'strain, sweat and jolt'. While the running of the Abbey Theatre was no doubt responsible for the decrease in the quantity of his poetry, it must also take some credit for the development of Yeats's style, with its greater clarity of thought and sharpness of focus. The title should not be overlooked for Yeats is, indeed, fascinated by his contact with the world of men, which stimulates more than it stifles his imagination. The extent of his determination to pursue his career as a poet is marked by the first person pronoun which starts the last two lines. Even without his vow, however, the qualities of the poem itself indicate that the 'bolt' has been removed and the muse is galloping free into the daylight world, not stumbling into another Celtic Twilight.

THE MASK

First Line: ' "Put off that mask of burning gold" '

Collection: 'The Green Helmet And Other Poems' (1910)

Original Title: A Lyric from an Unpublished Play

First Published: *The Green Helmet and Other Poems,* (1910)

Summary:
The poem takes the form of a dialogue between a man and a woman. The man asks the woman to remove her mask in order that he may know if the woman beneath is sincere or whether she will use him badly. The woman replies that he has become interested in the mask and not the woman and so she will not risk removing it. She asks him if it matters that she is to him only a mask so long as they are both capable of love.

Glossary:

1 'that mask'	In *Autobiographies* (p. 189) Yeats wrote: 'Among subjective men (in all those, that is, who must spin a web out of their own bowels) the victory is an intellectual daily re-creation of all that exterior fate snatches away, and so that fate's antithesis; while what I have called "the Mask" is an emotional antithesis to all that comes out of their internal nature.'
3 'make so bold'	Are so forward.

Commentary:
The poem, once more showing the influence of the drama on Yeats's poetry, suggests that, whatever the poet's feelings for Maud Gonne, he had by this time succumbed to the demands of his sensual nature and used his public mask not only in matters of theatrical business but in personal affairs as well. The clipped, epigrammatic style is starting to establish itself as his dominant mode — a kind of casual, conversational style that is, in fact, most carefully tuned to strike at the essence of a subject. The poem introduces an image, the mask, which was to develop into a major theme of Yeats's work with his adoption of an opposite public personality to the 'real' subjective man behind it.

UPON A HOUSE SHAKEN BY THE LAND AGITATION

First Line: 'How should the world be luckier if this house,'

Collection: 'The Green Helmet And Other Poems' (1910)

Original Title: To a Certain Country House in Time of Change

First Published: *McClure's Magazine*, December 1910, and *The Green Helmet and Other Poems* (1910). [Publication was virtually simultaneous].

Summary:
The poet asks what benefit it will be to the world if Coole Park is allowed to fall into ruins that will no longer be able to sustain the 'passion' and 'precision' of the high aspiring accomplishments of the nobility. The house has bred the kind of thinking which results from the close contact with an aristocratic past where only the 'best' features of existence have been admitted. Even if the lot

of the peasants were improved a little by the loss, they could never hope to inherit the qualities of government, still less the ability — a product of a materially easy life — to create works of art reflecting that noble way of life.

Glossary:

1	'this house'	Coole Park; Lady Gregory's house in Co. Galway.
4	'the lidless eye'	Only the eagle can gaze into the sun without blinking. The eagle is Yeats's symbol of the active, objective person.
5	'set sweet laughing eagle thoughts'	The thoughts of the aristocrat remembering his family's noble past.
8	'Mean roof-trees'	The cottages whose inhabitants would farm more of the estate.
10	'The gifts that govern men'	Sir William, Lady Gregory's husband, had served as Governor of Ceylon.
11	'a written speech'	Lady Gregory's plays and books of Irish legends.
11	'To gradual Time's last gift'	The space and 'ease' in which great art can be created.

Commentary:

This poem provides further evidence of Yeats's turning outwards to public events for the subjects of his work. Coole Park, where he had been welcomed as a poet might have been at a Renaissance Court, had come to symbolize for him all the ancient, heroic and aristocratic values which he saw threatened by the new spirit of democracy. In his view the inhabitants of the great houses gave more to life than they took from it and above all the environment provided the stimulation and time to create poetry in that easy, conversational style which Yeats had recently discovered.

AT GALWAY RACES

First Line: 'There where the course is,'

Collection: 'The Green Helmet And Other Poems' (1910)

Original Title: Galway Races

First Published: *The English Review,* February 1909

Summary:
The poem begins with a description of the races, paying attention to the single-minded concentration of the crowd. As the riders do now, so, long ago, the poets had a similarly large, attentive audience in the days of heroic deeds and aristocratic manners. But now the world owned by the middle-classes is not a fit place for the practice of his craft. However, he urges his fellow poets to continue in their work because their time will come again and the earth will once more be a place for bold deeds and reckless adventure of the kind now only found at the racecourse.

Glossary:

5 'We'	The poets.
6 'hearteners'	People who were stirred to the heart by the verses.

Commentary:
As so often in this collection, the poem introduces a thought and an image which are to prove of central significance to the later work. The thought is fully formulated in 'The Gyres', in the notion that a new subjective age will be born where the old, aristocratic values of the bardic age of pre-Christian Ireland will again be celebrated. Here the 'filthy modern tide' is characterized by the middle-class materialist existence of 'the merchant and the clerk' which makes no contact with the world inhabited by the poet. Yeats uses the verb 'sing' to stress that he sees himself in the oral tradition of the bards who were commissioned by an audience of aristocrats. The animal which symbolizes this world is the horse, since only the aristocrat could have afforded one and so the horse became a distinguishing feature of rank. Even in the poet's own day horse-racing was considered the sport of the aristocracy and those who thrill to its rhythms should not be beyond the reach of his verses. The rhythm of the poem is carefully worked to echo the rhythm of the galloping horses with sudden rising excitement, quickly giving place to a steadier movement. Again Yeats is con-

tent to develop one thought in one poem, enabling him to lead the reader through a coherent progression to a clearly articulated final point, and again the inspiration for this thought comes from the everyday world of contemporary Ireland.

ALL THINGS CAN TEMPT ME

First Line:	'All things can tempt me from this craft of verse:'
Collection:	'The Green Helmet And Other Poems' (1910)
Original Title:	Distraction
First Published:	*The English Review,* February 1909

Summary:
The poet is easy prey for any distraction from poetry; once it was 'a woman's face' or the apparently important call of nationalism. Even now, when the poet is used to the work of writing verse, he would rather do anything else as an excuse for not writing poetry. When he was a young man the poet would only lend an ear to poems that were written in a noble style about ancient deeds of bravery but now despite his success in the art, his experience of life makes him long for insensibility.

Glossary:

1 'tempt me'	Yeats wrote little verse as manager of the Abbey Theatre.
2 'a women's face'	Maud Gonne.
3 'my fool-driven land'	Ireland in the hands of political incompetents.

Commentary:
The simple language of this poem should not hide the complexity of its thought. The first sentence deals with his attitude to the content of his former works, the second with their form. He used to be distracted from the 'craft of verse' by love and politics which nevertheless provided him with the subjects for his verses. He used only to care for poems in an heroic idiom but now when the actual technique of composition has never been easier, he lacks the will and motive to write.

RESPONSIBILITIES
(1914)

John Unterecker has revealed the structural pattern by which the poems of this collection were arranged and the significance of the title in this organisation:

> 'Responsibilities of the Poet "close on forty-nine"
>
> Supernatural responsibilities
>
> Dead ancestors: "Pardon, Old Fathers"
> Dead friends who had been poets: "The Grey Rock"
>
> Social responsibilities
>
> Lane-pictures poems
> *Playboy*-riots poems
>
> The function of irresponsibility
>
> "Beggarman" poems
>
> Personal responsibilities
>
> Iseult Gonne poems
> Maud Gonne poems
> "Friends"
>
> Aesthetic responsibilities
>
> Supernatural models: "The Magi", "The Dolls"
> Style: "A Coat"
> Rededication: "While I, from that reed-throated whisperer" '

This collection represents in tone the utterances of the public man, the man now well aware of his status as a major figure in the cultural landscape of his country. As such he has a responsibility to both speak for and speak to the nation. The political poems reveal Yeats's deep interest in the Renaissance fostered by his visits to Italy in bitter contrast to his despair at the prevailing bourgeois standards of modern Ireland. He will have to rely increasingly on being properly valued and represented by a few like-minded souls who are to be found either among aristocrats or peasants but not among merchants and clerks.

The detail and concreteness of much of the writing in this volume indicates the nature of the influence of Ezra Pound upon Yeats. Much of the poetry is stripped of images and stark in its apparent simplicity.

TO A WEALTHY MAN WHO PROMISED A SECOND SUBSCRIPTION TO THE DUBLIN MUNICIPAL GALLERY IF IT WERE PROVED THE PEOPLE WANTED PICTURES

First Line: 'You gave, but will not give again'

Collection: 'Responsibilities' (1914)

Original Title: The Gift/To a friend who promised a bigger subscription than his first to the Dublin Municipal Gallery if the amount collected proves that there is a considerable 'popular demand' for the pictures.

First Published: *The Irish Times*, 11 January 1913

Summary:
The poet addresses a prospective patron of the city's arts who has made his bounty conditional upon the public also subscribing. The poet holds up the example of Renaissance Italy where the patrons, in imitation of classical Greece, benefitted the arts without reference to the people. The poet exhorts this patron therefore to give his money not to please the common people but for the future good of the country.

The first sentence of the first verse recapitulates the situation which has given rise to the poem. The 'wealthy man' will not give more money for the picture gallery unless the common people will also give money towards it, as if 'the blind and ignorant town' could be expected to understand the value of such things. Duke Ercole did not worry about the opinions of the 'onion-sellers' when he created his productions of Plautus. When Guidobaldo set up his court at Urbino as a model of refinement and culture he did not consult the shepherds about his plans. When Cosimo de Medici was exiled to Venice instead of being consumed by bitterness he busied himself with Michelozzo's plans for the San Marco Library, so that Italy might discover among those books the wisdom and art of ancient Greece.

In verse two the poet laments the unfavorable comparison between the Renaissance and the modern patron. He tells the man to leave the common people to their simple games and instead be able, like the eagle (emblem of nobility), to gaze upon the sun because he has made possible the hope for a better life through giving, not according to popular taste, but that which is necessary for a noble life.

Glossary:

1 'You'	Probably Lord Ardilaun, who had argued that no money should be given unless there was a clear public demand.
2, 3 'Paudeen's', 'Biddy's'	Terms for the common people.
9 'Duke Ercole'	Duke Ercole d'Este, Duke of Ferrara whose court was renowned for brilliant art and letters.
12 'his Plautus'	The Duke patronized productions of the Roman comic playwright, Plautus.
14 'Guidobaldo'	Guidobaldo di Montefeltro, Duke of Urbino.
15 'that grammar school'	The culture and refinement of his court is celebrated in Castiglione's *The Book of the Courtier.*
17 'Urbino's windy hill'	It enjoys a beautiful setting on the slopes of the Apennines. Yeats visited the city in 1907.
20 'Cosimo'	Cosimo de Medici who was exiled to Venice.
21 'rancour'	Spitefulness.
23 'Michelozzo'	The architect who accompanied Cosimo to Venice. T.R. Henn suggested that Cosimo stood for Hugh Lane, Michelozzo for Sir Edward Lutyens and the San Marco Library for the projected gallery.
28 'Sucking at the dug of Greece'	The poet sees Italy as a child drawing nourishment for her Renaissance from the classical example.

Commentary:

Yeats again pitches his verse into the arena of public debate and uses his typical device of setting the modern age against one of his favorite historical periods. Referring to the argument over the proposed Lane Picture Gallery, Yeats makes clear his attitude to art being dependent on popular taste by his derogatory references to 'Paudeen' and 'Biddy'. The central body of the poem then recounts the ways in which aristocratic patronage caused the arts to flourish in Renaissance Italy. Unlike Lord Ardilaun, Duke Ercole,

Guidobaldo and Cosimo de Medici did not feel constrained to seek the approval of the peasants for their aesthetic decisions. Using again the image from Blake of the eagle that can alone among creatures gaze unblinking on the sun to represent nobility of spirit, Yeats urges this modern-day patron of the arts to exhibit an unconditional generosity in the Renaissance spirit.

SEPTEMBER 1913

First Line: 'What need you, being come to sense,'

Collection: 'Responsibilities' (1914)

Original Title: Romance in Ireland/(On reading much of the correspondence against the Art Gallery)

First Published: *The Irish Times*, 8 September 1913

Summary:
The poet addresses middle-class nationalists whom he sees as being more concerned with business and sterile religious observance than the welfare of their nation. He contrasts these people unfavourably with the 'romantic' heroes of the Irish past. He ends by guessing that were such men to appear now their behaviour would be attributed to the passion of love, rather than ideals.

The first stanza describes with obvious contempt ('fumble in a greasy till') the new Catholic middle-class who are people of 'sense' rather than feeling, preoccupied with trade and religious observance. Such people have killed off the 'romantic Ireland' of the poet's desires which are closely associated with the figure of O'Leary. The second stanza turns to these older nationalists who were too active to spend much time at prayers and who ended being hung by the British, not even saving their lives, let alone their pence. In the third stanza the poet mentions specifically the exiles who fled to enlist in foreign armies ('the wild geese') together with Fitzgerald, Emmet and Tone — not men of sense but heroes who acted out of emotion and passion, sacrificing themselves for this new Ireland. In the final stanza the poet imagines being able to call these men back only to hear these unfeeling merchants misrepresent their passion as the working of an erotic impulse. The poet is glad they cannot be troubled by this modern age devoid of idealism.

Glossary:

1 'you'	The new Catholic middle-class.
8 'O'Leary'	John O'Leary (1830-1907), one of the leaders of the Fenian movement. Yeats was greatly influenced by personal contact with him and regarded him as the last nationalist hero.
17 'the wild geese'	Irishmen who went to fight in foreign armies after the passing of the 1691 Penal Laws. 120,000 left Ireland between 1690 and 1730.
20 'Edward Fitzgerald'	Lord Fitzgerald (1763-98), MP for Athy and Kildare, joined the United Irishmen in 1796 and died of wounds received while being arrested.
21 'Robert Emmet'	Emmet (1778-1803), led an abortive revolt, was tried for treason and executed.
21 'Wolfe Tone'	Tone (1763-98), founded the United Irish Club, led a French force to Ireland, was captured and condemned to death. He was said to have committed suicide in prison.
22 'delirium'	A passion like a fever.

Commentary:

Yeats's bitter mood created by the Lane controversy is the impulse behind the poem. He identifies the dominant occupation of the modern nationalists as trade and the church. They use their country's nationalist aspirations to line their own pockets, being men of 'sense'. They form a miserable contrast with the older group of men who died for Ireland with no thought for themselves. Yeats's names, Fitzgerald, Emmet and Tone, are all taken from the eighteenth century, the period which he increasingly felt was Ireland's greatest. The last verse of the poem suggests that the present would be incapable of understanding the motives of such men even if they were here now. The last link with 'romantic Ireland', the last man to carry in him the spirit of heroism was John O'Leary.

'September 1913' forms an interesting contrast with 'Easter 1916' where the poet is forced to recognize the partiality of his judgements on the new nationalists in a tone of humility as opposed to the arrogance of some of his opinions here.

THE THREE HERMITS

First Line: 'Three old hermits took the air'

Collection: 'Responsibilities' (1914)

Original Title:

First Published: *The Smart Set*, September 1913

Summary:
Three hermits, men who have lived away from the material concerns of the world, each face their impending death in a different state of mind. One whose efforts at prayer have been thwarted by sleep is afraid that his reincarnation will be in a monstrous form as a punishment. The second draws some comfort from their 'holy' profession to believe that their form in the next life will be human, although they will not escape into eternal life until transformed by passion. However, their love for God will reward them with a noble shape in their next incarnation. Meanwhile, the third hermit has sat alone, singing 'like a bird'.

Glossary:

4 'rummaged'	Searched.
20 'plagued'	Annoyed.

Commentary:
The conversational form of the poem is allied with an irreverend tone to give an earthy touch to this contemplation of the life to come. This tone is particularly strong in the treatment of the second hermit with his informal language, ('plagued') and his pursuit of the flea, contrasted with his dreams of being a 'poet', 'king' or 'witty lovely lady'. As far as Yeats's own position is concerned, however, the third hermit offers a more significant perspective and fittingly it is he who closes the poem. He is a singer which allies him to the poet; he is 'unnoticed' in this world, a further point of identification, and thirdly, he is associated with a bird — for Yeats the symbol of the isolated, majestic, subjective soul. This hermit has achieved a visionary gaiety of the kind which Yeats articulates frequently in later poems and which is associated with the 'tragic joy' of his final phase.

FALLEN MAJESTY

First Line:	'Although crowds gathered once if she but showed her face,'
Collection:	'Responsibilities' (1914)
Original Title:	
First Published:	*Poetry* (Chicago), December 1912

Summary:
Although when in her prime the woman celebrated here drew crowds of people to her, now that time has passed it is left to the poet, alone among men, to place on record the passion and beauty that once was. The woman still lives, though now grown old, but the poet speaks of her as she was when her beauty seemed almost supernatural. New crowds in years to come will not know they occupy the place where this extraordinary woman once spoke.

Glossary:

1 'she'	Maud Gonne.
2 'even old men's eyes'	Though preaching the kind of violence that older nationalists normally rejected, such was her power that even this group were moved by her words.
3 'courtier'	Frequenter of the royal court.
3 'gipsy'	Nomadic caravan dwellers originally of Indian descent.
4 'babbling'	Talking incoherently.
5 'lineaments'	A word taken from Blake meaning distinctive features.

Commentary:
In Yeats's imagination Maud Gonne had become something of a tragic figure, defeated by her unhappy marriage and the advancing years. The poet saw himself as a last remnant from a more noble age, an age of kings and beggars, recalling images from a past life to an uncomprehending audience. Now that Maud Gonne had almost entirely withdrawn from public life, Yeats was able to associate her with past ages of glory and dissociate her from the contemporary political movements with which he had no sympathy.

FRIENDS

First Line: 'Now must I these three praise—'

Collection: 'Responsibilities' (1914)

Original Title:

First Published: *The Green Helmet and Other Poems*(1912)

Summary:
The poem is written in praise of the three women who have most affected the poet's life. The first, Olivia Shakespear, is most notable for having never created any strife in their fifteen years' relationship despite the presence of cares and troubles which might have been expected to cause friction. The second is most praised for her role in the poet's professional development, helping him shed 'youth's dreamy load' (the Celtic Twilight) and discover the true passion (ecstasy) of the craftsman.

He then asks how he can praise the woman who stole his 'youth' without return. Then he remembers the sensations which still overpower him when the memory of her 'eagle look' steals upon him in the dawn.

Glossary:

4 'One'	Olivia Shakespear.
10 'And One'	Lady Gregory.
17 'her that took ...'	Maud Gonne.
25 'eagle look'	Signifying detachment and objectivity which Yeats associated with active not contemplative persons.

Commentary:
'Friends' shows Yeats making poetry out of his autobiography without the disguises of the mythological figures he had previously used to describe his most personal experiences. Here he attempts to summarize, in the now characteristic spare, direct language, the effect on his life of the three most important women in it: Olivia Shakespear, Lady Gregory and Maud Gonne. Olivia Shakespear has given him the experience of a shared mind, of a oneness not previously known. To Lady Gregory Yeats gives the credit for his artistic development. The case of Maud Gonne is less easy to deal with. Though he is almost surprised at himself for including her in the catalogue of praise, he acknowledges that the remembrance of her 'eagle look' is enough to create a different sort of 'ecstasy' to the one engendered by the craft of verse.

THE COLD HEAVEN

First Line: 'Suddenly I saw the cold and rook-delighting heaven'

Collection: 'Responsibilities' (1914)

Original Title:

First Published: *Responsibilities* (1914)

Summary:
The poet gazes upon a winter sky which, in its combination of extreme heat and cold, provokes a vivid memory of his youthful passion. He is shaken as if by a fever at the intensity of the recollection and the fierceness of the blame he puts on himself for the failure of that love. He ends by asking himself if he will be punished in his life after death for the folly of this passion by having to walk naked under this winter sky.

Glossary:

1	'rook-delighting'	The rooks are delighted by the freedom of the sky.
6	'crossed'	Not returned.
7	'out of all sense'	Meaning both 'senselessly' and 'beyond the reach of the senses.'
9	'riddled'	Meaning both 'shot through' and 'puzzled' as if by a riddle.
9	'quicken'	Come to life, that is life after death.
10	'confusion of death-bed'	The confusion of this life with the next when the soul belongs entirely to neither.

Commentary:
The density of the language and intensity of the vision reflect those metaphysical aspects which Yeats was taking from his recent reading of Donne. The specific memory is that of Yeats's unrequited passion for Maud Gonne but it is the strength of the poem that it uses this memory only as a starting point for the speculation on the after-life which will haunt the poet increasingly from now on, especially in the work which culminated in *A Vision*. The contrast of ice and fire provoked by the cold brightness of the winter sky, suggests that unity of the perfected being achieved by the instense evocation of a passion. However, the tremendous radiance which accompanies this moment of vision finds its

opposite in the speculation that the poet's ghost will experience an extreme of cold as a fitting punishment for his reckless and over-heated love during this life. The notion of the confusion between body and soul at the moment of death is one which Yeats exploits fully in his play *The Only Jealousy of Emer*.

A COAT

First Line: 'I made my song a coat'

Collection: 'Responsibilities' (1914)

Original Title:

First Published: *Poetry* (Chicago), May 1914

Summary:
The poet recalls how he cloaked his 'song' formerly in the ancient myths of Ireland so that no part was unadorned by them. But poor imitators carried off the 'coat', passing it off in front of others as their own. The poet concludes by telling his 'song' that it is better off without the 'coat' since 'there's more enterprise/In walking naked'.

Glossary:

1 'I made my song a coat' He means 'I made a coat for my song'.

3 'old mythologies' The Gaelic legends.

Commentary:
'A Coat' is appropriately positioned almost at the end of *Responsibilities* since it is the formal renunciation of Yeats's early style, now debased by pallid imitation. There is no regret in this loss of the 'coat' since it has ceased to serve its function for the poet and only cloaks his meaning from the sight of the reader. The decision to walk 'naked' has already been partially exemplified in the style of this collection.

THE WILD SWANS AT COOLE (1919)

The great variety of tone and subject matter of this collection reflects the contrasting and, at times, conflicting moods of the poet caused by the sudden and violent changes in his circumstances. In international and national politics conflict was the order of the day with the Great War and the Easter Rising with its aftermath of reprisal and bitterness. Yeats was touched personally by both for the Great War claimed Robert Gregory and the Rising several close friends. Yet during this same time Yeats was finally rejected by Maud Gonne, turned down by Iseult and married Georgie Hyde-Lees. He moved to the tower at Ballylee in his first permanent home and received from his marriage the unexpected gift of his wife's automatic writing which together with the poet's own studies was to culminate in the esoteric philosophical system presented in *A Vision*.

Much of this is present in the volume although there are also many poems which were excluded for lack of a suitable context, to be included in later collections where they were felt to be more appropriate. Many of the poems are linked by the common theme of death which from this time on became an increasing preoccupation with Yeats. The contemplative picture of the poet's aging presented in the title poem (p. 147) is given a sharp shock of violent actuality in the death of his dear friend. The poem 'In Memory of Major Robert Gregory' is an example of the personal, informal style of the mature Yeats at its best, the memories being the more vivid for being grounded in actual details from his life. Though sharing the same source for its inspiration 'An Irish Airman Foresees his Death' (p. 152) is a poem of a very different stamp with the poet adopting the mask of the dead airman in order to put his own thoughts on death into an actual context. This adoption of a persona or mask is used in several of the poems of the volume, enabling the poet to both dramatize and depersonalize his attitudes to love and death, thereby combining uniquely passion and detachment in a blend which was to become the hallmark of his later work.

The final section of the collection is given over to poems which reflect the beginnings of the work on *A Vision*. While some are little more than a rendering in verse of first draft material, others, notably 'The Double Vision of Michael Robartes', indicate the way in which the visionary material will become inextricably interwoven with the poet's self-image. Gradually the arena will change from the external public platform of his middle years to the private visions of his own mind in Yeats's old age.

THE WILD SWANS AT COOLE

First Line: 'The trees are in their autumn beauty,'

Collection: 'The Wild Swans At Coole' (1919)

Original Title:

First Published: *The Little Review,* June 1917

Summary:
Watching the water of the lake at Coole Park, the poet, revelling in the beautiful natural setting, counts fifty-nine swans there. It is nineteen years, he realizes, since he started to count them; as he did so, they scattered in a sudden flutter. But while they have remained here all this time, untouched by experience or even by time, the epitome of constancy, 'all's changed' and the poet himself has grown older and sadder. Finally the poet wonders where else the swans might bring pleasure to mankind if ever he should find one day that 'they have flown away'.

Glossary:

5 'brimming water'	Water that has filled up to the edge of the lake.
17 'bell-beat'	The poet likens the sound of the swans' wings against the air to the noise of a bell ringing.
18 'Trod'	Walked.

Commentary:
This rich, finely-tuned lyric proclaims a new sensuousness of image to combine with the direct style of the previous collection. Yeats speaks without self-conscious disguise in his own person and applies the images of Coole Park's landscape to the questions of aging and change which had begun to haunt him. The Park in general and the swans in particular seem not to have altered in the nineteen years since the poet first saw them. However, in his

life the curse of mortality, growing old, has been keenly felt. Unlike his earthbound self, the swans move between water and air, combining mortal and immortal elements. Their circular movement suggests that their presence is eternal. This illusion is made possible because they are always renewing themselves, the young replacing the old without the poet discovering the change. Through the strength of their mating urge, 'lover by lover', they preserve not only their numbers but also the vitality of their natures. They will still be building the nests to house the next generation when the poet has awakened to his life in the next world. The question on which the poem ends is rich in possibilities. It could be taken to mean that Yeats's life at Coole is a dream which must end with its passing, leaving the swans to find new habitats for they are 'wild swans', free and independent. The reference to 'men's eyes' suggests that like the swans' so the pattern of man is fixed and others will replace the poet in this landscape. So paradoxically the increased awareness of mortality also brings on a sense of man's place in the greater scheme.

Written after Maud Gonne's final refusal of him, Yeats contrasts the passion he once felt for her with the lack of passion with which he recently proposed to her. Unlike the swans, his heart is subject to the processes of change.

IN MEMORY OF MAJOR ROBERT GREGORY

First Line: 'Now that we're almost settled in our house'

Collection: 'The Wild Swans At Coole' (1919)

Original Title: In Memory Of Robert Gregory

First Published: *The English Review,* August 1918

Summary:
A twelve-stanza epitaph to dead friends of Yeats, in particular Lady Gregory's son, killed in the First World War.

I. The poet reflects on the friends and colleagues who might have spent time with him 'in our house' had they not died.

II. The poet's friends could also meet one another, hopefully without dispute, something of which the dead are incapable.

III. The first dead friend: Lionel Johnson, more scholar than philanthropist, who found his wished-for fulfilment in the classics.

IV. The second: J.M. Synge, a great dramatist whose failing health

coloured his descriptions of life, and who found his metier in dramatising the actual ways of 'passionate and simple' folk.
V. The third: George Pollexfen (Yeats's uncle), a good horseman in his youth, later an astrologist, having completely lost his sporting instinct and energy.
VI. These were particular friends of Yeats's and he reviews them like a reel of old film. But reconciled as he is to the fact of these friends being dead, the poet finds it hard to accept that Lady Gregory's youthful son should have joined them.
VII. Robert Gregory loved all things beautiful in nature and in art, and was the most sociable of men.
VIII. He was a swift and daring rider in the hunt but his alert mind was even quicker.
IX. He might have been 'a great painter' of the Irish landscape; as it was, he made a fine soldier, scholar and horseman, and his life story would make joyous reading.
X. He knew a great deal about structures and materials; he was soldier, scholar and horseman, each to perfection.
XI. Some have little fuel to 'burn', others burn up a great deal in their life-time. Being so skilled and active a man, perhaps Robert Gregory could never have reached old age anyway.
XII. The poet himself might be writing imaginatively of heroic or inspired lives, young or old, were it not for Robert Gregory's passing, which has made his heart heavy with regret.

Glossary:

1 'our house'	Thoor Ballylee, the Norman tower and cottages Yeats purchased in 1917.
17 'Lionel Johnson'	Dominant member of the Rhymers' Club who impressed Yeats with his learning.
25 'John Synge'	John Millington Synge (1871-1909) whom Yeats met in Paris in 1896. His plays were perhaps the greatest written for the Irish Literary Theatre.
30 'a most desolate stony place'	The Aran Islands where Synge went on Yeats's advice.
33 'George Pollexfen'	Yeats's maternal uncle with whom he used to spend his holidays in Sligo.
35 'meets'	Meeting of hounds and men for the purpose of fox hunting.
39 'trine'	The aspect of two planets 120 degrees apart.
40 'sluggish'	"He lived in despondency, finding in the most cheerful news reasons of discouragement" (*Autobiographies*).
46 'my dear friend's dear son'	Major Robert Gregory, son of Yeats's 'dear friend', Lady Gregory.

47 'Sidney'	Robert Gregory possessed a versatility similar to the Elizabethan poet, courtier and soldier, Sir Philip Sidney. They were both led to their deaths by love of action.
61 'perilous'	Dangerous.
74 'intricacies'	Obscure details.
77 'moulded plaster'	Smooth wall covering shaped into an ornamental pattern.
81 'faggots'	Bundles of sticks tied together for fuel.
82 'combustible'	Capable of being burnt.
87 'life's epitome'	A representation in his own person of life itself.

Commentary:
This elegy for Robert Gregory marks one of the high points of Yeats's poetic achievement. The sophisticated stanza form allows great variety within each one. The first five lines announce and develop the thought which is then given a twist by the last three as if each stanza was a miniature sonnet. The variety in the metric form creates the impression of conversation spoken in time to the speed of thought while, in fact, it is very tightly controlled by its fixed scheme.

The casual tone of the opening with its atmosphere of fireside chat enables an intimate relationship to form between poet and reader as if a private confidence was being entrusted to him. It is only with the last line of the first stanza with its repetition of 'all' and emphasis on 'being dead' that a change of tone is suggested. The change does not occur immediately, however, for the second stanza returns to the conversational mode between husband and wife. Even as Yeats recalls Johnson, Synge and Pollexfen, the mood is relaxed with the comfort of habit to make loss tolerable, even in a sense enjoyable. Instead of the emphasis on death, the last line of each of their verses is concerned with qualities by which they can be remembered. In stanza VI the mood intensifies and the poem draws towards its climax as its real subject comes into view. The easy momentum is destroyed in the breaking rhythm which signals the heightening of emotion: 'But not that my dear friend's dear son'. In retrospect it is clear that the earlier figures were evoked because they each represented an aspect of the personality of Robert Gregory. If the parallel with Sidney seems initially to be a wild over-statement, the direct, unadorned recollections of the Major's life come near to justifying it. The climactic stanza XI with its extended metaphor of a man's life burning like different types of fuel, draws attention to a complex density of the verses which echoes the sinewy quality of the metaphysical poets. Robert Gregory is to be added to that list of now dead heroes who belonged to the world of 'romantic Ireland'; aristocratic, passionate and possessing that immortal quality which can never live long in the body of mortal man.

AN IRISH AIRMAN FORESEES HIS DEATH

First Line: 'I know that I shall meet my fate'

Collection: 'The Wild Swans At Coole' (1919)

Original Title:

First Published: *The Wild Swans at Coole*, (1919)

Summary:
The poem is spoken through the voice of the airman who has received a premonition of his death in the air. He makes it clear that he is not driven by hatred for the enemy nor love of his own side. Those for whom he dares, the Irish peasant class will not be affected by the outcome of the war. He did not enlist for any of the usual reasons — conscription; patriotism; political rhetoric; mass hysteria. His reason is more private and personal than these. He has weighed his past and future in the 'balance' and found something appropriate and heroic in 'this death'.

Glossary:
5 'Kiltartan Cross' A landmark near Coole.

Commentary:
Though provoked by Robert Gregory's death, this lyric is not an elegy, nor is it about Gregory himself in the way that the previous poem was. The 'I' is Robert Gregory who did possess second sight which in a way enabled him to choose his death, but the poem spreads out to encompass any kind of solitary, heroic, detached death of the type which had always appealed to the imagination of the poet.

The essence of the poem is the idea of 'balance' reflected in both content and form. After the opening statement, the poem proceeds through balanced pairs reflected in the balance of the couplets until it reaches its climax with the only line that runs on into the following one:

A lonely impulse of delight
Drove to this tumult in the clouds;

After this the balance returns to the lines, recreating the cold, detached state of the airman's mind in deciding to choose a death which would balance his kind of life. The tightly rhymed, end-stopped lines give to the poem its sense of purpose and finality and its high incidence of monosyllables the feeling of simplicity and universal reference.

SOLOMON TO SHEBA

First Line: 'Sang Solomon to Sheba,'

Collection: 'The Wild Swans At Coole' (1919)

Original Title:

First Published: *The Little Review*, October 1918

Summary:
The poem is built up as a dialogue between Solomon and Sheba with Solomon speaking the first and last stanzas and Sheba the middle one. While Solomon kisses Sheba who sits on his knee, he tells her that they have spent all day talking only about the subject of love. She responds by saying that if he had raised a different subject he would have found out very soon that it was not the subject but her mind that was limited. Solomon answers by telling her that they are the wisest among all men but that the fruit of their wisdom is the understanding that love is the one universal theme that binds the world into a unity.

Glossary:

1	'Solomon to Sheba'	Yeats to Mrs. Yeats.
2	'dusky'	Dark coloured.
8	'pound'	Enclosure for stray animals.
11	'broached'	Brought up for discussion.

Commentary:
This poem reflects the changed mood in Yeats after his marriage. Adopting the persona of Solomon, he is now able to give much freer expression to his sensual feelings and to find in passion the

prime moving force of the human world. The dialogue form allows him a direct approach to his relationship with his wife who, in the form of Sheba, is thus able to talk back to the poet. Her unease in the face of her husband's learning is dismissed by him, for through her he has discovered more than learning has brought him, an understanding that the ultimate wisdom is passion. The sensuality which Yeats found in his reading of Arab literature is readily transferred to his own new-found freedom of the senses in marriage.

ON WOMAN

First Line: 'May God be praised for woman'

Collection: 'The Wild Swans At Coole' (1919)

Original Title:

First Published: *Poetry* (Chicago), February 1916

Summary:
The first stanza is a general hymn of praise to women for their special capacity for an utterly devoted friendship in which they submerge their own mind completely in a man's and feel no resentment in the process. After this introduction the poem moves to the specific area of sexual fulfilment, using as its example Yeats's favourite instance of Solomon and Sheba. First he chronicles the supreme sexual delight which Sheba brought to Solomon in the moment of their consummation, and then Yeats goes on to hope that he will experience a similar delight in his reincarnation, since he feels that he is now too old to hope for such an experience in this life.

Glossary:

9	'pedantry'	Dull scholarship.
18	'smithy'	Blacksmith's.
19	'It shuddered in the water'	The iron is a symbol for the male sexual organ, and the water a symbol for the female.
30	'the Pestle of the moon'	A 'pestle' is an instrument for pounding substances to dust. Thus the phases of the moon bring in the new incarnation.
39	'gnashing'	Grinding together.
41	'perverse'	Wilful.

Commentary:
In the context of Yeats's life the poem is ironic in that the poet sees himself too old for the ecstasy of passion, although it was written only a little time before his marriage when he again takes up the characters of Solomon and Sheba, this time attributing to Mrs. Yeats the traditional qualities of that queen. Perhaps the poem can be used as an indication of Yeats's readiness for marriage, since it derives its structure, rhythms and tension from the mechanics of the sexual act. The long second verse is made up of only two sentences. The first ceases at the moment of consummation after building to a hectic climax and the second repeats the same movement this time culminating in the erotic dance of Sheba being performed in the poet's imagined life to come. The reference to the phases of the moon shows into what metaphysical areas Yeats was moving, although the phrase 'if the tale's true' indicates that there is still work to be done to allay his scepticism.

THE FISHERMAN

First Line: 'Although I can see him still,'

Collection: 'The Wild Swans At Coole' (1919)

Original Title:

First Published: *Poetry* (Chicago), February 1916

Summary:
The poet tells us that though the image of the fisherman is still before him, fishing at dawn in a desolate countryside, the figure first appeared before him 'long since'. The man is seen as the ideal audience for the poet of the Irish race. 'The reality' has been that he has had to write for 'insolent', 'witty', 'clever' men who have betrayed their culture through their own self-seeking. In the second verse the poet says it is a year since he first called up the image of this skilful fisherman, who is a figment of his imagination. When he first called him into his mind's eye the poet told himself that he would write one poem fit for such an audience before he grew old.

Glossary:

4 'grey Connemara — The homespun tweed traditionally associated with

Line	Term	Note
	clothes'	Connemara.
14	'The dead man'	Probably J. M. Synge.
15	'craven'	Cowardly.
16	'The insolent unreproved'	The insulting man, carrying on without rebuke.
17	'brought to book'	Called to account.
24	'great Art beaten down'	Probably a reference to the Lane Gallery controversy or the riots over Synge's play, *The Playboy of the Western World*.

Commentary:
The theme is the familiar one of the gulf between the heroic, ideal Ireland which Robert Gregory represented, and the sordid real one of the aspiring middle classes locked in petty squabbles. The ideal image which exists only in the poet's dream is of a man who is in touch with his land, a man of simple feelings and instincts who both understands and feels his native culture. He is associated with a place 'where stone is dark under froth'. His mind, statue-like, is constant beneath the moving surface of daily life. Through his craft he is also associated with the faery powers who fish for the souls of men. Ultimately the image is of the poet himself and he promises to write at least one poem that will satisfy him by achieving at once, a detachment of style ('cold') and an intensity of vision ('passionate') which is found at dawn in the reconciliation of night and day.

BROKEN DREAMS

First Line: 'There is grey in your hair.'

Collection: 'The Wild Swans At Coole' (1919)

Original Title:

First Published: *The Little Review,* June 1917

Summary:
The woman being recalled by the poet has now grown old and is ignored by the young men, although the old bless her for past goodness and even the Day of Judgement is postponed by the power of her peaceful presence which has passed beyond the painful emotions of earlier years. Only uncertain images created

by a fallible memory remain, recalled to life by the questions of a generation too young to have known the lady at first hand but prompted to ask by the significance which the poet attaches to her memory. However, in the new life beyond the grave she will be reincarnated at the height of her beauty and the prospect has set the poet talking excitedly to himself. He remembers that her incomparable beauty was flawed by the smallness of her hands and fears that when she is a pure spirit in the life to come she will wipe away that flaw and so change the hands that have been kissed by him. So he begs her to leave them as they are. It is now midnight and the poet realises that he has spent the entire day sitting, talking to the image of his past love.

Glossary:

1 'your hair'	Maud Gonne.
4 'gaffer'	Simple country man.
18 'the poet'	Yeats.
19 'age'	Yeats was fifty at the time of writing this.

Commentary:

This poem on the familiar theme of Maud Gonne's memory and the poet's relationship to that memory reveals his growing mastery of sophisticated metrical forms that give the appearance of an easy, conversational manner but are, in fact, highly wrought to allow the most simple statements a directness of expression essential to the impact they create on the reader. The impression given is of the right phrase slipping into place without strain or striving for self-conscious effect. The use of the verb 'paddle' is significant in linking Maud to Helen via the symbol of the swans on the lake in Coole Park which dominates this collection. Notice also that Yeats speaks of the next life with growing confidence about the manner of its working.

A DEEP-SWORN VOW

First Line: 'Others because you did not keep'

Collection: 'The Wild Swans At Coole' (1919)

Original Title:

First Published: *The Little Review,* June 1917

Summary:
The poet admits to relationships with other women because his beloved broke her vow to him. Even so, at times of heightened awareness, it is her face that confronts his imagination.

Glossary:

1 'you'	Maud Gonne.
2 'That deep-sworn vow'	Not to marry.

Commentary:
Again, the simplicity is deceptive for the form in this poem is most carefully and tightly wrought. In a poem as short as this, the position of every word carries weight. The poet opens with a statement concerning his relations with 'others'; yet even before he makes it, he has excused himself by introducing the main sentence with the sub-clause in which the effect of haste in making the excuse is achieved through the internal rhyme of 'keep' and 'deep'. The moments when Maud appears to Yeats are then listed in descending order of seriousness, 'death', 'sleep' and 'wine'; linked by being states in which the usual restraints which daily life puts on the imagination do not apply. 'Suddenly' suggests he is taken unawares and the repetition of 'face' links Maud with the figure of Death, climaxing the tension which runs through the poem, arising out of the ambivalent feelings of Yeats concerning these encounters. Although they speak for the depth of his feelings for Maud, as in earlier years they are not easy to live with, acting as they do like a piece of grit in an oyster, provoking the painful pearls of poetic utterance.

IN MEMORY OF ALFRED POLLEXFEN

First Line: 'Five-and-twenty years have gone'

Collection: 'The Wild Swans At Coole' (1919)

Original Title: In Memory

First Published: *The Little Review,* June 1917

Summary:
The poem is a memorial to the Pollexfen family rather than to Alfred in particular although it is his death 'yesterday' which has prompted the poet to record their lives, starting with William twenty-five years before the poet is writing. He was laid to rest in a tomb of his own making beside his wife. His son George, twenty years after, was given a large, formal funeral by his fellow freemasons, in the place where he was also born. His fate contrasts with that of John Pollexfen who died at sea far away from this place. Alfred also died in his native place, having decided to come home ten years before. The poet asserts in conclusion that all these deaths were marked by the lament of a 'visionary white sea-bird' heard by the mourning women, to whose cry the poet adds his own.

Glossary:

1	'Five-and-twenty years have gone'	William Pollexfen, Yeats's maternal grandfather, died in 1890.
6	'after twenty years'	George Pollexfen died in September 1910.
8	'the astrologer'	One who studies the influence of the stars on human affairs.
9	'Masons'	Also known as 'Free Masons'; they are members of a widely established secret fraternity for mutual help with elaborate rituals and secret signs. Yeats describes the funeral on page 553 of his *Letters* (ed. Wade).
10	'Acacia'	Plant with sweet-scented white flowers.
11	'a melancholy man'	See pages 36 and 64 of this volume for a brief description of George Pollexfen.
15	'The Mall'	A street in Sligo.
29	'throng'	Crowd.
30	'journey home'	Alfred Pollexfen's wife and children had stayed in Sligo while he was away. He returned to Sligo at fifty

	and died ten years later.
37 'A visionary white sea bird'	Yeats records in *Autobiographies*: 'Only six months ago my sister awoke dreaming that she held a wingless sea-bird in her arms and presently she heard that he had died in his madhouse, for a sea-bird is the omen that announces the death or danger of a Pollexfen'.

Commentary:
This poem seems somewhat flat if compared with 'In Memory of Major Robert Gregory' but its purpose is quite different. Yeats's personal involvement is much less intense in this case, for his concern is to chronicle the passing of a whole family and to assert that family's significance in the history of Sligo. The formal, even set of the metre is well suited to this public function for the poem. In the last four lines the link is forged between this and the other world, particularly appropriate in the case of George, whose interest was in the supernatural. While the detail of the sea-bird is borrowed from his sister's dream, the significance of the solitary bird as a representative of the subjective soul is an archetypal symbol in the poetry. Yeats extends the image from a morally neutral position to one where it protests through its song against mortality.

THE SAINT AND THE HUNCHBACK

First Line: 'Hunchback. Stand up and lift your hand and bless'

Collection: 'The Wild Swans At Coole' (1919)

Original Title:

First Published: *The Wild Swans at Coole*, (1919)

Summary:
The poem is formed out of a dialogue between a Hunchback and a Saint. The Hunchback speaks first and asks for a blessing on himself. He is bitter because he has found his ambition thwarted by his physical deformity. The Saint, after first recognizing himself as part of God's plan, says that he will continue to bless even while beating out of himself any desire that might lead to personal ambition of the kind revealed by Alexander the Great, Augustus or Alcibiades. The Hunchback replies that he gives thanks to just

such people whom the Saint is seeking to expel from his flesh, most notably Alcibiades.

Glossary:

6 'a different plan'	The plan laid out in each of the twenty-eight phases of *A Vision*.
8 'taws'	A kind of birch used to punish children.
12 'Alcibiades'	A pupil of Socrates who had a disastrous political career.

Commentary:

This is one of those group of poems coming at the close of *The Wild Swans At Coole* which, like 'The Double Vision of Michael Robartes', is inspired by Yeats's work on *A Vision* and which cannot be fully understood without reference to that work. The figure of the Hunchback is the epitome of Phase twenty-six and the Saint of Phase twenty-seven. The Hunchback is characterized most strongly by ambition which devours all other qualities and isolates the possessor completely from other men. At this phase, however, the ambition is denied by physical deformity as the flesh is in a state of corruption and the consequence is that the Hunchback spends his life in bitter contemplation of figures from the past who have matched their personal ambition by their achievements. By contrast the Saint stands as a representative of the spirit of absolute renunciation. Yeats wrote in *A Vision*: 'His joy is to be nothing, to do nothing, to think nothing; but to permit the total life, expressed in its humanity, to flow in upon him and to express itself through his acts and thoughts.' Yeats uses the Greek philosopher Socrates as his example of the Saint, and the Hunchback stands to the Saint somewhat as Alcibiades stood to Socrates. The Hunchback prefers Alcibiades because Alcibiades was outstandingly *handsome*, as well as a lover of pleasure. Almost certainly referring to Alcibiades, Plato writes in *The Republic*: 'Will he not be filled with unbounded ambition, believing himself well able to manage the affairs of all the world, at home and abroad, and thereupon give himself airs and be puffed up with senseless self-conceit?'

THE DOUBLE VISION OF MICHAEL ROBARTES

First Line: 'On the grey rock of Cashel the mind's eye'

Collection: 'The Wild Swans At Coole' (1919)

Original Title:

First Published: *The Wild Swans at Coole,* (1919)

Summary:
The first section of the poem describes the first vision of Michael Robartes, that of the soul at the dark of the moon, the twenty-eighth phase, when it gives itself up to all external influences, until, without a will of its own, it allows itself to be formed into the shape of a human body. It is a body like a puppet, moving at another's volition, devoid of moral sense and even unaware of the universal laws which govern it.

The second section describes the other vision in which Robartes sees a sphinx and a Buddha. Between them he sees a girl dancing in a way which suggests she is not mortal. Though it is a vision what he sees seems stronger than reality, since he is seeing by the light of the full moon in the fifteenth phase when the soul is in a state of pure self-realization. The eyes of the sphinx roved over all the domain of the intellect while those of the Buddha were still, turned inwards to the domain of the emotions, a world of sadness not 'peace'. No relationship seemed to exist between the three figures of the vision for the dancing girl was in a condition beyond 'thought'. The sensations received through 'eye' and 'ear' cloud the pictures of the 'mind' with the intrusion of external reality but now when the mind is unhindered, it expresses the harmony of the 'spinning-top'. The vision is so strong that, for Robartes, the figures have become immortal and the moment of perceiving them eternal.

In the third section Robartes knows that the girl of the second vision is the one he has been seeking in his dreams, the one whose departing presence as he wakes is enough to stir him with a feverish impulse as if he had been in the company of Helen of Troy who cared not for the destruction she caused. Robartes then concludes by saying that the contrary visions 'of the dark moon and the full' have induced a state of madness in him causing him first to grieve, then, to affirm his links with his physical nature, kiss a stone, and then with his spirit in recreating the experience as 'a song' to celebrate the gift of understanding provided by the double vision which came to him in the chapel ruins.

Glossary:

Title:	'Michael Robartes'	In *The Wind Among The Reeds* Yeats wrote: 'Michael Robartes is the pride of the imagination brooding upon the greatness of its possessions.'
1	'the grey rock of Cashel'	The Rock of Cashel in Co. Tipperary has several ecclesiastical ruins.
2	'cold spirits'	Because they are born without the warmth of the moon's light.
4	'horn'	The new crescent of the moon.
9	'constrained, arraigned, baffled'	Compelled, accused, frustrated.
10	'wire-jointed jaws and limbs of wood'	The man is put together with physical materials like a puppet.
18	'A Sphinx'	Yeats's emblem for the introspective mind.
19	'A Buddha'	Yeats's emblem for the outward-looking mind.
20	'blest'	Gave a blessing.
28	'fifteenth night'	The phase of the full-moon when the soul achieves complete self-realization.
29	'lashed'	Struck violently.
31	'triumph of intellect'	The Sphinx represents pure intellect and the Buddha pure sanctity.
39	'she had outdanced thought'	She had put herself into a plane beyond human thought.
44	'a spinning-top'	It turns in circles so fast and so tight that it appears to be motionless.
56	'Homer's Paragon'	Helen of Troy, Yeats's symbol for Maud Gonne.
68	'Cormac's ruined house'	The chapel on the Rock of Cashel restored in the twelfth century by Cormac MacCarthy.

Commentary

This poem is among the first of those which Yeats created out of the material of *A Vision* in its earliest version. Michael Robartes is one of the poet's masks, the persona who expresses the heroic imagination. It is fitting that it should be he who is allowed a glimpse of what is hidden from mortal eyes, there being no life at the dark and the full of the moon. While examples of all the other phases can be drawn from past or present human life, a description of the twenty-eighth and fifteenth phases can only be achieved, if at all, through visions which put a man in touch with the immortal world.

The poem also introduces an important symbol in the later

poetry, the dancer. Ellmann in *The Identity of Yeats* points to her function in this poem:

'The Sphinx is the intellect, gazing on both known and unknown things; the Buddha is the heart, gazing on both loved and unloved things; and the dancing girl, most important of all, is primarily an image of art. She dances between them because art is neither intellectual nor emotional, but a balance of these qualities.'

MICHAEL ROBARTES AND THE DANCER (1921)

The poems in this collection can be divided into two sorts; the political poems carrying the poet's reflections on the Easter Rising and the more recent civil disorder; and the more personal poems dealing in the main with aspects of his work on *A Vision* or recreating personal situations through the medium of the mask.

Yeats had developed, by this time, his theory of the Mask of the Opposite by which a man, through the exercise of his will, is able to create a persona or identity of a figure comprising those qualities that are the opposites of the ones he possesses naturally. At this period of his creative life that figure is Michael Robartes, the tough, out-going lover and man of action. Not that Robartes is the correct mask for all occasions as can be seen in the poem 'Solomon to Sheba', a product of Yeats's Arab studies, where one reading of the poem takes the protagonists of the title as substitutes for the poet and his wife. The poem furnishes a good example of the confidence, almost nonchalance with which Yeats is now able to handle the most personal areas of his experience. The frank treatment of sexual themes which is a feature of his later work is attributable to a number of factors including his marriage, his reading in eastern literature and the device of the mask, all of which go into the creation of the conversational, deliberately down-beat, ironic tone of this poem.

This confidence in handling his material is reflected in 'Easter 1916' (p. 202) in the directness and simplicity clinched by the refrain. There is no pose or rhetoric as is discernable in the earlier political poems. He records frankly his misreading of the political and heroic capabilities of the fallen men without sentimentalising them.

These qualities culminate in this volume in one of Yeats's best known poems 'The Second Coming (p. 210) which is greatly enhanced by knowledge of the material of *A Vision* but which does not depend upon it to make its first impact on the reader. Two lines from the poem have often been quoted in times since the death of the poet to sum up the political climate in which we are placed today:

'The best lack all conviction, while the worst
Are full of passionate intensity.'

SOLOMON AND THE WITCH

First Line: 'And thus declared that Arab lady:'

Collection: 'Michael Robartes And The Dancer' (1921)

Original Title:

First Published: *Michael Robartes and the Dancer*, 1921

Summary:
'That Arab lady' (Sheba) speaks of having found herself shouting out in a language foreign to both her and Solomon while making love to him. Solomon, who understands all the languages of living creatures replies that it is the voice of a 'cockerel' speaking through her. This bird who last crowed 'before the Fall' has crowed again in the belief that in the union of Solomon and Sheba 'Chance' is 'at one with Choice' so that time may now be stopped and eternity restored. He tells Sheba about all the disappointments which love can bring when Chance and Choice do not coincide and the lovers' illusions are shattered. Nevertheless when all contraries are resolved in the perfect union the world ends. Sheba points out that the world has not ended. Solomon remarks that the cockerel was deceived, that image and reality did not quite coincide. Sheba's reaction is to urge him, with the help of the moon's increasing influence, to try again.

Glossary:

1	'that Arab lady'	Sheba.
6	'Who understood'	King Solomon.
9	'cockerel'	A young cock. In Hermetic tradition, it sits in the branches of the Tree of Life and crows to announce a new cycle.
15	'the brigand apple'	That Eve ate to bring death into the world.
17	'crowed out eternity'	Crowed to sound the end of immortality.
19	'love has a spider's eye'	The spider carries many associations such as the female destroying its mate after copulation and its uses in concocting poisons. The lens of the spider's

	eye is likened to a lover's capacity for distorting his images of his partner.
43 'the moon is wilder'	Because it is approaching the fifteenth night.

Commentary
The poem again demonstrates Yeats's mastery of the conversational form. The spare, uncluttered lines achieve resonance without pomposity and while there is much that invites reference to sources outside the poem, it stands up powerfully and effectively on its own.

On one level Solomon and Sheba are masks adopted by the poet for himself and Mrs. Yeats who was subject to the type of utterance described in the poem. Significantly, Yeats turns to the material of *The Arabian Nights* for a franker expression of his sexual feelings than he has been capable of previously. The theme of the poem, that of the relationship between Chance and Choice and the pain resulting from attempts to reconcile them might be expected to evoke a solemn atmosphere but the ease with which the poet handles his material allows for a great variety of tones from the poignant intensity of: 'And when at last that murder's over' to the colloquial nonchalance of 'Although he thought it worth a crow'.

Yeats does not treat his subject with complete seriousness and it is a mark of his maturing attitude in his relationships that he can write of the most personal areas of his life in this vein:

> 'O! Solomon! let us try again.'

EASTER 1916

First Line: 'I have met them at close of day'

Collection: 'Michael Robartes and the Dancer' (1921)

Original Title:

First Published: *The New Statesman*, 23 October 1920

Summary:
The rebellion against British rule of Easter week 1916, though in itself a futile gesture, became the symbol and rallying point for the Irish liberation movement in subsequent years. This impor-

tance was due almost entirely to the action of the British military authorities in executing fifteen of the leading rebels, turning them instantly from political extremists into martyrs. Public opinion which had been mainly unsympathetic to the Rising was henceforth committed to the cause of independence.

Before the Rising the poet never did more than acknowledge the presence of its subsequent victims. Now his regard for their leaders and their abilities is changed dramatically. They have played their parts and been changed by them even as the poet's perception of them is changed. One-track lives can seem like immutable stones when compared to ever-changing nature. Over-long suffering ('sacrifice') turns the heart to stone; when might it all end, and was it really even necessary? These heroes gave their all for love of Ireland, yet may have done it in vain after all; nevertheless they are transfigured and reborn as 'a terrible beauty'.

Glossary:

10 'gibe'	A sarcastic remark at the expense of another.
14 'motley'	A costume of many colours worn by a fool. Hence the expression of all shades of political opinion; none taken seriously.
17 'That woman'	Constance Markievicz.
23 'harriers'	Hounds used for hunting hares.
32 'vainglorious lout'	Excessively vain, insensitive man.
52 'plashes'	Breaks the surface of the water.
59 'suffice'	Be enough.

Commentary

The opening verse captures the mood of provincial Dublin with economy and directness. It is the world familiar from Joyce's short-stories, *Dubliners*, of routine work in dingy offices and escape at the end of the day into alcoholic conviviality in 'the club'. Those he meets, like the poet himself when wearing this mask, seem to lack substance; a race of jesters maintained at the whim of the British court. However, the final change of this 'motley' crowd is permanent, a change as in the poem from a comic to a tragic key:

> Being certain that they and I
> But lived where motley is worn:
> All changed, changed utterly:
> A terrible beauty is born.

The rest of the poem expands on the paradox of 'a terrible beauty', for that which has made these lives tragic has also given them beauty.

Even the despised MacBride is accorded his proper place in the pantheon of the great for the power of passion has transformed him. MacBride in fact provides the hinge for the poem. Up to this point the dominant tone is of regret at the waste of the lives of those who died for the cause. Now the poet accepts that such a response is too one-sided:

> Yet I number him in the song;
> He, too, has resigned his part
> In the casual comedy;
> He, too, has been changed in his turn,
> Transformed utterly:
> A terrible beauty is born.

The third verse widens the poem's frame of reference to encompass all human activity by means of Neo-Platonic symbols drawn from the natural world. 'The stone', though a part of nature, does not change 'minute by minute' but keeps its position and expression constant. The stone troubles the stream by diverting its course, even as the martyrs of the Rising have diverted the course of history. The turning of the heart to stone is a dehumanizing process, however, and the great cost of this change leads the poet into a hesitant, doubtful tone in verse four, shown by the frequent use of questions. Up to the last question the poem is poised on the tension of the poet's ambivalent response to the momentous events:

> And what if excess of love
> Bewildered them till they died?

However, England's later failure to 'keep faith' on Home Rule endorsed the poet's commitment to the nationalist cause which began in both his poetry and his life with the last lines of the poem and his return to Ireland to live at Thoor Ballylee. Whatever reservations and regrets the future might hold the stone held fast in the stream, channelling the poet's poetic style into a fiercer and more abrasive flow. The 'terrible beauty' belongs to both the political freedom of the new Ireland and the artistic freedom of the later poems of Yeats:

> I write it out in a verse —
> MacDonagh and MacBride

And Connolly and Pearse
Now and in time to be,
Wherever green is worn,
Are changed, changed utterly:
A terrible beauty is born.

September 25, 1916

THE SECOND COMING

First Line: 'Turning and turning in the widening gyre'

Collection: 'Michael Robartes And The Dancer' (1921)

Original Title:

First Published: *The Dial*, November 1920

Summary:
As the Christian dispensation of two thousand years draws to an increasingly objective close, and mankind grows deafer to the message of Christ, catastrophe is imminent. Only those steeped in wrongness have the will and urge to carry out their aims. The Second Coming must therefore be due, but it presents a terrifying vision to the poet: he sees a grotesque, sphinx-like figure making its clumsy way across the desert. Mankind can expect an ordeal, for the new Messiah must necessarily contrast dramatically with Christ; indeed, he will be a 'rough beast'.

Glossary:

1	'the widening gyre'	The outward-moving spirals reaching the widest point of a cone.
5	'The blood-dimmed tide'	The flood of irrational violence which marks the change of the cycles.
6	'The ceremony of innocence'	Innocence is the quality which opposes the military and sexual violence of the tide and ceremony carries associations of the Christian services.
12	'*Spiritus Mundi*'	Described by the poet as 'a general storehouse of images which have ceased to be a property of any personality or spirit'.
17	'Reel shadows'	The shadows cast around the 'shape' by birds flying above are seen to whirl unsteadily.
20	'vexed to nightmare by a rocking cradle'	Troubled with terrifying visions by the spirit of the Christian age.

22 'slouches' Moves slowly and ungainly.

Commentary
While the meaning of this poem is only apparent in consultation with the material of *A Vision*, its power and visual ferocity can be immediately felt. The first eight lines deal with the imminent destruction of civilization as prefigured in the violence attendant on the opening of the twentieth century in general and the Irish 'troubles' in particular. The Christian message and the figure of Christ are like a falcon and falconer who are no longer in touch with each other. Uncontrolled, the bird is left to prey on all men. The repetition of 'loosed' in the technical sense of letting a hawk off a leash gives the metaphor universal application. 'The falconer' and 'the centre' represent the power of a great civilization holding in check those anarchic forces which would otherwise break away. Despite the usual view the Irish held of British imperialism, Yeats was probably thinking of the British Empire as a force for order in the world.

The remainder of the poem proceeds to consider what these signs portend. The use of the phrase 'Second Coming' contains a savage irony since its form will be the exact opposite of the expectation that a Christian would give to it. The form, which is associated with the Sphinx, is the embodiment of callous, brute force of the type located at the dark of the moon; therefore the creature possesses:

> 'A gaze blank and pitiless as the sun'

The sphinx predates the Christian era and is therefore associated with the 'stony sleep' which, now roused from 'nightmare', manifests itself in the 'rough beast' about to vent its destruction. The terror evoked by the closing lines of the poem stems from the contrast of associations between 'stony sleep' and 'rocking cradle' and 'rough beast' and 'Bethlehem'. It is encapsulated in the inevitable, unfeeling, haphazard chaos of 'slouches'.

A PRAYER FOR MY DAUGHTER

First Line:	'Once more the storm is howling, and half hid'
Collection:	'Michael Robartes And The Dancer' (1921)
Original Title:	
First Published:	*The Irish Statesman*, 8 November 1919 and *Poetry* (Chicago), November 1919.

Summary:

The first two stanzas set the scene for the poem. As his child sleeps, the poet tries to gain relief from the depression which afflicts him by meditating on his daughter's future while the storm rages outside. Stanza three starts the prayer, the poet asking for beauty for her, but not that extreme of beauty which isolates the possessor from her ordinary humanity. Helen and Aphrodite are cited as examples of this type of beauty and both made bad marriages. Instead he wishes 'courtesy' and 'charm' for his daughter, for these qualities provoke stronger relationships. He hopes she will find permanence and continuity in her life while giving joy to others. Most of all the poet, as a result of his own experiences, hopes that hatred will keep from her mind, especially that 'intellectual hatred' which he has seen ruin the natural accomplishments of a beautiful woman. Happiness is possible for his daughter if she learns that it is to be found in following the promptings of her own soul. Finally her marital home will be vital in deciding her fate and so the poet hopes she will marry into a family where 'ceremony' and 'custom', the virtues of aristocracy and tradition are paramount.

Glossary:

Title. 'My Daughter'	Anne Butler Yeats.
10 'the tower'	Thoor Ballylee.
13 'reverie'	Day-dream.
18 'distraught'	Crazy with passion.
27 'that great Queen'	Aphrodite, Greek goddess of love, beauty and fertility.
29 'a bandy-legged smith'	A blacksmith with legs bent outwards at the knees. This is Hephaestus, the god of fire.
32 'the Horn of plenty'	The *cornucopia*, a common emblem in classical art, is a horn spilling out flowers and fruits.

Line	Word	Meaning
27	'beauty's very self'	Maud Gonne.
38	'a poor man'	Yeats.
38	'roved'	Wandered.
40	'a glad kindness'	Mrs. Yeats.
42	'the linnet'	Small heathland bird noted for the sweetness of its song.
45	'merriment'	Amused enjoyment.
47	'laurel'	Shrub with glossy leaves.
51	'Prosper but little'	Maud Gonne was imprisoned for her political activity.
55	'Assault and battery'	Attack and blows.
59	'the loveliest woman born'	Maud Gonne.
62	'Barter'	Sell by exchange.
64	'bellows'	Machine for pushing a jet of air to help a fire to start.
66	'radical'	Rooted.
68	'Self-appeasing'	Self-satisfying.
68	'self-affrighting'	Self-alarming.
75	'wares'	Goods.
76	'Peddled in the thoroughfares'	Sold in the streets.

Commentary

This poem inspired by the birth of his daughter illustrates many of the best features of Yeats's mature verse. Starting from a vividly realised, actual scene, the poem moves out to encompass a universal theme. The wide scope of the poem is contained by a combination of its imagery and its verse form which is the same as that used for 'In Memory of Major Robert Gregory' (see p. 135) where the stanzas are also formed around a rhyme scheme of *aabbcddc* and a stress pattern of 55545445 feet to the stanza. The result is a poem which reads with that now typically deceptive feeling of casual composition that disguises the scrupulous care with which the effect has been created. The physical reality of the storm is extended into Yeats's vision of the future, with 'the murderous innocence of the sea' echoing 'the blood-dimmed tide' of *The Second Coming*. A tension is maintained throughout between the wind and the tree with Helen/Maud being associated with the former through the bellows and Yeats's hopes for Anne being represented by the laurel and the linnet together struggling against the storms of 'arrogance and hatred' which typify the modern world for the poet. The Horn of Plenty, the other running image of the poem, climaxes with its contemporary realisation in the notion of 'ceremony' to which Yeats attaches all the virtues of the great house culture which have been gathering strength through such poems as 'Upon A House Shaken By The Land Agitation' (see p. 119). Here he sees the last repository for values which stand out against the ubiquitous materialism of a mercantile view of life; values which depend for their sustenance upon the strength that they draw from 'custom'. In other words from a respect for a tradition which predates the rise of the middle-classes in the nineteenth century.

A MEDITATION IN TIME OF WAR

First Line: 'For one throb of the artery,'

Collection: 'Michael Robartes And The Dancer' (1921)

Original Title:

First Published: *The Dial*, November 1920, *The Nation* (London), 6 November 1920

Summary:
In the time it takes for the pulse to beat once the poet experiences a vision of the eternal scheme which is normally hidden behind the cloak of mortal life.

Glossary:

1 'throb' — Beat.
5 'inanimate fantasy' — A lifeless imitation.

Commentary
The 'wind-broken tree' picks up the image from 'A Prayer For My Daughter' and indicates that the storm of world disaster has broken the frail tree of the poet's worldly hopes. There is, however, an important consolation for the prophet of global doom in the fleeting perception of the Reality of which man's life is only the shadow. This is a vital theme that Yeats carries into the last phase of his poetry, giving rise to the emotion of 'tragic joy'.

THE TOWER
(1928)

The collection, comprising much of Yeats's finest work, is only half of a total scheme that is completed by the subsequent volume, *The Winding Stair*. Both titles refer specifically to the tower at Ballylee with its spiral staircase where much of the verse of the mature Yeats was composed. However, the wide range of symbolic meanings which attach themselves to these features in all Yeats's work in general, and these two volumes in particular, provides a framework in which the overall scheme is set.

While the structure is parallel, the points of view are opposed. So where there are eleven poems in *The Tower* collected under *A Man Young and Old*, there are eleven in *The Winding Stair* under the title *A Woman Young and Old*. In fact, the male and female qualities are opposed throughout the collections, with the male principle with its symbol, the tower dominating the first, even as the female principle with its symbol, the winding stair, creating the shape of the gyre, dominates the second.

The opposition of mood is as marked as that of symbol with the violent, sterile and crumbling world of *The Tower* giving way to sexuality and regeneration in *The Winding Stair* as aesthetics replace politics.

The bitterness which sets the tone throughout the collection reflects on the political plane the desperate condition of Ireland in the Troubles and on the personal plane the failing health of the aging poet driving himself into nervous exhaustion through his determination to tap the rich vein of *The Tower* poems.

The scope and nature of the volume is announced in the opening poem, 'Sailing to Byzantium' (p. 217) where the life of this world is given up as the province of young men, while the poet seeks the soul's rather than the body's enrichment, as being more appropriate to his age. The same tension exists in the 'Meditations in Time of Civil War' (p. 225) where Yeats closes the door of Thoor Ballylee on the violence surging around it to continue his private, inactive contemplations. As in the previous collection there is a distinct grouping between the poems that relate to *A Vision* and the autobiographical poems whose meanings are extended beyond the personal to the universal through the carefully interwoven images of tower, tree, bird and dancer.

SAILING TO BYZANTIUM

First Line: 'That is no country for old men. The young'

Collection: 'The Tower' (1928)

Original Title:

First Published: *October Blast*, 1927

Summary:
The poet declares that Ireland is a young man's land, where sensuality takes precedence over intellect; not a place for the old. He has therefore sailed to Byzantium, where, among intellectual pursuits and historical magnificence, he can face the decay of old age. He prays to the 'sages' of Byzantium to free him from his old body and give him immortality, albeit of an artificial kind. Once immortal, the poet can choose his own form, ideally that of a golden songbird telling all Byzantium of past, present and future events.

Glossary:

Title: 'Byzantium'	In *A Vision* Yeats writes: 'I think if I could be given a month of Antiquity and leave to spend it where I chose, I would spend it in Byzantium, a little before Justinian opened St Sophia and closed the Academy of Plato.'
1 'That is no . . .'	Ireland.
7 'Caught in . . .'	Lured away by the music of nature which appeals to their senses, the young neglect works of art whose appeal is intellectual.
9 'a paltry thing'	A contemptible object.
10 'a tattered coat'	A coat torn to rags.
19 'perne in a gyre'	Move with a spinning motion through the cone from apex to base.
24 'The artifice of eternity'	The work of art exists outside the laws of time.
28 'enamelling'	Inlay.
29 'drowsy'	Sleepy.

Commentary:
This is the first of many poems expressing the poet's concern with

the theme of aging. The tension between mortality and immortality, life and art has been with him, however, since his earliest poems. Ireland is here associated with the young and the concerns of mortal life from which the poet feels detached on account of the declining powers of his body. To learn the music of the soul rather than the body, he will travel to Byzantium where he can be in touch with those who will free him from his mortal body and help him to take on the shape of an immortal golden bird. The flourishing of Byzantium occurs half-way through the two thousand year cycle of Christianity and half-way through the moon's phases when it is at its brightest and the body can dissolve, leaving the soul free to recast itself in pure form. The simple verse structure leaves the stress to fall on the final couplets with the rhyme of verse II being inverted in verse IV to emphasize that in Byzantium the poet can lift himself beyond the laws of time. The contrast with the real world that Yeats inhabits is made in the phrase:

> 'Whatever is begotten, born, and dies'

which is echoed and transcended in the final line of the poem:

> 'Of what is past, or passing, or to come.'

THE TOWER

First Line: 'What shall I do with this absurdity —'

Collection: 'The Tower' (1928)

Original Title:

First Published: *The Criterion*, June 1927, *The New Republic*, 29 June 1927

Summary:
The poem is written in three sections. The first sets out the theme of the poem; the second relates the theme to memories evoked by the poet's immediate surroundings; the third looks beyond the death of the poet in an attempt to establish a tradition of like-minded people to whom he can bequeath his personal qualities. Section one lays out the theme of the body's decay contrasting with the vigour of the imagination which is now even more

passionate than in the days of his boyhood. So he must either renounce poetry in favour of the abstractions of philosophy, more appropriate to his age, or else be laughed at for writing poems with an imaginative vigour mocked by his physical condition.

Section two places the poet on the top of Thoor Ballylee at dusk casting his imagination onto the surrounding countryside in order to call up 'images and memories' to whom he wishes to address the same question. The first is an aristocratic lady, Mrs. French, whose wish to have a farmer's ears clipped was carried out with literal devotion by a servant. The next image from the past is that of a beautiful peasant girl whose memory was still known to some in those parts when the poet was a boy. Such was her beauty that men fought with each other to get a sight of her. Some men, being intoxicated by the song about her and by drink, went to look for her. They confused night with day, and lost their way, and one of their number was drowned in a bog. The poet (Raftery) who composed the song was blind, which set him in the same tradition as Homer, also a blind poet who celebrated extreme feminine beauty in creating Helen. So Yeats hopes he can occupy a place in this tradition and also succeed in making men lose their senses as a result of singing his songs. He moves on to recall one of his own creations, Hanrahan, whose story he starts to tell. This, too, is a matter of the imagination's power to create reality out of fantasy. The poet forgets the conclusion to the story as he remembers a previous owner of the tower who died a bankrupt. He thinks now of all the ghostly figures from the past who have come in contact with the tower and who still haunt there. He lists all those he has mentioned and then asks them the question which is preoccupying him. Did they cry out, either publicly or privately, against the process of growing old? Finding his answer in the expression of their eyes which show them in a hurry to reach the next world, Yeats dismisses all except Hanrahan. He has a more particular question to ask Hanrahan who now carries the wisdom of the grave and who experienced in his life an enormous range of relationships with women. Is the imagination caught more by a lost love than a love achieved? As he attempts an answer he moves from Hanrahan to his own experience with Maud Gonne, a memory which has the power to turn day into night.

In section three the poet writes out his will in poetic form. His inheritors will be the solitary fishermen of the region who recall his own activity as a younger man. He associates himself through the quality of pride with a free-spirited Anglo-Irish inheritance, even if it is destined to die. The quality is akin to the swan's beautiful song sung just before death. He returns now to the tension of the poem's opening, rejecting the philosophers' abstract in favour of the concrete reality of man whose soul has called the universe into being and which lives on after death in a newly created form. The poet has prepared himself for his death by contemplation of the art of Renaissance Italy and Classical Greece and by the creations of his own imagination and memories of past loves. All these combine into a dream of life outlasting life itself. As a parallel he cites the jackdaws who seem to throw sticks together carelessly, yet end up with a nest on which the next generation can be nurtured. Then he returns to the mountain-climbing fishermen of whom he was one, until the profession of poet made him out of condition. Finally the poet will prepare himself for death by studying until his physical decay and the loss of friends and lovers become as remote to him as clouds at sunset or a bird-call before sleep.

Glossary:

2	'caricature'	Grotesque representation.
3	'Decrepit'	Enfeebled.
8	'rod and fly'	Fishing-rod and fly for bait.
11	'the Muse'	The Muse of Poetry.
12	'Plato and Plotinus'	Greek philosophers.
15	'derided'	Scoffed at.
16	'battered kettle at the heel'	Meaning the poet's physical frame. The image refers to a cruel way of teasing a dog, by tying a tin can to its tail.
17	'the battlements'	Of Thoor Ballylee.
25	'Mrs. French'	In his note to the poem Yeats states that: 'Mrs. French lived at Peterswell in the eighteenth century and was related to Sir Jonah Barrington who described the incident of the ears.'
26	'sconce'	Bracket-candlestick.
39	'jostled'	Pushed for a view.
48	'one drowned in the great bog of Cloone'	Yeats wrote in his notes: 'The peasant beauty and the blind poet are Mary Hynes and Raftery, and the incident of the man drowned in Cloone Bog is recorded in my *Celtic Twilight*.'
49	'the man who made the song'	Anthony Raftery (1784-1834), the blind Gaelic poet. His poem on Mary Hynes is recorded on page 24 of *Mythologies*.
57	'Hanrahan'	Character invented by Yeats who appeared in *Stories of Red Hanrahan* (1904).
60	'juggleries'	Tricks.
65	'bawn'	The original story has 'barn' but 'bawn' means either a fortified enclosure or a cattle ford.

Line	Phrase	Note
76	'harried'	Harassed.
85	'the Great Memory'	*Anima Mundi*. In Platonic thought all knowledge is a recollection drawn from this store.
90	'old, necessitous, half-mounted man'	The bankrupt former owner of the Tower.
91	'beauty's blind rambling celebrant'	Raftery.
92	'The red man'	Red Hanrahan.
93	'Gifted with so fine an ear'	The phrase would normally be a figure of speech meaning a sensitive ear. Here the reference is to Denis Bodkin who lost his ears.
105	'Old lecher'	Hanrahan, marked out by his sexual exploits.
114	'woman lost'	Maud Gonne.
125	'Drop their cast'	Put out their bait on the water.
132	'of Burke and Grattan'	See p. 18.
136	'fabulous horn'	See note on line 32 of 'A Prayer For My Daughter'.
137	'sudden shower'	Compare this with the image in the first stanza of 'Meditations In Time Of Civil War'.
140	'the swan'	Yeats's note acknowledges a debt to T. Sturge Moore's *Dying Swan*.
150	'lock, stock and barrel'	Idiom meaning all the parts, literally of a gun.
156	'Translunar'	Beyond the moon.
158	'learned Italian things'	Visits to Italy, Dante, Castiglione, painters and sculptors.
159	'stones of Greece'	Greek sculpture, especially Phidias.
165	'Mirror-resembling dream'	The dream created by a man's imaginative power bears the same relation to life as the image in a mirror bears to the thing itself except in this case it is 'superhuman'; above the reach of mortality.
166	'the loophole there'	In the tower.
167	'daws'	Jackdaws.
177	'drop a fly'	As bait into the water to catch a fish.
180	'This sedentary trade'	Of writing poetry. 'Sedentary' means sitting down.
181	'make my soul'	Irish expression meaning to prepare for death.
186	'testy'	Short-tempered.
191	'a catch in the breath'	Whose beauty made him gasp.

Commentary:

This poem establishes the tower as the central symbol for Yeats himself, dominating the last phase of his poetic output. After an introductory section which reiterates a theme common to this period, that of the conflict between the failing powers of the body and the growing powers of the imagination, the question of how to cope with old age is set in terms of Thoor Ballylee, both tower and poet alike in a state of decrepitude but both sharing memories of a passionate past. Especially potent is the image of the blind poet who compensates for the physical deficiency of blindness by the vividness of his mind's eye in conjuring up beautiful women. It is the description of Mary Hynes in Raftery's poem and not the girl herself which drives men to distraction, just as it is Homer's description which has made Helen the archetypal image of feminine beauty. Of his own creations, it is to Hanrahan that Yeats is now drawn, for he seems closest to the poet's own state of imaginative distraction. The question asked of Hanrahan is one which he uses his own experience to answer as best he can. The assertion of the vitality of human experience climaxes in Yeats's favourite symbol for the isolated soul of subjective man, the swan. He interprets the death song as a defiant cry against death such as his own rage at the onset of physical decay for the passage on the swan gives way to his own declaration of faith in the concrete reality of the passionate life. After the declaration, thoughts of the grave begin to assert themselves as Yeats reckons up what he has with which to make his 'peace'. However, those things which take a man beyond himself are first of all born in the imagination of man. The tensions of the third section are exemplified in the image of the jackdaw preparing for protection on a crumbling tower and in terms of the section's structure, between the two references to the dying swan. There is no resolution of the tension, only a final inclining towards the peace of the grave in the last verse, as this world and its sufferings fade from consciousness. As elsewhere in his longer poems, Yeats here uses a repeated, varied image to contain the thoughts which threaten to spread out of control. From the opening of the first stanza of section II to the last line of the poem the most vivid incidents all occur in the half light between day and night or night and day. This is the poet's realm for his imagination acts on the minds of his hearers to create a world where fantasy and reality are free to act on each other. It is also the moment of transition between this world and the next. At the climax of the second section when memory of this life is at its most intense the light of day gives way to darkness and the end of the poem subsides into the gathering blackness of the grave.

MEDITATIONS IN TIME OF CIVIL WAR

First Line: 'Surely among a rich man's flowering lawns,'

Collection: 'The Tower' (1928)

Original Title:

First Published: *The Dial*, January 1923

Summary: *Ancestral Houses*
The poet thinks that life for the wealthy in their 'ancestral houses' must be rich and full since they are provided with an abundance of what life offers and do not have to put themselves under an obligation to anyone else to get it. In the second verse this thought is relegated to the status of 'dreams'. However, it had once been true because Homer based his art on such an abundant nobility. But now the poet finds the 'glory of the rich' only a facade, a beautiful shape without substance like an 'empty sea-shell'. The men who built these houses were 'violent' and 'bitter' for it was these qualities which brought 'the sweetness' of their way of life into being. But their inheritors, having enjoyed a life of ease are 'mice'.

The poet is moved to ask if the creation of all this noble beauty did not perhaps exhaust the 'greatness' as well as the 'violence' of the nobility so that now they are gentle they are also ineffectual.

Glossary: *Ancestral Houses*

12 'The abounding glittering jet'	The fountain is a symbol for intense joy in living.
33 'escutcheoned'	Surrounded with shields displaying armorial bearings.
34 'a haughtier age'	A prouder age.

Summary: *My House*
The poet describes his home and its immediate surroundings, both natural and supernatural ('the symbolic rose'). Description moves from the country to the interior of the tower and the poet's own study where isolated like Milton, he sees all through the fever of his imagination while late travellers on the road gaze on 'his midnight candle'. The tower has two founders; the first a man of war who, with a small band, defended the place against all comers; the second is the poet who holds it for his children

that they may see in the tower and its surroundings reminders of the poet's struggle against the world.

Glossary: My House

14	'*Il Penseroso*'s Platonist'	A reference to an illustration of Samuel Palmer in *The Shorter Poems of John Milton* (1889) entitled 'The Lonely Tower'.
30	'Befitting emblems of adversity'	The poet's work will have turned the physical surroundings in which he created into the 'emblems' of his stand against the prevailing ethos of his day.

Summary: My Table

Coming now to the table at which he works, he considers the history of the curved Japanese sword lying on it and how it can act as an inspiration by reminding him of another age and culture. Though shaped like the moon, it is not subject to change for it has been made by one who has longed to escape the bonds of his mortality. It has been passed down the generations as a symbol for the 'soul's beauty' since it shares the soul's immortality. The 'inheritor' of the sword, the poet, is also one who is trying to achieve an image of eternity in his art before the body dissolves in the sleep of death.

Glossary: My Table

2	'Sato's gift'	Yeats was given the sword by Junzo Sato, a Japanese admirer of his work.
7	'sheath'	Close-fitting cover for blade of sword.
32	'Juno's peacock'	In *A Vision* Yeats writes that 'the loss of control over thought comes towards the end; first a sinking in upon the moral being, then the last surrender, the irrational cry, revelation — the scream of Juno's peacock'.

Summary: My Descendants

Being the inheritor of the 'vigorous mind' of his family, the poet cannot prevent himself speculating on the future awaiting his children when he has gone. The brevity of life's beauty resembles the flower of the rose whose petals are torn by the winds almost as soon as they bloom. He wonders if his 'descendants' like those of the 'Ancestral Houses' will allow their souls to become corrupted by the transitory aspects of life and so cause the tower to fall into an owl-infested ruin. In the last verse he comforts himself with the knowledge that the shaping force of the universe will operate even then. His own life has been 'enough' since he has known the friendship of Lady Gregory and the love of his wife, both factors in his choosing to live in the tower whose 'stones' will outlast these troubled times.

Glossary: *My Descendants*

7 'petal'	The petals are the segments of the rose's flower, symbol of the soul's beauty.
17 'Primum Mobile'	The First Mover, that which sets the universe in motion.

Summary: *The Road at My Door*

A member of the I.R.A. comes past the poet's door and passes the time with 'jokes of civil war' as if the deadly struggle he is engaged in was a game. Next come soldiers of the National Army with whom the poet converses about the weather. He envies these men of action and tries to console himself with images of the world of nature. He returns to the solitude of his room to continue his dream of heroic deeds.

Glossary: *The Road at My Door*

1 'an affable Irregular'	A good-humoured member of the Irish Republican Army.
2 'Falstaffian'	With the appearance of Falstaff, the fat, jocular character from Shakespeare's plays.
6 'A brown Lieutenant'	An officer of the National Army.

Summary: *The Stare's Nest by My Window*

The poet notices that bees are using the cracks in the tower wall as hives and birds are feeding their young in nests they have built there. As the wall crumbles, the poet invites the bees to use an empty starling's nest. The poet is cut off from information about the outcome of the fighting. Men die, houses burn and the poet wants the bees to carry on their proper function. The war has raged for two weeks. A dead soldier has been wheeled past in the night, yet the bees must come. 'The heart' has been made hard from its dreams of freedom so that hate is proving stronger than love. Still the bees should come to his tower.

Glossary: *The Stare's Nest by My Window*

1/2 'crevices/Of loosening masonry'	Cracks in the crumbling stone.
5 'the empty house of the	

stare'	The empty nest of the starling.

Summary: *I see Phantoms of Hatred and of the Heart's Fullness and of the Coming Emptiness*

At the top of his tower on a moon-lit misty night, the poet falls a prey to nightmares and dreams that float before 'the mind's eye'. His imagination calls up the medieval age of Jacques Molay and the hand to hand fighting of the men-at-arms of the Knights Templar. The frenzy of the fighting is so real that the poet almost joins in the cries. The next vision is derived from a painting and evokes phantoms 'of the Heart's fulness' in contrast to the images which precede and succeed it. The ladies are the embodiment of the ultimate self-contemplation of the subjective soul.

Both visions now give place to the 'brazen hawks', the creatures of logic and destruction which herald the coming age, an age which is conceived at the dark of the moon when the bronze wings of the hawks have shut out the beauty of the soul's light. The poet comes down from the top of the tower and as he descends the stairs he speculates on whether an active participation in his country's troubles might not have better shown his 'worth' to others. Then he realizes that any immediate benefits from such a policy would not have satisfied his soul. The spiritual fulfilment of the creative life is enough for 'the aging man' as it was earlier for 'the growing boy'.

Glossary: *I see Phantoms of Hatred and of the Heart's Fullness and of the Coming Emptiness*

10 'Jacques Molay'	In his notes to the poem Yeats writes: 'A cry for vengeance because of the murder of the Grand Master of the Templars seems to me fit symbol for those who labour from hatred, and so for sterility in various kinds'.
20 'almanacs'	Calendars with months, days and astronomical data.
25 'unicorns'	Mythical animal with a horse's body and single, straight horn.
29 'brazen hawks'	Symbolizing 'the straight road of logic, and so of mechanism'.
32 'clanging wings that have put out the moon'	The destruction and abstraction of the coming cycle without benefit of the moon's subjective light.
39 'The half-read wisdom of daemonic images'	The images evoked by Yeats's occult research whose sense he cannot entirely divine.

Commentary:
The poem which embraces a wide variety of topics, is held together by the personality of the poet, the focus of the tower and the now familiar theme of the mortal artist and his immortal art. Amongst the disorder and confusion of the troubled times, the poet seeks images which can keep him in touch with the qualities of gentleness and nobility found in former ages. Sato's sword acts on him in this way and he tries to use the patient creativity of the honey-bees in a similar way. However, since the present violence is a herald of the destruction to come, they provide only temporary comfort. While he can shut the door and return to his own world of immortal art, his heirs will have to live in the violent world. The tower, though in the midst of the confusions of war, allows the poet to retreat to a position above the daily action so that he can view the longer perspective in which the events must be set. The detachment is only achieved at the cost of some longing to join the fighting but in the end he knows he will only find 'joy' in his chosen path, no matter what the world will make of it.

NINETEEN HUNDRED AND NINETEEN

First Line: 'Many ingenious lovely things are gone'

Collection: 'The Tower' (1928)

Original Title: Thoughts upon the Present State of the World

First Published: *The Dial*, September 1921

Summary:
The first stanza of the first section records the glories of ancient Athens that have been destroyed by subsequent ages though at the time they were considered immortal. The poet finds a parallel in his own lifetime for there was a period in his youth when men thought that the days of violence and evil had been left behind forever. The war-like instincts had been removed from men and their armies had become show-pieces detached from any aggressive purpose. The fourth stanza pitches the reader fiercely into the present time of terrifying, mindless brutality as Ireland fights its civil war and the generation of fine philosophers is reduced to 'weasels fighting in a hole'. The man who, like the poet, has witnessed all this destruction of man's best endeavours can hold

on to one source of 'comfort': the lonely introspection of his spirit has withstood all that the world has thrown at it. Then he asks if this is a real comfort when man commits himself to the transitory elements of life. Like the glories of ancient Greece, the civilization centred on the great houses of Ireland has been destroyed.

In the second section the poet finds an image for the movements of the spheres in the patterns of a group of dancers. As the dancers obey the rhythms of the dance, so men obey the 'barbarous' movements of the present age. The cosmic system likewise blows a new age out on a spiral which repeats a former civilization. Men must perforce dance to its tune.

In the more private third section the poet is content, if a 'solitary soul' resembles 'a swan', for it to reveal its essence once in its life as it flies in defiance of the encroaching darkness. In this life a man's preoccupations can shield him from unpleasant contact but the Platonists assert that these activities become the distractions of the next incarnation and keep a man from his introspection. The swan is able to achieve release from the concerns of this world and, seeing this, the poet is tempted to give up his own efforts at creating a perfect form. Before, however, it had seemed possible to improve the world; now those ideas have degenerated into displays of petty aggression. We are invited to 'mock' at greatness, wisdom and goodness for they are set at nothing by the cycles of the ages, shown in the violence of the 'wind'. The 'mockers' of these qualities are also to be mocked for failing to help those who try to combat the 'foul storm' even though the effort be futile. The violence of the coming age with its herald in the chaos of 'evil' is blown in on the wild 'wind'. When the 'dust' thrown up by the wind subsides, it reveals an incubus summoned by a witch to satisfy her lust, as confusion gives way to the uttermost evil.

Glossary:

7	'Phidias' famous ivories'	The most famous Athenian sculptor, none of whose work has survived.
25	'Now days are dragon-ridden'	The monstrous violence which evokes this image is the fighting in Ireland.
32	'weasels'	Small rat-like creature, known for its ferocity in fighting.
45	'Incendiary'	Person setting fire to property.
45	'bigot'	Someone who holds an irrational opinion.
46	'The Acropolis'	The hill on which the citadel of Athens was founded.
49	'Loie Fuller'	An American dancer at the *Folies Bergères* in the 1890s.

54	'Platonic Year'	The Great Year derived from Plato when the constellations return to their original positions in the heavens.
118	'Herodias' daughters'	A name given to the winds in the Middle Ages when witches were said to ride upon them.
128	'That insolent fiend Robert Artisson'	Yeats reported that 'My last symbol, Robert Artisson, was an evil spirit much run after in Kilkenny at the start of the fourteenth century.'
129	'Lady Kyteler'	Dame Alice Kyteler was charged with carnal knowledge of the demon and the sacrifice of peacocks and cocks to it.

Commentary:

This poem covers the same ground as 'The Meditations in Time of Civil War', but is not at all meditative in tone. Though placed later in the collection, it is an earlier composition reflecting more the poet's despair at the events among which he lives, rather than the stoicism which grows later. The destructive forces in the world seem so great that even the immortality of art whose image is again conveyed in the figure of the dance, is threatened. The 'dragon of air' although associated with the 'dragon-ridden' days and the violent winds of section VI is an image created by the artistic perfection of man and though the dancers seem like mankind dancing to the whirling movement of the Platonic Year, the shape is in the hands of man, the artist. In this poem, though, the dance seems a frail thing caught between the irrational force of the 'drunken soldiery' and the 'fiend' that 'lurches' like the slouching monster evoked at the end of 'The Second Coming'. The conclusion of the poem is weakened by the esoteric, local reference which is unable to carry the sense of horror intended. Nevertheless, the use and placing of the symbol indicates the state of instability and fear that characterized Yeats at this moment. The carefully integrated symbols of 'dragon' and 'wind' of the earlier parts of the poem have given way to a confusion which relates the poet's mind to the state of the world.

THE WHEEL

First Line: 'Through winter-time we call on spring,'

Collection: 'The Tower' (1928)

Original Title:

First Published: *Seven Poems and a Fragment*, 1922

Summary:
Man spends his life looking forward to the next season but, having experienced the full cycle, does not see the return of spring. During this process man fails to realise he is being pushed through life by a desire to reach the grave.

Glossary:
3 'hedges ring' With the sounds of birds singing.

Commentary
This epigrammatic poem picks up the idea in 'The Tower' of those images 'impatient to be gone'. Here the constant tension between soul and body, life and death is resolved in favour of death, at least for the moment. Perhaps frustration at the failing of the body's powers is responsible.

YOUTH AND AGE

First Line: 'Much did I rage when young,'

Collection: 'The Tower' (1928)

Original Title:

First Published: *The Cat and The Moon and Certain Poems*, 1924

Summary:
As a young man the poet cried out against the world for oppressing him. Now as an old man the world speaks well of him in order to hurry him into the next.

Commentary:
The thought is the same as that expressed in 'The Wheel' with the

implication, unusual in Yeats, that man's home is not in this life where he is only a temporary guest. The epigram illustrates a sardonic tone in Yeats's work which is not often associated with him. 'Welcome the coming, speed the parting guest' (Pope) carries the same sense in a proverb.

LEDA AND THE SWAN

First Line: 'A sudden blow: the great wings beating still'

Collection: 'The Tower' (1928)

Original Title: Book III/Dove or Swan/I. Leda; Book V: Dove or Swan/I/Leda

First Published: *The Dial*, June 1924

Summary:
The swan comes upon Leda with 'great wings beating', holding her neck in his bill. She is helpless to push off the swan as he comes between her thighs, and she feels his 'strange heart beating' next to her own. Coitus is completed in a fire of passion. The poet asks rhetorically whether the swan passed on his 'knowledge' as well as his 'power' to Leda in the brief, violent moment of their union.

Glossary:

6	'The feathered glory'	The poet is drawing on the Greek myth in which Leda, Queen of Sparta, coupled with Zeus disguised in the shape of a swan.
7	'rush'	Violent movement onto Leda.
9	'A shudder in the loins engenders . . .'	The result of Zeus's intercourse with Leda was two eggs, one giving birth to Helen of Troy, the other to the twins, Castor and Pollux.
11	'Agamemnon'	Agamemnon was the most powerful ruler in Greece and leader of the expedition to reclaim Helen. On his return to Greece he was murdered by his wife, Clytemnestra. He was Helen's brother-in-law.
12	'the brute blood of the air'	The swan belongs to the element of air and is also composed of both blood and air being both a living creature and a spirit.
14	'beak'	The mouth of the swan which has been holding Leda by the neck.

Commentary
In *A Vision* Yeats set out his theory of history running in 2000-year cycles. The union of Zeus and Leda gave birth to the cycle whose high point was the Greek civilization. This was succeded by the epoch of Christianity which was announced in a similar way by the appearance of the Holy Ghost to the Virgin Mary. Now the Christian civilization is breaking up as the poet indicates in his poem 'The Second Coming'. The new age will reverse the direction of the present one as the swan, Yeats's symbol for subjectivity heralds its demise.

The poem is one of Yeats's few sonnets yet he exploits the form expertly. He uses the traditional break between the first eight lines and the last six to alter the direction of the poem and to expand its significance. The first octave uses violent physical imagery as it focuses on the circumstances of the rape. The violent contrasts of the sounds match the images with hard 't's contending with heavy 'b's and the sibilation of the swan's rustling feathers. The encounter is given time to make its own impact on the reader so that it can later bear the weight of the symbolic attributes which are attached to it in the second part.

Even at the moment of its inception the epoch is already doomed. The egg will hatch both the greatest love and the greatest strife in the person of Helen. Does the poet find a parallel here with his own Helen, Maud Gonne, who is similarly divinely blessed in her beauty yet through her political activities the source of strife? The destruction of Troy occupies a similar place in his imagination as the destruction of the great houses of Ireland. The poem ends by asking whether at the moment of union the woman has become for an instant divine, whether she has been blessed and cursed with the god's knowledge of all that is to come. Zeus may be 'indifferent' to the history he will create but even he is powerless to alter its course once begun.

The poet is able ultimately to draw comfort from the chaos of the age he inhabits for it assures him that a change of cycles like that inaugurated by Leda and Zeus is about to take place.

AMONG SCHOOL CHILDREN

First Line: 'I walk through the long schoolroom questioning;'

Collection: 'The Tower' (1928)

Original Title:

First Published: *The Dial*, and *The London Mercury*, August 1927

Summary:

I. The poet stands in a classroom, and the teacher ('a kind old nun') tells him what the children learn there; they all stare at the aging, genial 'public man'.

II. He dreams of a child resembling Leda, telling a story of how harsh words once affected her deeply, and his heart goes out to her.

III. Looking around at these children, he wonders whether they have ever suffered so, and feels the girl he dreamt of is now before him.

IV. He sees her form in detail, lean and spare; he himself was young and handsome once, if not quite a match for Leda, but now he must be content with the image of an 'old scarecrow'.

V. Would women become mothers, the poet asks, if they knew the torment of birth pangs and upbringing eventually resulted in old age?

VI. Plato, Aristotle and Pythagoras each achieved eminence in his own way, and were unattractive old men.

VII. Religious images, though not alive, have power to 'break hearts', as they mock at 'man's enterprise'.

VIII. The children at work seem entirely natural — no age or infirmity hinders them.

Glossary:

8	'public man'	Yeats the Irish senator.
9	'a Ledaean body'	Maud Gonne who is associated with Leda through her symbol, Helen of Troy, Leda's daughter.
28	'a mess of shadows for its meat'	Maud has grown thin by trying to live on the insubstantial fare of her political activity.
32	'scarecrow'	A figure made from sticks and old clothes to frighten birds away from growing seeds.
34	'Honey of generation'	An image from Porphyry's *On the Cave of the Nymphs*. It is the sweetness associated with the process of

	generation.
41 'spume'	Foam.
42 'a ghostly paradigm of things'	Plato held that this life was only a shadowing of the 'real' life to come.
60 'blear-eyed wisdom out of midnight oil'	The wisdom achieved by studying deep into the night until the eyes are strained.

Commentary:

This poem is one of Yeats's best dealing with the ever-present obsession with aging. As with the other poems of this collection, he looks to art as a means of escape from the cycles of decay and regeneration. The art that is referred to is one which can provide images of man's Unity of Being that can assign to the aging body a role in the creative purpose. The school children who have provoked the memory of the young Maud Gonne also embody aspects of her that enable the immortal image of her to be married to their mortal figures like the wild swans at Coole. While it is through the creation of images that man achieves his intimations of immortality, those images which are of an ideal and do not touch the reality of life, 'break hearts' by the impossibility of being realized or transcended through 'man's enterprise'. The cost of the soul's 'pleasure' or of 'beauty' or of 'wisdom' on the mortal parts of man, mind and body, takes away from its image of perfection. This sense of loss is only defeated in the contemplation of the organic unity of the tree whose whole is more than the sum of its parts, or in the image of the dancer. To make a dancer it is necessary to harmonize the abstract, immortal form of the dance with the concrete, mortal form of the human being. Only in this figure of the dancer can the seeming pain and futility of aging be reconciled with the perfection of art.

The poem is built up in series of three after the initial image of Maud is displaced in the attempt to generalize from it. Plato, Aristotle and Pythagoras are ranged alongside the lover ('passion'), the nun ('piety'), and the mother ('affection'), each united by the need to create images which endow mortal life with an immortal purpose. The operation succeeds with the figure of the 'chestnut-tree' of Life whose three elements unite to create an image which owes its existence to its real components and whose unity of being heralds the dancer.

THE WINDING STAIR AND OTHER POEMS (1933)

After the dissolution of the flesh in *The Tower* this collection swings back to an acceptance of life with all its faults. Yeats had been made vividly aware of the preciousness of life by his own recent illness and felt that the time left to him was a kind of reprieve. He was concerned not to close the book with the bitter flavour of the previous volume leaving the reader with a partial and distorted understanding of the poet's view of this world. Thus the volume represents what Yeats termed 'the return to life', with all the gaiety he felt in spite or even because of the physical pain. It is the condition which he calls in 'Byzantium' (p. 280) 'death-in-life and life-in-death'.

Some of the earlier gloominess still attaches itself to the first poems of the collection, the recollections of important friends from the past. However, he draws strength from the evocation of them and manipulates the now familiar pattern of symbols to assign universal significance to the shape of their lives, to make of their mortal lives an immortal art form.

'Byzantium' carries the speculations about the life of the soul to a stage beyond 'Sailing to Byzantium' where the soul is not set in opposition to the body but made a part of an interrelated scheme in which each is dependent upon the other. It is no longer a matter of escape from life to death but an eternal movement between the two.

After achieving this balance at the apex of the collection, Yeats moves on to an affirmation of the flesh contained in the two groups of poems within the collection, *Words for Music Perhaps* and *A Woman Young and Old*. Here acceptance of life is carried from philosophy into actuality by means of characterization, of masks or characters through which the poet can extend his personal intuitions into a universal context.

In a letter to Mrs. Shakespear Yeats expressed this sense of the triumph of affirmation over denial when he wrote: 'The swordsman throughout repudiates the saint, but not without vacillation.'

IN MEMORY OF EVA GORE-BOOTH AND CON MARKIEWICZ

First Line: 'The light of evening, Lissadell,'

Collection: 'The Winding Stair and Other Poems' (1933)

Original Title:

First Published: *The Winding Stair and Other Poems*, (1933)

Summary:
The poet pictures the sisters as young girls in their family home, beautiful and elegant. However, time has brought changes and the withering of their beauty is related in the poet's imagination to their involvement in politics. The poet often thinks of looking them up again to talk over old times. Now 'shadows', both of their former selves and because they have entered the realm of shades, they know that the real enemy they should have confronted was time. Like the mob who set a match to the great houses, the poet asks the sisters to incite him to set a match to time itself and destroy the process of ageing.

Glossary:

1 'Lissadell'	The Gore-Booths' house in Sligo.
4 'one a gazelle'	Eva, who wrote poetry and later committed herself to social work.
7 'The older'	Constance, who joined the Citizen Army, fought in the Rising and later became a minister in the Irish government.
12 'skeleton-gaunt'	Thin as a skeleton.
28 'conflagration'	Fire.
30 'gazebo'	A summer-house in the grounds of Lissadell.

Commentary:
One of several lyrics related to personal memories in this collection, it is written in memory of the Gore-Booth sisters as they were in their youth. The poet is again concerned here with the process of ageing and the destruction it causes. The young girls are bound up in his mind with the great house society where Yeats first encountered them. Their change to old women corresponds with the change in Irish society which they themselves fought to bring about. Thus they have in fact assisted Time in its attacks on them. His attitude to their political commitments parallels his feelings about Maud Gonne's career. With the benefit of their wisdom

achieved either in old age or death, they can now direct him to burn up the real enemy, Time, instead of the one they fought in their lives.

A DIALOGUE OF SELF AND SOUL

First Line: *My Soul.* 'I summon to the winding ancient stair;'

Collection: 'The Winding Stair and Other Poems' (1933)

Original Title:

First Published: *The Winding Stair and Other Poems*, (1933)

Summary:
In the opening stanza the poet's soul invites him to ascend the winding stair that is the path of escape from this life into the great dark of eternity with no return. It is the dark of the moon when the possibility of escape from the cycle of incarnations is offered for in this phase the spirit is totally 'objective' and pliant to the pull of external circumstances.

But in reply the Self prefers to meditate on Sato's sword which Yeats introduced in the third section of 'Meditations in Time of Civil War'. He finds in it an appropriate symbol for conflict, love and the masculine principle in life, enveloped by the sheath of material from the dress of a court lady which though tattered like the poet's own body can nevertheless still protect that life force.

The Soul tells him he is past the time when such emblems of love and war should attract. It is more appropriate for him to concentrate on the dark that can release him from the punishments of continual reliving. But the Self affirms its right to opt for the day of the sword rather than the night of the tower which contains the winding stair. Though life is a 'crime' he will 'commit' it again. The Soul persists in brooding on eternity and knows that the surfeit of life that spills into the mind forces an acute awareness of the mortality of the physical being. The ascent to Heaven can only be undertaken by one who becomes absorbed by the supernatural through loss of will and only the dead can be forgiven because only they pass through the stages of purification from life. However, the contemplation of this process strikes the Soul with a fearful dumbness.

The second section of the poem is spoken only by the Self who goes over in his thoughts the painful experiences of his past life, and most painful of all believing he is the thing that malicious opinion claims him to be. Even so, the Self wants to live again. He knows to live is to be blind to the prospect of eternity and to suffer the torment of unrequited love. He ends in a state of beatitude, blessing himself and blessing life itself that has given him all experience, fair or foul.

Glossary:

1	'the winding ancient stair'	The spiral staircase in Thoor Ballylee.
3	'crumbling battlement'	The wall around the top of the tower.
5	'the hidden pole'	At this phase of the moon man escapes this life by moving past the Pole Star.
7	'That quarter'	The dark of the moon.
9	'The consecrated blade'	The sword given to him by Junzo Sato, in token of admiration for his work.
13	'That flowering, silken, old embroidery'	Yeats wrote to Olivia Shakespear in October 1927 to say he was writing 'a new tower poem "Sword and Tower", which is a choice of rebirth rather than deliverance from birth. I make my Japanese sword and its silk covering my symbol of life.'
15	'scabbard'	The sheath of the sword.
18	'his prime'	The most vigorous period of his life.
19	'emblematical'	Being used as emblems for.
25	'Montashigi'	The maker of the sword.
28	'Heart's purple'	A wild flowering pansy of purple colour.
37	'*Is* from the *ought*, or *Knower* from the *Known*'	The reference is to the Four Faculties of the spirit in *A Vision*. Will represents 'is', Mask 'ought', Creative Mind 'Knower' and Body of Fate 'Known'.
45	'ignominy'	Dishonour.
56	'the wintry blast'	Death.
59	'frog-spawn'	Frog's eggs and the jelly-like substance which surrounds them.
61	'fecund'	Fertile.
64	'A proud woman'	Maud Gonne.

Commentary:

The poem was written in the spring of 1928 during a long illness in which Yeats had to face up to the possibility of imminent death. All the more remarkable, then, is his resolve not to seek the path of the soul in eternal life but to opt for a return to self in the experience of this life. Thus the poem marks a crucial development in the later poetry, paving the way for that undaunted, life-accepting mood which dominates the *Last Poems*. There are a number of verbal premonitions in this poem of that collection, in particular the repeated question 'what matter?' which is used again in 'The Gyres' (p. 337) and the phrase 'I am content' anticipating the poem 'Are You Content?' (p. 370).

The first section can hardly be called a dialogue for the Soul and the Self are really talking past each other, the eyes of the one fixed on the tower and of the other on the sword. The Soul's contemplation of the purgatorial states on the way to the purification of the spirit reduce it to silence so that in section two the Self pours out an uninterrupted affirmation of life. It is not a sentimental statement but an acceptance of this life with all its imperfections. Indeed, it is the imperfections that are dwelt on with violence as the poet wrestles with his illness as in the fierce alliterative line 'A blind man battering blind men'. The blind man is a common figure in Yeats's work representing the fate of man on earth. The poem is notable as an example of the way in which Yeats creates universal symbols out of the objects important in his own life, in this instance Thoor Ballylee and Sato's sword. It is also a further illustration of the working of the material of *A Vision* into poetic form. Most important of all the poem sets the dominant mood of the final phase of the poetry, in spite of all, rejoicing.

COOLE PARK, 1929

First Line: 'I meditate upon a swallow's flight,'

Collection: 'The Winding Stair and Other Poems' (1933)

Original Title:

First Published: *Coole*, by Lady Gregory, (1931)

Summary:
The poet ponders on Lady Gregory and her home which inspired 'great works' and which achieved in the crumbling world that harmony of art and artist symbolized in the dance. The second verse evokes some of the persons who used to visit the house and though these people used it like the swallows flying in and out on their summer migration, the strength of Lady Gregory's personality caused them to make Coole Park the focus of their artistic lives in order to benefit fully from its capacity to inspire. The poet asks them all, the travellers Shawe-Taylor and Lane, the scholar Hyde,

and the poets Yeats and Synge, to come back as ghosts when the house has been destroyed to pay honour to the memory of Lady Gregory.

Glossary:

2	'an aged woman and her house'	Lady Gregory and Coole Park.
9	'Hyde'	Dr. Douglas Hyde, Irish poet and scholar, first president of Eire.
10	'That noble blade'	The gift of poetic utterance. Yeats imagines the sword of poetry being beaten into the ploughshare of prose.
11	'There one that ruffled'	The young Yeats striking a pose out of Castiglione.
14	'Shawe-Taylor and Hugh Lane'	John Shawe-Taylor and Hugh Lane were Lady Gregory's nephews.
21	'to whirl upon a compass-point'	These men are seen as being held in the circle of their lives, like a pencil-line controlled by a compass, by the harmonizing force of Lady Gregory.
24	'withershins'	In an opposite direction.
32	'that laurelled head'	Lady Gregory, honoured with Apollo's laurel bough for her literary achievements.

Commentary:

Yeats again blends the personal with the symbolic as Lady Gregory's position at the hub of a group of creative minds is likened to the axis of a gyre which holds the flights of certain souls on a circular path around it. The poem, too, is shaped in a circle, 'the swallow' of the opening line being required to cease its flight and take a stand in the closing stanza where the magnificent trees of the house in its prime have been replaced by 'saplings' growing in the broken walls. However, these 'saplings' perhaps suggest a future growth into a tree of life made possible by the inspiration of the memory of the 'dance-like glory', appropriately celebrated by those who are beyond the mortal pleasures of this life.

COOLE PARK AND BALLYLEE, 1931

First Line: 'Under my window-ledge the waters race,'

Collection: 'The Winding Stair and Other Poems' (1933)

Original Title:

First Published: *The Winding Stair and Other Poems*, (1933)

Summary:
The first stanza describes the flow of the stream outside the poet's window which then disappears below the ground to reappear in Coole Park where it forms a lake before disappearing again. The water's journey resembles that of the soul. As he stands in the wood beside the lake, he finds its wintry aspect reflecting his own state until he hears a swan flying up from the lake into the sky. The swan is another emblem for the soul, this one containing a loveliness which can restore this chaotic world. From the sticks of the wood, Yeats turns to the sound of the dying Lady Gregory's stick as she moves about the house with difficulty. She is the last of a line of noble and wise people to whom Coole Park has brought joy. The poet thinks of the past times of the house as a continual summer of satisfied desires unlike the restlessness of an existence without such traditions. Lady Gregory and the poet are the final representatives of an earlier age which valued the poetic traditions established by Homer who kept his soul pure in the face of world events.

Glossary:

1	'my window ledge'	At Thoor Ballylee.
4	' "dark" Raftery's "cellar" '	Raftery was a blind Gaelic poet.
6	'demesne'	Estate; land actually occupied by the owner.
12	'Nature's pulled her tragic buskin on'	Nature is being thought of as an actor getting into his costume for a tragic role.
13	'rant'	Loud declaiming.
46	'that high horse'	Pegasus, the horse of poetry.

Commentary:
Another poem of thanks to Lady Gregory, 'Coole Park and Ballylee'

is carefully bound together by its two emblems for the poet's soul, the water and the swan. Taking the Neoplatonic symbol, Yeats sees a figure for the union of his soul with the world of Coole Park in the underground river flowing from his home to the estate. Like the soul, the water lives for a moment before disappearing into the dark only to emerge reincarnated as the lake at Coole before returning to the dark again. Although this emblem may not seem propitious, it does lead to the swan which carries with it the hope of redemption for the fallen world:

> And is so lovely that it sets to right
> What knowledge or its lack had set awry,

Though the second half of the poem moves from the swan to Lady Gregory, from the grounds to the house, we are intended to locate the qualities of the swan in her.

BYZANTIUM

First Line: 'The unpurged images of day recede;'

Collection: 'The Winding Stair and Other Poems' (1933)

Original Title:

First Published: *The Winding Stair and Other Poems*, (1933)

Summary:
In the night-time streets of Byzantium the poet experiences an emptying of his mind which is reflected in the clearing of the streets. The dome of the cathedral looks down on the petty concerns of mortal men. Thus prepared, a figure from the spirit world appears before him which has already dreamed its way back through its previous incarnations to achieve a condition of pure spirit able to call up those spirits whose mortality still keeps them from the pure state.

The golden bird, sitting on the Emperor's golden tree is the next image to appear to the poet, condensing in its being the eternal quality of the art form. Its song expresses the need to escape from the cycles of human generation. At midnight, the time when the spirit quits the body, the flame which needs no natural fuel appears on the marble floor to purge the impure spirits that dance in the fire of their mortal consciences. The spirits keep fetching up on the Byzantine shore carried on the dolphins of the body. As they come, the goldsmiths of the emperor recast them in purer forms but still more come across the sea of life and time.

Glossary:

3	'night-walkers'	Prostitutes.
5	'A starlit or a moonlit dome'	The dome of St. Sophia.
11	'Hades' bobbin bound in mummy-cloth'	A bobbin is a spool for holding material, in this case the cloth used to embalm a corpse. Taking his lead from Plato, Yeats uses Hades' bobbin as an emblem for the purified soul.
32	'An agony of flame that cannot singe a sleeve'	The fire cannot burn anything since it is not a real fire. It is the image of the soul's consciousness of its most intense mortal experiences and the means by which the soul frees itself from them.
33	'Astraddle on the dolphin's mire and blood'	The spirits are pictured travelling on the dolphin's back through the trials of mortal life to reach the purifying fires of Byzantium.
40	'that gong-tormented sea'	Because the sea represents mortal life, it is tormented by the awareness of time passing which is marked off by the gong.

Commentary:

Though described by Yeats as an exposition of his earlier poem 'Sailing To Byzantium', the content and tone of the poem is markedly different. The poet had suffered a serious illness and wrote the poem 'to warm myself back into life'. Byzantium is now not the serene place of all reconciliations viewed from outside but a place of the soul's agony whose flame the poet has begun to feel. While the richness of its densely associative language sets the reader severe problems in untangling its levels of meaning, the force and energy climaxing in the last stanza exert an immediate grip on the imagination. The themes are not new but they are set in new relationships. While the first and third stanzas supply images of the perfected art form that stands aloof from the 'complexities' and 'fury' of mortal life, the alternate stanzas with their ebb and flow of motion suggest the struggle of the human soul to achieve the status of 'the superhuman'. The two strands are interwoven in the final stanza where life crashes against art, unpurged spirit against pure essence. Ultimately the two states are interdependent for the process of spiritual purification by flame results in the return of the cleansed spirit to inhabit a new body in a new age. Appropriately the poem ends back in the mortal world.

VACILLATION

First Line: 'Between extremities'

Collection: 'The Winding Stair and Other Poems' (1933)

Original Title: Sections at first printing were as follows: I What is Joy; II The Burning Tree (II and III of subsequent versions); III Happiness; IV Conscience; V Conquerors; VI A Dialogue; VII Von Hügel.

First Published: *Words for Music Perhaps and Other Poems,* (1932)

Summary:
Section one states that man's life is lived between opposites until death wipes out all distinctions. But is the grave a place of death and 'remorse' if life has given experience of 'joy'?

Section two represents the opposites in the symbol of the tree, half on fire with the flame of the soul, half green with the vigorous life of the body. Each half, however, does not know of the presence of the other and takes itself to be the whole. One who, like the priest, hangs an image of the god between the two halves experiences a revelation of the total pattern more profound than he can realise which takes him beyond a condition of sorrow at the state of the world.

Section three examines the problem in terms of a man's life. Man is exhorted to live a worldly existence to the full but not to lose sight of the contradictions of this life, such as women loving men who do nothing although their children need a father who can work to secure their future. By the time a man gets to forty he can no longer afford to lose himself in daily existence, but must think on what is to come and rid himself of those elements in his life that will not carry him in a state of joy into the grave.

Section four deals with a specific incident which occurred sometime after the poet was fifty, when in the most ordinary surroundings, he was gifted with a revelation which seemed to consume his usual bodily torment and leave him in a state of blessedness, loving all mankind.

Section five brings in the opposite of the mood of the previous section. Now the poet cannot enter into the contrasted beauty of the natural world for his mind is full of his worldly preoccupations; in particular the memories of past words or deeds which were thought, spoken or performed to the later discomfort of the poet.

Section six glances at those who have not been seduced by the significance of their deeds but have understood that all their achievements will vanish. The tree itself, the life of both soul and body is rooted in the human heart and not only the singer but the song itself is mutable.

Section seven is in the form of a dialogue between 'The Soul' and 'The Heart'. The Soul advocates the way of the saint, man being purified by the flame of salvation, the burning half of the tree. The Heart who has the last word, opts for the way of the poet which necessitates an impure life to provide material for his art.

Section eight moves on from the Old to the New Testament, placing Christianity in opposition to Homer. The poet acknowledges Christianity as a temptation for the heart and indeed accepts the miraculous elements in the faith, but returns at the last to his place in a pre-ordained pattern of reincarnation which lies outside Christianity. He dismisses Von Hügel, with his blessing, and opts, as the heart had in the previous section, for Homer.

Glossary:

5 'antinomies'	Contradictions.
11 'A tree'	This tree, taken from Lady Charlotte Guest's translation of *The Mabinogian*, is mentioned by Yeats in his essay 'The Celtic Element in Literature' in *Essays and Introductions* (p. 176).
16 'he that Attis' image hangs'	At the ancient festival of Attis the priest hung the god's image on the sacred pine tree.
21 'trivial days'	Perhaps those spent working for the Abbey Theatre.
23 'dote upon'	Are passionately fond of.
27 'Lethean'	Lethe means oblivion in classical Greek.
29 'fortieth winter'	The time by which Yeats had developed his spare, direct, conversational style.
36 'I sat'	This experience is described in '*Anima Mundi*' (Mythologies pp. 364-5).
59 'the great lord of Chou'	Probably Chou-Kung, twelfth-century member of the Chou dynasty of Chinese emperors.
63 'Babylon or Nineveh'	In an essay called 'The Symbolism of Poetry' in *Essays and Introductions* Yeats wrote: 'A little lyric evokes an emotion, and this emotion gathers others about it and melts into their being in the making of some great epic; and at last, needing an always less delicate body, or symbol, as it grows more powerful, it flows out, with all it has gathered, among the blind instincts of daily life, where it moves a power within powers, as one sees ring within ring in the stem of an old tree. This is maybe what Arthur O'Shaughnessy meant when he made his poets say they had built Nineveh with their sighing . . .' (A

	reference to O'Shaughnessy's poem 'Music and Moonlight'.)
74 'Isaiah's coal'	The reference is to chapter vi of Isaiah.
75 'simplicity of fire'	In *Per Amica Silentia Lunae* (*Mythologies* pp. 356-7) Yeats wrote: 'There are two realities, the terrestrial and the condition of fire. All power is from the terrestrial condition, for there all opposites meet and there only is the extreme of choice possible, full freedom. And there the heterogeneous is, and evil, for evil is the strain one upon another of opposites; but in the condition of fire is all music and all rest.'
78 'Von Hügel'	Yeats was reading the Catholic Baron Friedrich von Hügel's *The Mystical Element of Religion*.
82 'lettered slab'	The carved tombstone.
82 'self-same hands'	Of the spirits of ancient Egyptian embalmers sent to preserve the body of Saint Teresa.
88 'The lion and the honeycomb'	The reference is to Samson's riddle in chapter xiv of Judges.

Commentary:

As before with longer, sectionalized poems, Yeats uses the opening section to state the theme which is to be expressed with different emphases in the following sections. As in 'The Tower' a question is posed which the main body of the poem will attempt to answer. The key image is introduced early on, in this instance, the tree, the first major symbol to be developed in Yeats's verse, although by this point the associations have enriched it. The same tension, that between heart and soul, is again the poet's theme, though here the resolution is different. As the title implies, the poet is vacillating between the soul's preference for preparing itself for eternity and the body's continuing attempts to live a full life in the present in pursuit of artistic rather than religious perfection. While the debate is real, the conclusion is decisive. From henceforth the poet will continue his poetic calling until the end. In a letter to Olivia Shakespear Yeats wrote: 'The swordsman throughout repudiates the saint, but not without vacillation'. The swordsman is Yeats's symbol for the man who leads the traditional aristocratic way of life to the full. The tree imagery goes some way to providing an overall pattern for the theme to be worked out but the great variety in the types of experience and styles of the different sections gives rise to a lack of continuity. Even so the significance of the 'heart' as an image for all that ties a man to earthly life becomes clearly apparent. After its introductory mention, the heart is crucially involved in the development of the significance of the tree in section six, forms one pole for the dialogue of section seven, and is used twice as the end rhyme-word in section eight, anticipating its climactic position at the end of 'The Circus Animals' Desertion'.

CRAZY JANE TALKS WITH THE BISHOP

First Line: 'I met the Bishop on the road'

Collection: from 'Words for Music Perhaps' in *The Winding Stair and Other Poems* (1933)

Original Title: Crazy Jane and the Bishop (LM), Cracked Mary & the Bishop (NR)

First Published: *The London Mercury*, November 1930, *The New Republic*, 12 November 1930

Summary:
Crazy Jane, the 'I' of the poem falls into conversation with the Bishop. He describes her aged form and tells her to look to things spiritual rather than physical now that she is close to death. She replies that the 'fair' of the spirit needs the 'foul' of the body, a lesson that both body and soul have taught her. She says further that a woman can adopt a haughty manner when her mind is set on love but the actuality of passion is a much more physical affair. The soul cannot achieve its unity of being without exposing itself to violent experience.

Glossary:
Title. 'Crazy Jane' She was based on 'Cracked Mary', an old woman described by Yeats as 'the local satirist and a really terrible one'.

Commentary:
The mask of 'Crazy Jane' was adopted by Yeats to express those feelings of vitality and lust with which he felt himself increasingly afflicted. While the Bishop expresses the orthodox dichotomy between body and soul, Crazy Jane has understood the need to reconcile the opposite demands of each as expressed in the two puns of the penultimate line:

> For nothing can be sole (soul) or whole (hole)
> That has not been rent.

The experience of sexual passion is a necessary ingredient for a whole soul. The simplicity of the language is supported by a directness of form which lends the poem an air of the traditional ballad.

TOM AT CRUACHAN

First Line: 'On Cruachan's plain slept he'

Collection: from 'Words for Music Perhaps' in *The Winding Stair and Other Poems* (1933)

Original Title:

First Published: *Words for Music Perhaps*, (1932)

Summary:
Old Tom sleeps on the plain of Cruachan. He sings of the creation of the world by the male principle of immortality and the female of mortality.

Glossary:
6 ' 'Gat' Begat, engendered.

Commentary:
The figure of Old Tom the lunatic, a sort of male counter-part to Crazy Jane, is used by Yeats to reconcile the contrary forces of Eternity and Time acting on man. Not only can the world only be understood as dependent on both forces, he states here that both are responsible for its genesis. The image of the mating horses echoes the earthy, physical directness of the Crazy Jane poems.

A FULL MOON IN MARCH
(1935)

Yeats was never satisfied with the overall design of this collection which he never succeeded in shaping in the way he had achieved with the two previous volumes. In a letter to Dorothy Wellesley he called it 'a fragment of the past I had to get rid of'. After a barren period following the death of Lady Gregory Yeats forced himself to work on 'Parnell's Funeral' (p. 319), an expression of his view that Ireland stood at the forefront of that chaos and anarchy which was the inevitable harbinger of a new cycle of civilization.

The songs from plays and the political meditations which make up two of the groups of poems in the volume have a forced, struggling quality about them, suggesting that the disorder of the political theme is a reflection of the poet's mental state. However, these give way to the group of 'Supernatural Songs', written after Yeats's gland operation, which display his renewed creative energies that carried him through to his death. In these he moves back to a simplicity and directness of style that echoes the prophetic, epigrammatic atmosphere of Blake. But the reader is held up in places by the obscurity of the sources of thought from which Yeats draws.

PARNELL'S FUNERAL

First Line: 'Under the Great Comedian's tomb the crowd,'

Collection: *A Full Moon In March* (1935)

Original Title: A Parnellite at Parnell's Funeral

First Published: *The Dublin Magazine*, June 1932

Summary:
The poet recalls the legend that a star fell out of the heavens at the moment of Parnell's funeral in Glasnevin Cemetery. He asks what this signifies and portends for the trembling crowd that witness

it. The poet uses a dream of his concerning a woman shooting at a star to try to explain the phenomenon. The dream connects with an ancient Cretan ritual of renewal and Parnell is implicitly linked with the saints and sages who unlike the meandering lives of ordinary mortals, are capable of moving in a straight line towards the sun. Yeats compares Parnell's death with those of earlier Irish nationalist heroes, Emmet, Fitzgerald and Tone. They died with the Irish people as spectators but, to their shame, the Irish themselves hounded Parnell into his grave. Yeats asks to be accused of Parnell's murder along with all the Nationalists who turned their backs on him. Consequently all the political rhetoric that has followed in the democratic generations 'is a lie'. The Irish are guilty of making their own chaos. If de Valera had had any of the qualities of Parnell, he would have been able to prevent the civil war. Had Cosgrave been of Parnell's stamp, he would have instituted stronger government that might have prevented an outrage such as the murder of O'Higgins. Perhaps O'Duffy if he had only been cast in an heroic mould — but there were many such political opportunists and only one great man. Parnell experienced the same disillusion in the end as that bitter satirist, Swift, had before him.

Glossary:

1 'the Great Comedian'	David O'Connell (1775-1847), Irish M.P.
7 'the Cretan barb that pierced a star'	The reference and all the following verse concern the details of a dream whose mythological significance for ancient Crete the poet later explored. The falling star at Parnell's funeral is imagined as being the same one shot out of the heavens or down from the Tree of Life in the old fertility ritual. The action brings renewal to the cycle of the seasons.
21 '*Hysterica passio* dragged this quarry down'	Parnell was brought low by the hysteria of an irrational mob. The reference is *King Lear*II.4.57
23 'devoured his heart'	A pagan or barbaric custom.
27 'Bred out of the contagion of the throng'	Created by the infectious malice of the crowd.
33 'de Valera'	Eamonn de Valera, one of the leaders of the Rising and later President of Eire.
36 'Cosgrave'	William T. Cosgrave, first President of Dail Eireann.
39 'O'Higgins'	Kevin O'Higgins, Vice-President of the Executive Council of the Government of the Irish Free State was assassinated in 1927. See 'Death' (p. 264).

40 'O'Duffy'	Eoin O'Duffy, head of police in the Irish Free State. Subsequently, he lead a fascist movement which attracted Yeats briefly.
51 'Jonathan Swift'	Eighteenth century Irish satirist and Dean of St. Patrick's, Dublin.

Commentary:
After the last poems of *The Winding Stair*, Yeats believed his poetic drive had deserted him. With the death of Lady Gregory and the loss of Coole it seemed for a time as if he had lost the focus of his inspiration. 'Parnell's Funeral', based on the text of a lecture given in America, marks his return to the verse form. The passion has not been lost and the apparently casual, conversational style maintained:

> The rest I pass, one sentence I unsay.

There is, however, a sense of forcing the pieces by contrivance into a whole. The second verse is largely self-contained and could be taken out of the poem without much loss of coherence. Even after elaborate exegesis, the connections between the myth and the fact remain tenuous. The Irish material is much stronger and reflects the period of political involvement that Yeats was once more caught up with in Dublin. The proud aristocrat and hater of democracy speaks out in clear, ringing tones.

A PRAYER FOR OLD AGE

First Line: 'God guard me from those thoughts men think'

Collection: *A Full Moon In March* (1935)

Original Title: Old Age

First Published: *The Spectator*, 2 November 1934

Summary:
The poet asks God to preserve him from solely intellectual activity, for poetry that lasts comes not from the mind by itself but is felt in the depths of the body. He has no wish to be thought wise by behaving as old men are supposed to, but is happy to be considered a fool for the sake of continuing to write with passionate reality. So he prays to appear to the world, even though old, foolish and passionate.

Commentary:
This was one of the first poems to be written after Yeats's operation, and reaffirms his determination to ground his poetry in the sensual realities of this earthly life. However, the statement is not simple. Firstly it is written in the form of a prayer, appropriate to the age of the poet and not a passionate song. Secondly, Yeats is anxious to 'seem' (the word is repeated) rather than to *be* 'a foolish, passionate man'. In other words he is adopting a mask from behind which he can enter the last phase of his poetic work; a self-conscious intellectual choice that expresses his distrust of intellectual poetry.

CHURCH AND STATE

First Line: 'Here is fresh matter, poet,'

Collection: *A Full Moon In March* (1935)

Original Title: A Vain Hope

First Published: *The Spectator*, 23 November 1934

Summary:
The first verse offers a vision of a well-ordered, authoritarian political structure of the Church and the State working together to control 'mobs'. It is a situation which an old man can enjoy celebrating in his poetry. The second verse dismisses that vision as a dream and its celebration in poetry as 'cowardly'. For Church and State are themselves made up of the 'mob'.

Commentary:
The poem probably signals the finish of Yeats's brief interest in O'Duffy's fascist movement (see 'Parnell's Funeral'). From this time on Yeats withdrew from any political involvements and kept himself a private man. His loathing of uncontrolled crowds is again evident here: he knows that the times are against him and his views. The last two lines of each verse, drawing on the symbols of the Christian Communion, clearly link the era of Christianity with that of the growth of a levelling, democratic movement in world politics.

LAST POEMS
(1936-1939)

This collection comprises two parts. The poems from 'The Gyres' (p. 337) to 'Are You Content?' (p. 370) were arranged and shaped by Yeats for his volume *New Poems* published in 1938. The remaining poems were organised by the editors after the poet's death, according to a notion of his probable intentions.

The dominant mood of the collection is one of 'gaiety', achieved paradoxically by contemplating both his own decline and the wider destruction in the world around him. A typical situation in these poems is that of the old man climbing to some high place to enable him to look down, dispassionately on the 'blood and mire' below. He is not involved in the outcome of events in this life as he was when younger. There is still anger and sorrow for the misguided ways of his country, but now he is viewing the violence and waste in a larger context of historical inevitability.

Above all there burns a fierce energy, a refusal to die until he is ready encapsulated in the line: 'But I am not content'. The volume contains the familiar blend of personal poems, political observations and metaphysical speculations, all now informed by the passion of an old man raging against the approaching night. Many of the sources are the same as those used at earlier points in his career, but Yeats knows now that no life can be breathed into his structures of thought if they are not kept in touch with 'the foul rag-and-bone shop of the heart'. (The Circus Animals' Desertion p. 391).

The ballad form exerts considerable influence over several of the poems, in the simple, urgent rhythms and the use of a refrain. It is the form appropriate to the hero and the mask of the *Last Poems* is most often that of the aristocrat as the poet sees the world sinking into the democracy which heralds the end of the gyre and the hope for a new civilisation residing in the models furnished by the great men of the past.

THE GYRES

First Line: 'The Gyres! the gyres! Old Rocky Face, look forth;'

Collection: *Last Poems* (1936-39)

Original Title:

First Published: *New Poems*, (1938)

Summary:
The detached impassive face of the spectator who has reconciled all, looks out on a world which has destroyed its ancient beauties in a flood of mindless violence. An epoch was once marked by the flames of burning Troy as another now finishes in the flames of the great houses. Yet the inactive spectator can see through it to a state of 'tragic joy'. He asks if it matters that the world is given over to war and destruction and that a better age has passed. He used to long for the return of ancient civilizations but now he hears the voice from the great darkness urging him to 'rejoice'. No matter how bad the state of the world, when the dark of the moon comes round again the former, now despised, age will be reinstated. The hour of 'the workman, noble and saint' will come round again when the cycles are reversed.

Glossary:

1 'Old Rocky Face'	The mask adopted by Yeats for the *Last Poems*.
4 'ancient lineaments are blotted out'	Ancient architectural features are destroyed. The immediate reference is to Coole Park.
6 'Empedocles'	A Greek philosopher who thought that the elements of life were mingled by love or separated by strife.
9 'numb nightmare ride on top'	The irrational violence at the moon's dark and specifically the Irish civil war.
22 'disinter'	Unearth.
24 'that unfashionable gyre'	The subjective cycle currently out of favour.

Commentary
This poem sets the tone for the *Last Poems* with its clear change from the bitter mood of poems such as 'The Second Coming' and 'Nineteen Hundred and Nineteen'. Yeats's observations on history

have not altered but his response has. He now views events with a cold detachment which enables him to laugh at the condition of all mortal life. The dominant tone is conveyed in the repeated question: 'what matter?' The poet accepts his place and his role in the cycles of history and can now comment condescendingly on the younger man who tried to imagine himself back into another age. The 'Rocky Face' sees all, but cannot be changed by what it sees unless it be the final change of slow crumbling to extinction.

LAPIS LAZULI

First Line: 'I have heard that hysterical women say'

Collection: *Last Poems* (1936-39)

Original Title:

First Published: *The London Mercury*, March 1938

Summary:
Women in the grip of war hysteria have said that 'they are sick of' works of art, music and poetry that express gaiety at odds with the prevailing mood of panic at the impending destruction. The actors involved in the characterization of tragic figures who experience the worst that man can, do not break down in tears while they perform but rather adopt a detachment which makes them able to see the pattern beyond the tragedy. The character is fixed and unchanging no matter how often performed or to how many people or if the theatre should fall down. The destroyers of 'old civilisations' appear in every age. Nothing remains of Callimachus' work in marble even though it was known to be of the finest quality. But something of that artist's soul is handed on to another, so that his work can exist again in another form. This is why the artist achieves a state of gaiety.

The poet now describes the scene carved on a piece of lapis lazuli he has been given. The scene presents two Chinese and their servant. The imagination of the observer turns the changes wrought by time on the piece into part of the scene so that cracks and dents become rivers and snow-covered hills. He then imagines the figures resting on their way up the slope and gazing in serene contemplation on the tragedies below. With the aid of skilfully performed music they are also lifted into that condition of gaiety.

Glossary:

Title: 'Lapis Lazuli'	Stone of bright blue colour used for sculpture and jewellery.
6 'Zeppelin'	Large airship, using hydrogen bags to provide lift, designed by Graf Von Zeppelin, and used by the German army in the First World War, principally for dropping bombs.
7 'King Billy bomb-balls'	Cannon-balls shot by the army of William of Orange at the Battle of the Boyne in 1690.
10 'struts'	Exaggerated walk of the actor on a stage. The word is used in this sense by Shakespeare.
22 'drop-scenes'	Curtain at the end of the final scene.
29 'Callimachus'	Athenian sculptor known for his use of the drapery effect in marble.
40 'longevity'	Long life.

Commentary:

This poem continues the theme of 'tragic joy' announced in 'The Gyres'. It is created out of the contrast between the vision of the artist and the blindness of those consumed in their own daily affairs. At first sight the stanzas seem disconnected but it is left to the reader to supply the links which are not fully revealed until the poem is complete. The opening verse expresses the view of those who deny the validity of any art form ('palette', 'fiddle-bow' and 'poets') which does not relate to the present state of the world; an art that can find gaiety in the midst of destruction whether caused by King Billy or Kaiser Bill.

The subsequent verses consider the contributions to civilization of those three categories of art. The position of the poet as expressed through the medium of drama is perhaps the most complicated because there are both actor and character to be accounted for. To the actor belongs that spirit of detachment which prevents him sharing in the break-down of the character (an attitude in marked contrast to the hysterical women) and to the character belongs the immortality of the changeless form. Even where the whole output of the artist has been destroyed, the genius is reincarnated elsewhere so that all that falls can be rebuilt. The lapis lazuli is at a mid-point between its original concept and destruction. Time has acted on it but the changes merely aid the imagination of the observer who is able to invest the scene with a meaning important for him, even to the extent of imagining the effect of the third art form, music, on the figures. Thus the charges levelled against the arts at the beginning are answered by the end.

SWEET DANCER

First Line: 'The girl goes dancing there'

Collection: *Last Poems* (1936-39)

Original Title:

First Published: *The London Mercury*, April 1938

Summary:
The poet watches a girl dancing on his garden lawn and sees in her dance an escape for her from the oppressions of the world. He asks that if people come to take her away, they may be detained until the girl finishes her dance.

Glossary:

1 'The girl' — Margot Collis whose pen name was Margot Ruddock. Yeats wrote an Introduction to her volume of verse *The Lemon Tree*. He describes the event which inspired the poem in a letter to Olivia Shakespear (*Letters* p. 856).

Commentary
Yeats reintroduces one of his most potent symbols from an earlier phase, the dancer (see 'The Double Vision of Michael Robartes'). Out of the confusion and disorder of her 'bitter', 'black' life the girl has created a perfect work of art, her dance, which has put her in touch for as long as she dances, with the pattern which shapes itself beyond our daily understanding. This ecstasy does not lead to happiness, only an awareness of order which consoles us for the painful disharmony of life. This is why it is important that she be allowed to finish. The use of a refrain points to Yeats's interest in the ballad during this period, when he strove to found his art more overtly in a folk tradition. The effect here is to give the poem a kind of formality and distance which, together with the symbol, moves it beyond the personal. Though founded on an incident in Yeats's life, the poem in no way depends on a knowledge of this incident for its effect.

THE MUNICIPAL GALLERY REVISITED

First Line: 'Around me the images of thirty years:'

Collection: *Last Poems* (1936-39)

Original Title:

First Published: *A Speech and Two Poems*, (1937)

Summary:
The pictures which surround the poet in the Municipal Gallery recall the incidents and personalities of recent Irish history with which Yeats has grown up. Particularly arresting is the portrait of Yeats's friend O'Higgins, revealing the soul of the man. He feels that what he is seeing is not Ireland as he experienced it when growing up but an imaginative recreation of the 'poets'. He confronts a portrait of Maud Gonne in an attitude which he only encountered for a fleeting moment in her life. The emotions raised by these familiar ghosts almost overwhelm a heart which is anyway recovering from serious strain. The images continue to crowd in upon him; Robert Gregory, Hugh Lane, Hazel Lavery and most important of all for him, Lady Gregory. For all that it is a fine picture even if it does not come up to Synge's description of it, how could any artist hope to present the great contrasts in her character? He fears that the future will contain people who fit the mould that society designates for them but not those who rise above the 'patterns'. He recalls his earlier hope that his own children, when he had them, would be exposed to the long traditions of Coole Park for he did not then envisage its destruction. But he will not despair for at least no unworthy successor can bring dishonour to the heritage. He sees himself united with Synge and Lady Gregory in keeping art in contact with its roots in the land itself. They form an unfashionable group in the present age, insisting in a feudal manner on the link between noble and peasant. Finally he comes to a portrait of Synge and concludes from all the memories evoked by these pictures that we should not be content to assess the merits of Yeats from his own work alone, but should ourselves go to the Municipal Gallery and understand him better for knowing something of his friends.

Glossary:

2 'An ambush'	Possibly Sean Keating's 'The Men of the West'.
2 'pilgrims'	'St. Patrick's Purgatory' by Sir John Lavery.

Line	Word/Phrase	Note
3	'Casement upon trial'	Lavery's 'The Court of Criminal Appeal'. Sir Roger Casement was executed for treason in 1916.
4	'Griffith'	Arthur Griffith was one of the leaders in 1916 who was not shot. President of the Executive Council of the Government of the Irish Free State, he had proclaimed loudly against Synge's *The Playboy of the Western World*.
5	'Kevin O'Higgins'	See note to 'Parnell's Funeral'.
23	'Hazel Lavery'	Second wife of Sir John Lavery, she died in 1935.
27	'ebullient'	Bubbling with energy.
39	'No fox can foul'	An image from the poet Edmund Spenser referred to in Yeats's essay 'Edmund Spenser' (1902). Foxes are reputed to be as unhygienic in their personal habits as badgers are meticulous in theirs.
44	'Antaeus-like'	Antaeus, son of Poseidon and Earth, drew strength from his mother when he touched her.

Commentary:
Rather like 'In Memory of Major Robert Gregory', this poem is written in an easy, conversational style to the memory of his friends. Yeats pays them the highest tribute of asking to be judged by our impression of them. While there is no doubt about the power of the past to move him greatly, Yeats indicates that his feelings about the role of art in the cycles of civilization are perhaps not quite as unequivocal as the previous poems have suggested. The poets and painters have created images of Ireland that are 'terrible and gay' but they have also selected attitudes from life that they were able to record and no matter how skilfully done these cannot express the whole soul.

ARE YOU CONTENT?

First Line: 'I call on those that call me son,'

Collection: *Last Poems* (1936-39)

Original Title:

First Published: *The London Mercury* and *The Atlantic Monthly*, April 1938

Summary:
Yeats asks all the ancestors by whom he was created to judge his

work. They have the benefit of transformation into pure spirit and can thus see more clearly than his mortal eyes. Whatever the judgement, he is not 'content'. In the second verse he refers to particular recent members of his family to whom he will be held accountable. He is now of an age when he could reasonably be expected to retire from his profession into a life of passive contemplation and 'good company'. This he will not do because he is still 'not content' with what he has achieved so far.

Glossary:

9	'He that in Sligo'	The Rev. John Yeats (1774-1846).
11	'That red-headed rector'	The Rev. William Butler Yeats, son of the Rev. John.
13	'Sandymount Corbets'	The poet's great-uncle Robert Corbet owned Sandymount Castle.
14	'Old William Pollexfen'	Yeats's grandfather.
15	'That smuggler Middleton'	Yeats's great-grandfather who had a depot in the Channel Islands.
22	'What Robert Browning meant'	The reference comes in Browning's 'Pauline'.

Commentary

With death approaching the poet's mind turns to his ancestors whom he will soon be joining. He invites them to judge his present by their past but whatever their judgement he does not feel in his own judgement that he has satisfied himself as a poet. It is this dissatisfaction which compels him to work on. In this poem we feel something of the energy and restlessness which makes the poems of his later years a unique combination of detachment and stoicism on the one hand and vitality and frustration on the other.

THE STATUES

First Line: 'Pythagoras planned it. Why did the people stare?'

Collection: *Last Poems* (1936-39)

Original Title:

First Published: *The London Mercury*, March 1939

Summary:
The statues of ancient Greece were made according to Pythagoras's system of measurement and number. Young people gripped by the 'passion' of an ideal love can recognize the ideal in the statues and so impose 'character' which might otherwise be supposed to be lacking in them. The most credit in the system must go, not to its inventor, however, but to the sculptors who transformed the system into art. It was their vision of perfect beauty which defeated the Asiatic invasion, not the military power of Greece. Phidias gave women an ideal to which they could aspire through his forms. The Greek system was transported to India and was responsible for the form given to the Buddha, the symbol for the consummation of subjectivity through the exclusion of the external world, that hall of mirrors of infinite illusions.

When Pearse called on Cuchulain during the Rising in the Post Office, Yeats saw the figure which came before his imagination as being based on the Pythagorean system. So the Irish, by keeping alive an ancient tradition, place themselves alongside the Greeks and out of step with the 'modern' objective world. When the cycle changes, they will find their rightful place on the forms of the ancient statues.

Glossary:

2	'His numbers'	The Pythagorean system of numbers and proportions on which the Greek sculpture system was based.
8	'a plummet-measured face'	A face constructed by exact, mathematical method.
14	'The many-headed foam at Salamis'	Where the Persian fleet was defeated by the Athenians in 480 B.C. Yeats pictures the single ideal image routing the many real ones worshipped by the Asiatics.
16	'gave women dreams'	The forms of Phidias have provided women with a single image, a 'collective unconscious' through

		which to channel and combine their sexual and religious passions.
19	'No Hamlet thin'	Yeats thought that Shakespeare's view of Hamlet was of a contemplative, Buddha-like figure rather than the neurotic impersonations of the modern stage.
24	'Grimalkin crawls to Buddha's emptiness'	The witches' deformed cat, the image of the objective soul, is nevertheless drawn to the place of perfect contemplation at the hour of death. The place is empty because it is beyond human capacity to give it form.
25	'When Pearse summoned Cuchulain'	Pearse was well versed in the ancient stories of Ireland. When the Post Office was rebuilt a statue of Cuchulain was erected in it.

Commentary:

'The Statues' is another of those poems in which the density of Yeats's thought is in danger of crushing the verse form. Several of the allusions are essentially private but crucial to the development of the thought. Central to the poem's meaning is Yeats's idea of an Indo-European form of perfect or divine beauty spread through its sculptural image to the East to combat the cultures of diverse forms which the poet terms 'Asiatic'. Yeats has been accused of racism and fascism by some critics but, while it is not necessary to perceive him as being freer from such prejudices than other men, Yeats is dealing in essence with religious not racial ideas. No simple contrast between East and West is possible anyway. While it may have once been true that the ideal of Unity of Being was held by the Greek civilization in the face of Asiatic opposition, in his own day Yeats felt that the Asiatic spirit had conquered almost everywhere. The ideals encapsulated in the ancient statues were to be found only in an occasional, isolated 'rocky face'.

As has been noted in other poems where the thought is complicated, Yeats provides links through repeated, albeit changing images. The most important linking image of the poem is obviously the statue itself. It moves through four phases reflected in the four-verse structure. In the first verse it is the blue-print or abstract contained in the plans of Pythagoras; in the second it becomes the actual statue of ancient Greece based on the model; in transition via the armies of Alexander it becomes the fat, dreaming Buddha of the East; finally it is recreated in the heroic passion of the Irish spirit in revolt, the 'plummet-measured face' returning the poem back to its first word, 'Pythagoras'.

LONG-LEGGED FLY

First Line: 'That civilisation may not sink,'

Collection: *Last Poems* (1936-39)

Original Title:

First Published: *The London Mercury*, March 1939

Summary:
In order that Julius Caesar may secure civilization through military conquest, it is vital to preserve a silence around him so that 'his mind' can move 'upon silence'. If it is necessary to move at all near the presence of Helen of Troy, do not disturb the beauty as she dances spontaneously believing herself unobserved. In order that Michael Angelo can paint the figures that will stir young girls to passion, the door of the Sistine Chapel must be shut to them while he works. Caesar, Helen and Michael Angelo must all be given the isolation and silence in which to summon their superhuman power.

Glossary:

11 'the topless towers'	From Marlowe's *Dr. Faustus*.
17 'a tinker shuffle'	The made-up, probably drunken, dance of an itinerant pot- and kettle-mender.
23 'the Pope's chapel'	The Sistine Chapel whose roof Michael Angelo painted by lying on his back on a scaffold.

Commentary:
Yeats here investigates three aspects of genius which have enabled their possessors to wield great power over the mass of men — political power, the power of supernatural beauty and the power of the artist to move others through his work. In each case, for the mind to exert its power, absolute concentration is essential. The isolation of the hero from the world of men has always been a plank in the poet's philosophy. He clearly draws with vital intensity on his own experience of the creative process.

THE CIRCUS ANIMALS' DESERTION

First Line: 'I sought a theme and sought for it in vain,'

Collection: *Last Poems* (1936-39)

Original Title: The Circus Animal's Desertion

First Published: *The London Mercury* and *The Atlantic Monthly*, January 1939

Summary:
The poet writes of his inability to find a theme now that he is an old man. In the past he had been able to show off his work like a series of acts in the circus, always ready to be produced on demand. Therefore he is reduced to going over his 'old themes'. 'The Wanderings of Oisin' now appears to be the product of a young 'embittered heart', not really connecting with the frustrations of its youthful creator. Again in the creating of the play *The Countess Cathleen*, the autobiographical motive was the strongest. In the Countess, Yeats created an emblem for Maud Gonne whom he saw destroying herself with politics. The 'dream' which resulted from this inspiration soon consumed all his energy and attention. Similarly, when he wrote his play *On Baile's Strand*, although its conception was linked closely to his own emotions, it was the form of the drama itself which delighted him. Then the mechanics of the theatrical performance took him even further from the emblematic sources of the play. The images of these plays achieved their form in art because they were finished and consistent but the poet wants to know how they arose in the first place. He knows they emanate from the meanest, simplest, dirtiest scraps of life and so now that he is without the 'ladder' of his lofty themes, he must start again at the beginning with 'the heart'.

Glossary:

19 'pity-crazed'	Cathleen is driven mad with pity for the starving peasants.
25 'And when the Fool'	The climax of Yeats's play *On Baile's Strand*.
40 'rag-and-bone shop'	Traditionally one of the lowest jobs on the social scale.

Commentary:
This poem is often taken to be an expression of the inability to

write poetry and placed by critics alongside Coleridge's 'Dejection: An Ode'. However, the use and placing of the word 'heart' thoughout the poem until it achieves its final emphatic position, suggests that the poem may in fact have more to do with the origin of the impulse to create than a lack of the impulse itself. The description of his earlier achievements as 'circus animals' implies a sense if not of disgust, at least of predictability and stereo-type in the trained, programmed working of the intellect. In recapitulating the past opus, he indicates how far the works in question grew from their initial, very personal origins. The autobiography became so disguised that all his interest was diverted onto the disguise at the expense of the feeling which prompted it in the first place. Where dramatic production was concerned the process was extended even further so that interest centred not on the written work itself but only on its dramatic realization. As the trend of his later work suggests Yeats was trying to find ways of putting the heart's intuitions as directly as possible into verse. Like the scarecrow of 'A Coat', the rag-and-bone man, though frail and exposed, though deserted by 'the circus animals' of his youthful displays, has put himself back in touch with the source of the energy without which there could have been no circus.

THE MAN AND THE ECHO

First Line: 'In a cleft that's christened Alt'

Collection: *Last Poems* (1936-39)

Original Title:

First Published: *The London Mercury* and *The Atlantic Monthly*, January 1939

Summary:
The poet climbs into a hollow in a mountain side to shout out his secret to the emptiness, a secret that now he is old and ill has become a question which he attempts nightly to answer without success. He asks if a play of his was responsible for getting men shot by the English; or if his criticisms of a girl's poetry drove her mad; or if he could have said something to prevent the destruction of a great house. Only death would seem to release him from evil. But such a death would only be an avoidance of the goal of his

'spiritual intellect' and a useless avoidance for such a death would not be a proper 'release' which cannot take place until he has made his work a meditation on his past life. While a man is still able to go to sleep he thanks God for it, but when he dies he will not be able to sleep until his mind has organized his past life, as the poet is trying to do at the moment. Only then will he be able to judge his own soul and find out 'the night'. He asks the Echo who has commanded him to die whether he will 'rejoice' when 'the great night' comes. The question goes unanswered, for the train of the poet's thought is lost in the death cry of a rabbit being killed somewhere on the mountain by a hawk or an owl.

Glossary:

1	'a cleft that's christened Alt'	A rift in the rocks of Knocknarea, chosen as the Irish equivalent to Delphi.
11	'that play of mine'	Cathleen ni Houlihan (1902).
12	'Certain men the English shot'	Perhaps the leaders of the Easter Rising.
14	'that woman's reeling brain'	Margot Ruddock's.
16	'a house lay wrecked'	Coole Park.
20	'shirk'	Avoid through cowardice or laziness.
22	'bodkin'	Needle. Symbol of suicide from *Hamlet* III, 1.
24	'man's dirty slate'	On which is written the misdeeds of his life.
37	'Rocky Voice'	Functions in a similar way to 'Old Rocky Face' of 'The Gyres' (see p. 200).

Commentary:

For this most personal, confessional poem Yeats returned to the setting of his boyhood, the slopes of Ben Bulben, since it is to the earth of those parts that he is ultimately to return. He is using this time before death, at least death of the body, to go over the main actions of his past life, since this is the occupation he will have to engage in after that death. As in the days when he paced the top of Thoor Ballylee ('The Tower'), so now his musings form themselves into questions — in this case all questions which give rise to a feeling of guilt. His desire for death as an escape changes into a command in the mouth of the Echo. In the middle section Man (Yeats) realises that such a notion of death does not conform to his understanding of what is really involved, for the intellect, not the body, prepares the soul for the rebirth into the spirit world. Again the last phrase is transformed by Echo from a wish to a command, as the Man's question at the start of the last section seems to acknowledge. This imperative 'Rocky Voice' recalls 'Old Rocky Face' from the opening poem of the collection and is similarly associated with the urge to 'rejoice'. For although the meditation is unfinished, interrupted significantly by a cry of death — the 'stricken rabbit' being a more urgent reminder of death than the measured cry of the swan — had the Echo had the opportunity to answer the question, it could only have responded with that single word of command 'rejoice'.

UNDER BEN BULBEN

First Line: 'Swear by what the sages spoke'

Collection: *Last Poems* (1936-39)

Original Title:

First Published: *The Irish Times*, *The Irish Independent* and *The Irish Press* (section VI only), 3 February 1939

Summary:
The poet orders the reader to commit himself to the wisdom of those who have understood the mysteries of the occult and of those who have freed themselves from mortal life to become the faery people or Sidhe who ride the landscape around Ben Bulben. The poet follows the order with a summary of this superhuman wisdom in the rest of the poem. A man experiences many incarnations within the contrary, whirling gyres of 'race' and 'soul' as was understood in the old Ireland of the legends. The worst thing to fear from death whether it is violent or comes from old age is the short farewell from loved ones. For although the process of burial is arduous for the grave-digger, those they bury return to inhabit another form. If a man responds to the call to fight, he experiences a fulfilling of the soul through being in touch with a momentary sensation of supernatural reality which enables him to commit a decisive action. The experience of heroic action which puts the soul in touch with God can be produced also by the artist if he has maintained the tradition which created him. In this way appropriate images can be set before the next generation. The images of perfection began with Egyptian mathematics and moved through Greek sculpture to the painting of the forms of

the Italian Renaissance, forms which can still move a modern spectator to passion since the soul of man is revealed in them. The fifteenth century Italian painters created landscapes which are otherwise only experienced at the moment of waking from a dream. The visions seem to put a man into the presence of the divine. With the decline of the gyre, artists of more recent times have produced less potent visions in the same tradition, until in the modern age the tradition itself has given way to chaos. The poet tells those Irishmen who come after in his profession to have nothing to do with their contemporaries but instead to turn their minds to the subjects of former days, the nobles, peasants and saints of the Middle Ages. By keeping up the stories of the former heroic ages, the Irish nation will be able to hold onto its fighting spirit.

The poet pictures the grave-yard where he wants to be put to rest, thus maintaining the ancestral links. Using local stone he dictates the unconventional epitaph that is to be carved above him.

Glossary:

2	'the Mareotic Lake'	The temple of Osiris was situated on Lake Mareotis in Egypt. The priests were the guardians of their religion's occult wisdom.
3	'the Witch of Atlas'	From Shelley's poem where she symbolized the beauty of wisdom. She should not be thought of as a witch.
11	'Ben Bulben'	The mountain was associated with the Fianna.
12	'the gist'	The substance.
25	'Mitchell'	The quotation is from the *Jail Journal* of John Mitchell who led a rebellion, was transported and escaped to America before returning to be an M.P.
64	'Calvert'	Edward Calvert (1799-1883), English visionary, artist.
64	'Wilson'	Richard Wilson (1714-82), landscape painter.
64	'Claude'	Claude Lorrain (1600-82), artist of picturesque landscapes.
66	'Palmer's phrase'	Samuel Palmer (1805-81), disciple of Blake and visionary artist of ideal landscapes.
77	'randy'	Lusty.

Commentary:

The poem was being corrected by Yeats right up to the time of his death. Into its short four-stressed couplets he packs many of the major themes of his verse. The tone is in the main peremptory with the imperative form of the verb dominant, as at the opening of the poem ('Swear'). Sections I, III, IV and V all reflect this mood of assertion as the old sage issues his last will to his disciples. The tone returns at the end of the quieter section VI in the first and last words of the epitaph ('Cast' and 'pass by'). Like the career stretching out behind it though, it is a poem of contrasts and contrasting tensions announced in the opening section and carried on through the poem in fulfilment of the poet's dictum of man's life comprising the contrary movements of the interpenetrating gyres. He has lived according to the movements towards the 'two eternities'; that of 'soul', represented by the occult wisdom of the sages and that of 'race', represented by the horse-backed women of the Sidhe. Sections III, V and VI deal with the claims of 'race', the longer section IV with those of the soul; taken together they demand his fulfilment as an Irish poet at once in the visionary tradition from Egypt to Blake and in the Celtic tradition of the ballads of Cuchulain's time, celebrating heroic deeds.

NARRATIVE AND DRAMATIC POEMS

Between 1889 and 1923 Yeats published six narrative poems which he elected to place together at the back of *Collected Poems* rather than place them in their chronological positions where they might have unbalanced the collection through their length and differences of style. The three selected for analysis are representative of the developments in both substance and form which are reflected in these six poems.

'The Wanderings of Oisin' shows that desire of the young poet for a world of perfect and timeless form beyond this world and the route he chose to pursue this ideal, that of pre-Christian Irish mythology.

'The Shadowy Waters' treats the same area of material and pursues the eternal in that material. In this case the revisions applied to the different versions of the poem provide a fascinating insight into that process whereby Yeats developed from a Victorian to a modern poet. Those features which mark his style out for special notice in the poems of his maturity begin to appear in the later revisions, charting the passage from self-indulgent emotionalism to passion.

'The Gift of Harun Al-Rashid', though very different in setting and substance, is nevertheless concerned with the pursuit of an ideal, meant to be achieved here in this world. It supplies a unique biographical insight into the poet's view of his relationship with his wife as well as an important introduction to *A Vision*.

These poems also show the increasingly dramatic qualities of Yeats's writing, whether in poems or plays. The conversational style so characteristic of the later work becomes more and more prominent in the long poems where characters are used as poles of a symbolic pattern whose tension supplies the vitality for the verse.

THE WANDERINGS OF OISIN

First Line: 'S. *Patrick*. You who are bent, and bald, and blind,'

Original Title:

First Published: *The Wanderings of Oisin and Other Poems*, 1889

Summary:

Book I

The old Oisin recounts his story to Saint Patrick. He tells of meeting a 'high-born lady' by the sea while he was out hunting with his family. She reveals that she is Niamh, an immortal from the country of the Young, and has come to claim the love of Oisin whose reputation stands high in the poems she has heard about his deeds. Oisin falls instantly in love with her. She invites him to ride with her to the land which is beyond the laws of Time. He accepts despite the grief of his family at his departure and records the passing of his fellow Fenians who are left behind in Time. St. Patrick reproves him for mourning heathens long dead. Oisin is brought to the country of the Young where the men and girls dance and sing continuously. When Oisin sings of 'human joy', however, the company is filled with sorrow and he is stopped. He is taken to hear the song of a Druid who sings of the contrast between human and eternal joys. Oisin then joins in the song to celebrate changeless youth. He tells Patrick that he spent a hundred years on this island, hunting, playing and fishing with Niamh as his wife. Then one day a broken piece of a warrior's spear is washed up by the tide and takes Oisin's thoughts back to the land of humans and separates him from the Immortals who sing of the injustice of the human world where everything is destined to die. He leaves with Niamh.

Book II

After the passing of an indefinite period they come to the Isle of Many Fears where they are led through towers and statues by the sound of a woman's sad song. They find the lady chained to 'two old eagles'. She tells of the demon that holds her prisoner and urges them to flee. But despite Niamh's protest, Oisin refuses flight and unchains the lady without disturbing the eagles. After journeying through a vast hall so high that a sea-gull under the roof cannot hear Oisin's cry, he encounters the demon and, after a long fight in which the demon changes shape many times, Oisin kills it. He celebrates his victory with the women and then sleeps.

But on the fourth day after, the demon rises up again. Oisin does battle with it and slays it again and the event repeats itself every fourth day for a hundred years. Then the branch of a beech tree recalls the human world to Oisin and it is time for him to move on with Niamh. She tells him they are going from 'the Islands of Dancing and of Victories' to 'the Island of Forgetfulness', but she cannot tell him which is the Island of Content.

Book III

This third island is a place without living forms; only a huge, dense forest and the sound of moisture dropping from the trees until they come to a valley of giant bird-men, asleep. Oisin takes Niamh's horn and blows a note to awaken the chief; but though he wakes he does not speak. Oisin and Niamh lie down in the valley and pass a century in oblivion. He dreams of all the great figures and events of early Irish history. After a hundred years a starling falls in the meadow where he sleeps, and draws Oisin back to mortal life. He mounts the horse, carrying the starling, and tells Niamh of his longing for the human world. Niamh tells him to ride through the mortal lands but not to touch the ground, for then he will never return to her. The wind blows the starling from Oisin's grasp. As he comes back to the world he is surprised by the effect of Christianity on the landscape and the people in his three-hundred-year absence. They are now devout, peace-loving farmers, not the warriors of his own day. When he learns that the Fenians and their gods 'a long time are dead', he longs to return to Niamh and turns from the human world. He sees two men struggling with a sack of sand and leans down from his horse to help them. The girth breaks and he falls to the ground, immediately becoming his actual age of three hundred. St. Patrick tells him the old Fenians are in Hell. But Oisin rejects the Christian way of prayer, and says that when he dies he would rather be with his friends even if they are in Hell.

Glossary:

Book I

1	*'S. Patrick'*	Patron saint of Ireland and by tradition the bringer of Christianity to its shores.
4	'dalliance'	Love-making.
5	*'Oisin'*	Son of Finn and Saeve of the Sidhe. His name means 'the little fawn'.
13	'Caoilte'	Caoilte Mac Ronain, Finn's favourite warrior.
13	'Finn'	Chief of the Leinster Fianna and father of Oisin.
13	'Conan'	Conan Mail, a loud-mouthed, boastful warrior.
15	'Bran, Sceolan,	Bran and Sceolan were Finn's cousins; Lomair was

and Lomair' one of their three offspring.

16 'Firbolgs' Prehistoric invaders of Ireland, supposedly buried at Ballisodare.

17 'cairn-heaped' A 'cairn' is a heap of rough stones used as a burial marker. The hill is Knocknarea (see p. 69).

18 'Maeve' Queen of the western Sidhe.

21 'findriny' An alloy like white bronze.

24 'citron' Lemon-coloured.

41 'Oscar's pencilled urn' The urn containing the ashes of Oisin's son Oscar has words carved on it.

43 'Gabhra's' The Fianna was defeated in battle here in 284, effectively ending its era.

47 'Aengus and Edain' Aengus, god of love and beauty who lived in the country of the Young. Edain was a legendary queen who went to live with the Sidhe.

48 'Niamh' The name means both brightness and beauty.

53 'the birds of Aengus' The kisses of Aengus turned into birds and flew round his head.

63 'Danaan' Of the Tuatha de Danaan, the fairy people who lived in Ireland before man.

71 'brazen bell' These bells were introduced into Ireland by St. Patrick.

79 'dun' Fortress.

123 'the foeman's bucklers' The shields of the enemy.

156 'Almhuin's' Finn's hall.

192 'bitterns' Marsh birds.

192 'stoats' Small vermin like weasels.

229 'honey-marts' Places where honey is traded.

239 'this strange human bard' Oisin.

249 'wattles, clay, and skin' Wicker-work, clay and outer skin, an old building method.

263 'sluggard' Lazy person.

266 'peewit' A name derived from the call of the lapwing.

272 'barrow' Ancient grave-mound.

303 'osprey' A fish-hunting eagle.

Book II

1 'man of croziers' St. Patrick. The crozier is the pastoral staff of a bishop.

30 'mace' Heavy, spike-headed weapon.

30 'pole-axe' Battle-axe.

47 'unvesselled' Emptied of ships.

55 'pare' Trim down.

69 'tapers' Candles.

72 'ruddy' Glowing red.

82 'jabber' Chatter volubly.

84	'the Seven Hazel Trees'	In *Poems* (1895) Yeats wrote: 'There was once a well overshadowed by seven sacred hazel trees in the midst of Ireland. A certain lady plucked their fruit, and seven rivers arose out of the land and swept her away. In my poems this is the source of all the waters of this world, which are therefore sevenfold.'
87	'Aedh'	Irish for Hugh. He was the god of death.
93	'jot'	Small amount.
95	'Heber's'	Eber, son of Milesius, ruler of Southern Ireland.
102	'basalt'	Dark green or brown rock.
111	'cumbered'	Weighed down.
118	'phosphorous'	Yellow, slow-burning.
128	'Ogham'	Ancient alphabet of twenty characters used in Ireland.
128	'Manannan'	Manannan Mac Lir, god of the sea.
134	'milk-pale face'	The face of Christ.
144	'jags'	Sharp points of rock.
156	'runnel'	Small stream.
161	'Bacchant'	Like a reveller.
178	'livid chop'	Bluish cheek.
185	'unguents'	Soft substances used as an ointment.
204	'anvil'	Iron block on which a blacksmith works.

Book III

9	'grisly'	Causing terror.
35	'mural'	Like a wall.
36	'curds'	Solid part of the milky substance used in making cheese.
53	'bell-branch'	In *Poems* (1895) Yeats wrote of it as 'a legendary branch whose shaking cast all men into a gentle sleep'.
53	'sennachies'	Story-tellers.
70	'moil'	Drudgery.
73	'sorrels'	Sour-leaved herbs.
80	'the name of the demon'	Culann, the blacksmith who made the sword, spear and shield for Conchobar.
82	'osier'	Willow.
87	'the kings of the Red Branch'	The kings in the Ulster cycle of tales as opposed to the Fenians.
89	'Blanid'	The wife of the king of Munster, in love with Cuchulain.
89	'MacNessa'	Conchobar, son of Nessa, king of Ulster.
90	'Cook Barach'	The man who invited Fergus to the feast.
89	'tall Fergus'	Fergus, Conchobar's stepfather who was not allowed to refuse a feast so had to leave Deirdre and the sons of Usna who were under his protection. They were then murdered by Conchobar's men.
91	'Dark Balor'	A Formorian king, leader of the forces of darkness.

94	'Grania'	She fled with her lover Dermot to escape her aging husband, Finn. Finn slew Dermot at Sligo and took her back to the assembly of Fenians.
116	'Conan's slanderous tongue'	Warrior renowned for his loose tongue.
117	'Meridian isle'	Island in the equatorial zone.
159	'wroth'	Angry.
160	'from Rachlin to Bera of ships'	From the island of Rathlin to Dunboy (i.e. the length and breadth of Ireland).
163	'rath'	Irish fort.
164	'mattock'	Tool similar to a pickaxe.
167	'the straw-death'	Dying in bed.
179	'On Crevroe or broad Knockfefin'	Small townlands in county Sligo.
184	'where Maeve lies'	Knocknarea (see note on Book I, line 17).

Commentary:

The poem was extensively revised by Yeats at various times throughout his career. Shortly before his death he decided to place it at the front of the *Definitive Edition*. This is an appropriate position for the poem, in many respects, maps out the later development of Yeats's poetic themes. That fundamental tension between Eternity and Time — the very action of writing poetry is in part an attempt to immortalize an aspect of transient being — underpins all Yeats's finest work and is the subject of this poem. The secondary tension, providing the framework for the main body, is that between Christianity and the ancient, pre-Christian warrior existence represented by the Fenians. While this matter provides the subject for the end of the poem it is not the thematic centre. It is something of a structural fault that the debate between Oisin and Patrick suddenly assumes prominence after the climax of the poem, the parting of Oisin from Niamh. The last section of the poem, despite the defiant tone of Oisin's concluding words, is therefore somewhat mechanical. The problem lies with the previous scant treatment of Patrick who, until this late point in the poem, has been little more than a device to enable Oisin to recount his story. Consequently the reader's interest is in the story rather than in the confrontation between Oisin and Patrick.

Yeats based the plot of his poem on Bryan O'Looney's adaptation of Michael Comyn's Gaelic poem *The Lay of Oisin and the Land of Youth*. However, the sagas of the Fenians are among the oldest and most important in the mythology of both Ireland and Scotland.

The Fianna was a band of warriors, something like the Knights of the Round Table, who acted as protectors for the whole of Ireland except Ulster. Their chief and hero was Finn Mac Cumhail, soldier, magician and poet, and his son Oisin or Ossian who escaped from the battle of Gabhra in which the Fenians were defeated in 284 to spend three hundred years with Niamh, daughter of Manannan. There is a tradition that these deeds were recounted in a dialogue with Saint Patrick. In the eighteenth and early nineteenth century these stories enjoyed a burst of popularity inspired by the 'discovery' of the *Translated Poems of Ossian, Son of Fingal* (1760-63); in fact the work of their so-called translator, the Scot James Macpherson. These poems inspired personalities as diverse as Goethe and Napoleon. In his choice of material Yeats is staking his claim as foremost bard of the Irish nation by reaching back to a time when the Irish were truly their own masters. In an era of scientific materialism, he strives to reinstate the idealism of myth in the national consciousness.

Critics have exercised themselves at length in expounding the symbolism of the poem, paying particular attention to the location of the three islands and the identity of the main figures, especially the demon of Book II. Notwithstanding Yeats's own acknowledgement of the symbols, the poem serves as a warning or touchstone for the whole of Yeats's poetic work. Attempts to locate symbols in the world outside the poem, while perhaps satisfying some instincts for detection, do not improve the quality of a reading of that poem and may indeed cause the reader to miss the essential qualities through a concern for what is peripheral. It is the function of the symbol in the poem which is important, for, as with the images, they are not isolated ornaments but rather the means by which Yeats structures his longer works. The pattern of images is vital for the coherence of a poem when the same word reappears in different contexts acquiring new associations with each appearance. The images of birds and trees together with those of water and the moon are the means by which this poem is held together. For instance, Niamh is from her first appearance associated with birds, and a bird or bird image is crucial to all the climactic incidents of the poem, culminating in the starling which brings Oisin back to mortality in contrast to the painted Asian birds of the first book. Far more useful for an understanding of Yeats's poetic method than tracking down a single meaning for a symbol, would be to trace the development of a major image throughout the poem. Notice, as an example, how the word 'wandering' is used structurally in the poem. Already associated with Oisin from the title, the link is reinforced in the second line of the poem where his mind is described as 'wandering' and in the second verse where he describes his tale as being 'like the wandering moon'. So when the immortals sing of 'the grey wandering osprey sorrow' we are conditioned to associate Oisin with 'wandering', and by extension with the sadness of mortality. Not only those remembrances of past life which move him on from island to island, but the very fact of his nature being 'wandering' dooms him to the mortality which Niamh assigns to him at the climax of the poem:

> . . . 'O wandering Oisin, the strength of the bell-branch is naught
> For there moves alive in your fingers the fluttering sadness of earth.'

The idea is still being used at the end of the poet's life, in the scream of the slaughtered rabbit which interrupts his immortal speculations at the end of 'The Man and the Echo'. St. Patrick's instructions to Oisin at the end fit just as aptly when applied to Yeats himself at the end of his life and make this poem worthy of a place at the head of his work:

> 'But kneel and wear out the flags and pray for your soul that is lost
> Through the demon love of its youth and its godless and passionate
> age.'

THE SHADOWY WATERS (first version)

First Line: 'I walked among the seven woods of Coole:'

Original Title:

First Published: *Poems 1899-1905*, (1906)

Summary:
The introductory lines dedicated to Lady Gregory describe how the poet walked in the grounds of Coole Park and found there a sense of the eternal life which lies behind the human and from which all human life derives its transitory forms. This is the context in which the story of Forgael and Dectora came to him. 'The Harp of Aengus' briefly tells of Aengus and Edain, the immortal figures who lie behind Forgael and Dectora to establish the primacy of the immortal context into which the story he is about to present should be placed. The 'waters' are 'shadowy' because they are the realm inhabited by the shadows — in other words the immortals.

As the poem opens the sailors on Forgael's ship are plotting to throw him overboard while he is asleep and to head the ship for home because they are tired of sailing deserted seas far from treasure, wine or women. They are, however, afraid of Forgael on account of the magical powers of his harp to bring the shapes of phantoms before their eyes. They say they have seen Aengus and Edain set before them in this way and suspect that they are the powers who have caught Forgael in their net. They approach Aibric to take command of the ship on the death of Forgael. Aibric refuses to raise his arm against his 'master from my childhood up'. Forgael then wakes up asking if the birds which are the dead souls of men who are guiding him have passed overhead. Aibric tells him of the plot and asks why Forgael has led them to this desolate sea. Forgael explains that he is seeking eternal love of a type not known in the human world. Aibric warns him that he is being lured to his death, but Forgael does not mind if death is the gateway to the love he seeks with a woman of the 'Ever-living'. They are interrupted by the sighting of another ship carrying a king and a queen. Under Aibric's direction the sailors fasten the other ship with a rope and board it. Forgael remains on his ship staring at the birds with heads of men that circle over the mast. The sailors bring the queen (who is Dectora) to Forgael. She demands to be released but Forgael tells her even if he released her, her ship would be washed back against his. Dectora still refuses to stay with him and is about to throw herself over the side when the sailors tell her they will kill Forgael if she will take them home. She offers riches to the man who slays Forgael. Thrusting Aibric aside, they are about to kill Forgael when he starts to play his harp and they are put in a trance. The sailors go to the other ship to mourn the dead king and call Aibric to them. Dectora stands before Forgael, about to murder him. But she also drops the sword and starts to mourn as in a dream. Forgael tells her she is weeping for him. Then he stops playing and challenges the birds by asserting that all the 'Ever-living' have used such devices to achieve their passion. He tells Dectora of the deception, but she says she no longer cares about it, for she loves with that changeless love that he was seeking. Forgael points to the birds showing them the path they are to follow. The sailors return speaking of the vast hoard of treasure that the captured ship contains. Aibric tells Forgael they are going to return home, but Forgael says he is going on. Aibric insists it will be to his death and accuses Dectora of taking her revenge on Forgael. She asks Forgael to take her to a place where they can be alone together, but Forgael says he must answer the call of the spirits. Aibric tells the sailors to board the other ship for home. Forgael tells Dectora to go with Aibric but she chooses to stay with Forgael. Aibric goes to the other ship and cuts the rope. Forgael and Dectora are left to sing of their eternal love for each other, freed from the world of men.

Glossary:

Introductory Lines

1	'Coole'	Coole Park, home of Lady Gregory.
2	'Shan-walla'	Old road.
4	'Kyle-dortha'	The dark wood.
4	'Kyle-na-no'	The nut wood.
7	'Pairc-na-lee'	The calf field.
9	'Pairc-na-Carraig'	The rock field.
11	'Pairc-na-tarav'	The bull field.
13	'Inchy wood'	The wood of the islands.
14	'marten-cat'	Type of weasel hunted for its fur.
15	'Biddy Early'	A famous witch in County Clare.
20	'cloven'	Split in half.
22	'Forgael'	An ancient Irish sea-king.
31	'coneys'	Rabbits.

The Harp of Aengus

1	'Edain came out of Midhir's hill'	Yeats wrote in a footnote to 'Baile and Aillinn': 'Midhir was a king of the Sidhe, or people of faery, and Etain his wife, when driven away by a jealous woman, took refuge once upon a time with Aengus in a house of glass, and there I have imagined her weaving harp-strings out of Aengus' hair. I have brought the harp-strings into "The Shadowy Waters" where I interpret the myth in my own way.'
6	'opal'	Milk-white precious stone.
6	'ruby'	Crimson-coloured precious stone.
6	'chrysolite'	Olive-green precious stone.

The Shadowy Waters

Stage Directions:

	'tiller'	The lever which turns the rudder to steer the ship.
	'bulwark'	The side of the ship above the deck.
	'stern'	The back of a ship.
5	'A good round sum'	A large amount of money.
11	'billows'	Large waves.
15	'gunnel'	Upper edge of the ship's side.
27	'westward'	For Yeats the direction of death.
70	'flagons'	Vessels with handle and spout for holding liquor.
99	'man-headed	

	birds'	The souls of the dead.
123	'cozening'	Cheating.
132	'burnished'	Polished.
166	'besotting'	Making stupid.
169	'hurley'	Old Irish game similar to hockey.
214	'chrysoprase'	Yellowish-green precious stone.
215	'chrysoberyl'	Apple-green precious stone.
215	'beryl'	Green precious stone.
216	'juggleries'	Tricks.
221	'ambergris'	Wax-like substance from whales used for making perfume.
221	'sandalwood'	Wood with a strong scent.
222	'opoponax'	Gum-resin used in perfume.
222	'cinnamon'	Yellowish-brown aromatic bark of the cinnamon tree.
224	'on the nail'	Promptly.
236	'bandy'	Bending outwards at the knees.
257	'laggard'	One who lags behind.
381	'to wake'	To hold a party for the soul of a recently dead person.
389	'the keen'	The funeral song sung by the mourners at a wake.
410	'Iollan'	Son of Fergus MacRoy; Finn's uncle by marriage.
451	'hale and hearty'	In excellent health.
492	'sod'	Literally, a small piece of turf.
538	'amethyst'	Purple precious stone.
597	'ancient worm'	The essence of change and decay; the spirit of mortality.
608	'bird among the leaves'	Purified soul in the topmost branches of the Tree of Life.
609	'silver fish'	The object of a quest. (See 'The Song of Wandering Aengus' p. 97).
610	'morning star'	A symbol of love, wisdom and beauty.
611	'white fawn'	A symbol of love.

Commentary:

In programme notes and other references to this work, Yeats made clear the symbolic content of the poem. The sea represents the material world with the boat as the soul of man. The rope which ties the two ships becomes the symbol of their human needs and frailties. This is the tie which holds the lovers back in the mortal world. It is clear therefore that Dectora must make the same sacrifice as Forgael, renouncing the world, before she can achieve the perfect state of the conclusion. The harp is the poetic imagination, the means by which an intimation of the immortal world is carried into the senses of those still in the world of change and decay. Forgael stands for 'mind' and Dectora for 'will', the sea-fight being the struggle of the one for supremacy over the other. The struggle, however, produces not a victor, but a unifying harmony of soul and body without which the spirit world cannot be reached.

The first version of the poem (1900) is the culmination of Yeats's nostalgia for a dream-world, captured in the spirit of the introductory lines. The poet is drawn irresistibly from everyday material existence to an idealized world of the imagination. This version contained no action at all but was poetry without drama. It lacked any effort at characterization and each character spoke in exactly the same manner, hero and sailors alike. The version of 1906 shows a severe reduction in the symbolism, which now fulfils a structural rather than ornamental role. The character of Dectora is now allowed to emerge as that opposite to Forgael which the symbolic interpretation requires, although her original words were almost interchangeable with Forgael's. The events of Yeats's own life between the two dates also leave their mark on the revisions, notably the marriage of Maud Gonne and the poet's daily struggles in running the Abbey Theatre, both of which must have done much to dispel the mists of the earlier idealism. This sense of reality clashing with the ideal is reflected most sharply in the revised treatment of the sailors who are now given their own voice, though still a poetic one, and who now represent much more fully a concern with the material desires of the flesh — alcohol, money and women. They now also experience something of Forgael's visions, thereby authenticating them and suggesting the power of the imagination in acting on unlikely receivers. Aibric also is greatly developed as an individual. He belongs to the world of the sailors but unlike them is capable of abstract thought and moral distinctions. He is the practical man who undertakes all the actions of the poem and makes possible the separation of this world from the next for Forgael. The most dramatic element introduced into his presentation is the jealousy which he now feels at Forgael's successful seduction of Dectora, a feature which increases the tension of the climax and gives a degree of understandable selfishness to his desire to separate the lovers and thwart Forgael's destiny.

The 1906 version also shows the emergence of Yeats's theory of the tragic hero, the almost superhuman figure whom history has placed in an age which opposes the values he lives by. So here Forgael develops in the later versions into an ideal figure opposing the forces of a real world, even as Oisin is a pagan figure thrust back into a Christian world where he does not belong.

The 1907 acting version shows considerable stylistic changes, most notably the use of prose for the sailors' speech, but the material is essentially the same as that of the poem of 1906. Yet despite the radical changes which the treatment underwent, the original story is basically undramatic in a way which prevents the reader from ever experiencing Forgael and Dectora as fully human. Examining the changes undergone by this poem provides a fascinating insight into a vital transitional phase in Yeats's poetic development which also reflects a wider change in the development of English poetry between the nineteenth and twentieth centuries. The product of a pre-Raphaelite imagination has been brought into collision with a style which more nearly encompasses the experience of modern realism.

THE GIFT OF HARUN AL-RASHID

First Line: 'Kusta Ben Luka is my name, I write'

Original Title:

First Published: *English Life and the Illustrated Review*, January 1924

Summary:
The poem is presented in the form of a letter from Kusta Ben Luka to Abd Al-Rabban, Treasurer to the Caliph of Baghdad, Harun Al-Rashid. He asks that the letter be hidden among 'the Treatise of Parmenides', for that is sure to be preserved until the end of time. Otherwise the 'mystery' contained in the letter would be known only to the wise, wandering Bedouin of the desert. In the year when the Caliph had Vizir Jaffer put to death he came to Kusta and engaged him in conversation. The Caliph says that he and his new young bride are troubled by the fact that Kusta is without a wife. Kusta replies that he is getting old, to which the Caliph responds that neither seem old for they, both hunter and poet, lead a life which keeps them young. Kusta replies that indeed their souls, if not their bodies, are young. He explains that he follows a different faith from that of the Caliph and once he has chosen a bride he must remain with her, no matter how she treats him. The Caliph asks him what he would say if he was told that the Caliph had found him a bride who, though young, nonetheless shared his enthusiasm for mystical learning and contemplation of Eternity. Kusta says that if such a one existed then he would have been accorded the ultimate happiness of a

companion in experiencing the unique quality of his own soul. The Caliph acknowledges such a changeless relationship is possible for a philosopher, even though his notion of passion is the opposite one which highlights man's animal nature. The Caliph does indeed provide him with such a bride. Kusta asks himself if she came to him for love of him or of 'that mystery', or a confusion of one with the other. As soon as they were married she buried herself in his books. While he was working at night and she slept, she sat up in bed and began to expound to him the meaning of the mysteries he had been struggling to interpret. When she woke next morning she knew nothing of what had passed. At full moon she arose again in sleep and made marks on the desert sand to explain the signs he had been working on. All this occurred seven years before this date and now she does not pursue that early enthusiasm for his books and loves him only for himself. Now he is afraid that if she realizes what she has given him, she will think he only loves her for those voices which have provided the nourishment of his aging years. If he lost her love or she lost faith in his, he would be deprived of all, for her love and the wisdom from her unconscious voice are as one, the voice being the expression of the love. Wisdom is found where woman's beauty is and he has been given the experience of that ultimate understanding.

Glossary:

1	'Kusta Ben Luka'	One of the masks adopted by Yeats to stand for himself.
2	'fellow-roysterer'	One who joined with him in noisy party-going.
3	'The good Caliph'	Harun Al-Rashid, Caliph of Baghdad (786-809).
6	'night-coloured'	According to Yeats they are mourning in remembrance of those who died fighting to establish the dynasty.
12	'Sappho's song'	Sappho of Lesbos, famed as a poetess.
14	'love-lorn'	Pining with unrequited love.
16	'the Treatise of Parmenides'	Parmenides, born in 513 B.C., was founder of the Eleatic school of Philosophy. Extracts, which are all that remain of his treatise, *The Way of Truth*, give the sphere as the symbol of perfect harmony and ultimate reality. The symbol was adopted by Plato.
20	'the parchment'	Animal skin treated to be used for writing on.
22	'Bedouin'	Adjective used for the nomadic Arab tribes of the desert.
32	'Vizir Jaffer'	(Wazir Giafar) in *The Thousand and One Nights*. 'Vizir' is Arabic for Minister of State.

45	'colloquy'	Conversation.
48	'honeycomb'	The place of greatest sweetness.
53	'jasmine'	Shrub with a white or yellow flower, heralding the spring.
57	'falcon'	Small hawk trained for sport.
58	'ringed mail'	Chain-mail worn for protection in battle.
62	'mimicry'	Imitation.
64	'this pure jet'	The jet of water from the fountain where they sit.
78	'the Byzantine faith'	Byzantium was the centre for eastern Christianity.
101	'stag'	Male deer.
101	'doe'	Female deer.
124	'faggots'	Bundles of dry sticks used for fuel.
135	'Djinn'	A spirit capable of appearing in human form.
142	'implacable'	Not capable of being satisfied.
143	'the vegetative dream'	Daily life without the experience of higher truths.
184	'gyres and cubes and midnight things'	Yeats's footnote in *The Dial* read: 'This refers to the geometrical forms which Robartes describes the Judwali Arabs as making upon the sand for the instruction of their young people, and which, according to tradition, were drawn as described in sleep by the wife of Kusta-ben-Luka'.
193	'the armed man'	From earlier drafts of the poem this would seem to be the figure of Wisdom, the metaphor possibly originating in *The Song of Solomon*.

Commentary:
In both substance and style this poem stands on its own. The primary source for it is *The Thousand and One Nights*, many of which have the Caliph Harun Al-Rashid as their protagonist, although an immediate inspiration may also have been James Elroy Flecker's play *Hassan* published in 1922, the year before this poem was written. In this play Hassan's bride is called Yasmin, the name perhaps giving rise to Yeats's use of 'jasmine' as an image for the approach of love. The major problem for most commentators on the poem has been the justification of the eastern setting, which seems to many an elaborate and unnecessary way into a poem about the effect of Yeats's marriage on his work. The more direct substitution of Solomon and Sheba for Yeats and Mrs. Yeats might perhaps have fitted as well, though it is interesting that Yeats opts for the same part of the world when dealing with his relationship in this poem. Clearly he associated the Arab world very strongly with images of sensual passion leading to the insight of total wisdom. As an introduction to *A Vision* the poem affords a fascinating insight into the way in which Yeats's feelings

for his wife were interwoven with the unexpected development in his work provided by her gift of automatic writing. Even allowing for the poet's need to adopt a disguise, however obvious, it is not clear why the poem could not have started at the point where the conversation begins. The introductory framework is never referred to at the end of the poem, so it is difficult to make much of the references to the 'wild Bedouin' or 'Vizir Jaffer' in terms of relevance to the central body of the poem.

A note written by Yeats in *The Cat and the Moon and Certain Poems* (1924) indicates how closely he thought of the material in the terms of his own life:

> According to one tradition of the desert, she had, to the great surprise of her friends, fallen in love with the elderly philosopher, but according to another Harun bought her from a passing merchant. Kusta, a Christian like the Caliph's own physician, had planned, one version of the story says, to end his days in a monastery at Nisbis, while another story has it that he was deep in a violent love affair that he had arranged for himself. The only thing on which there is general agreement is that he was warned by a dream to accept the gift of the Caliph, and that his wife a few days after the marriage began to talk in her sleep, and that she told him all those things which he had searched for vainly all his life in the great library of the Caliph and in the conversation of wise men.

Whatever amusement this device affords Yeats in revealing his autobiography in this way, the difficulty for the reader is that whereas in *The Wanderings of Oisin* and *The Shadowy Waters* this element serves to enrich a story with universal application, this tale can only apply quite narrowly to the circumstances of the poet. In other words this is allegory, where the others are symbol.

Nevertheless the blank verse form does allow for a fluid build-up to the climax of the poem, as the reader is made to share some of the excitement that Yeats must have felt during these revelations. Unlike the studied pose of the opening, the poet's anxiety and tumult of emotion seems genuine and is well reflected in the running-over of lines and the half lines that suggest thoughts crowding in on each other until they all dissolve in the image of the naked bird, the creature Yeats usually summons when his emotions are most profoundly stirred:

> Were she to lose her love, because she had lost
> Her confidence in mind, or even lose
> Its first simplicity, love, voice and all,
> All my fine feathers would be plucked away
> And I left shivering.

That compromise between eternity and the mortal world that eluded the poet in *The Wanderings of Oisin* and *The Shadowy Waters* is at last achieved through the medium of his wife's voices, that allow him a vision of the other world without Yeats having to renounce his place in this one.

SUGGESTIONS FOR FURTHER READING

It is hoped that the inquisitive and interested student for whom these notes have been prepared will first and foremost read the poetry itself. Then, with the help and guidance of the notes in the foregoing pages, it is to be hoped that he will be better able to understand the demands that Yeats makes upon his readers.

Several major critical works are available in most libraries and any list to cover them all would be beyond the scope of this introductory work. However, the following titles, listed under appropriate headings, should direct the student to the general and specific areas of Yeats scholarship.

W. B. Yeats — Standard Editions

The Variorum Edition of the Poems of W. B. Yeats, ed. P. Allt and R. K. Alspach (New York, Macmillan, 1957)

The Variorum Edition of the Plays of W. B. Yeats, ed. R. K. Alspach (London; New York, Macmillan, 1966)

Collected Poems (London, Macmillan, 1950; New York, Macmillan, 1951)

The Poems: A New Edition, ed. R. J. Finneran (New York, Macmillan, 1983; London, Macmillan, 1984)

Collected Plays (London, Macmillan, 1952; New York, Macmillan, 1953)

Autobiographies (London, Macmillan, 1955)

The Autobiography (New York, 1953)

Mythologies (London, Macmillan, 1962)

Essays and Introductions (London; New York, Macmillan, 1961)

Explorations, selected by Mrs W. B. Yeats (London, Macmillan, 1962; New York, Macmillan, 1963)

Memoirs, ed. D. Donoghue (London, Macmillan, 1972)

A Vision (London, Macmillan, 1937)

The Speckled Bird, ed. W. H. O'Donnell, 2 vols (Dublin, Cuala Press, 1973, 1974)

The Senate Speeches of W. B. Yeats, ed. D. R. Pearse (London, Faber & Faber, 1960)

Uncollected Prose I. First Reviews & Articles 1886-1895, ed. J. P. Frayne (London, Macmillan; New York, Columbia UP, 1970)

Uncollected Prose II. Reviews, Articles & Other Miscellaneous Prose 1897-1939, eds. J. P. Frayne & C. Johnson (London, Macmillan, 1975; New York, Columbia UP, 1976)

Selected Poems, ed. A. N. Jeffares (London, Papermac, 1962)

Poems of W. B. Yeats: A New Selection, Selected, with Introduction and Notes by A. N. Jeffares (London, Macmillan, 1984)

Selected Plays, ed. A. N. Jeffares (London, Papermac, 1964)

Selected Prose, ed. A. N. Jeffares (London, Papermac, 1964)

Selected Criticism, ed. A. N. Jeffares (London, Papermac, 1964)

The Letters of W. B. Yeats, ed. A. Wade (London, Hart-Davis, 1954)

The Collected Letters of W. B. Yeats, I, *1865-1895*, ed. J. Kelly, assis. E. Domville (Oxford, OUP, 1986)

Letters on Poetry from W. B. Yeats to Dorothy Wellesley, intro. K. Raine (Oxford, OUP, 1964)

Ah Sweet Dancer: W. B. Yeats — Margot Ruddock, ed. R. McHugh (London, Macmillan, 1970)

(Editor) *Fairy and Folk Tales of Ireland*, containing *Fairy and Folk Tales of the Irish Peasantry* (1888) and *Irish Fairy Tales* (1892), foreword by K. Raine (Gerrards Cross, Smythe; New York, Macmillan, 1973)

(Editor) *Representative Irish Tales*, foreword by M. H. Thuente (Gerrards Cross, Smythe, 1979)

Letters to the New Island, ed. H. Reynolds (Cambridge, Mass., Harvard UP, 1934)

Bibliography

A Bibliography of the Writings of W. B. Yeats, Allan Wade, 3rd ed. rev. Alspach (London, Hart-Davis, 1968)

W. B. Yeats: A Classified Bibliography of Criticism, K.P. S. Jochum (London, Dawson, 1978)

Commentaries

A Commentary on the Collected Poems of W. B. Yeats, A. N. Jeffares (London, Macmillan, 1968)

A New Commentary on The Poems of W. B. Yeats, A. N. Jeffares (London, Macmillan, 1984). The 1968 edition revised, enlarged, and keyed to *Collected Poems* (1950) and *The Poems: A New Edition* (1984).

A Commentary on the Collected Plays of W. B. Yeats, A. N. Jeffares and A. S. Knowland (London, Macmillan, 1975)

A Reader's Guide to W. B. Yeats, J. Unterecker (London, Thames & Hudson, 1959)

Criticism and Biography

Biersby, B., *The Interpretation of the Cuchulain Legend in the Works of W. B. Yeats* (Uppsala, 1950)

Bushrui, S. B., *Yeats's Verse Plays: The Revisions 1900-1910* (Oxford, Clarendon Press, 1965)

Bushrui, S. B., and Munro, J. M. (eds.), *Images and Memories* (Beirut, Dar El-Mashreq, 1970)

Ellmann, R., *The Identity of Yeats* (London, Macmillan, 1954)

Ellmann, R., *Yeats: The Man and the Masks* (London, Faber, 1961)

Harper, G. M., *Yeats's Golden Dawn* (London, Macmillan, 1974)

Henn, T. R., *The Lonely Tower: Studies in the Poetry of W. B. Yeats* (London, Methuen, 1965)

Hone, J., *W. B. Yeats 1865-1939* (London, Macmillan, 1942)

Jeffares, A. N., *W. B. Yeats: Man and Poet* (London, Routledge, 1949)

Jeffares, A. N., *W. B. Yeats* (Profiles in Literature Series) (London, Routledge, 1972)

Jeffares, A. N., *W. B. Yeats, A New Biography* (London, Hutchinson, 1988)

Kermode, F., *The Romantic Image* (London, Routledge, 1951)

Koch, V., *W. B. Yeats: The Tragic Phase* (London, Routledge, 1951)

Malins, E., *A Preface to Yeats* (London, Longman, 1974)

Melchiori, G., *The Whole Mystery of Art: Pattern in the Work of W. B. Yeats* (London, Routledge, 1960)

Miller, L., *The Noble Drama of W. B. Yeats* (Dublin, Dolmen; Atlantic Highlands, Humanities, 1977)

Moore, V., *The Unicorn: William Butler Yeats's Search for Reality* (New York, Macmillan, 1954)

Parkinson, T., *W. B. Yeats: Self-Critic* (Univ. of California Pr., 1971)

Parkinson, T., *W. B. Yeats: The Later Poetry* (Univ. of California Pr., 1971)

Raine, K., *Yeats, The Tarot and the Golden Dawn* (Dublin, Dolmen, 1972)

Stallworthy, J., *Between the Lines: Yeats's Poetry in the Making* (Oxford, OUP, 1963)

Stauffer, D. A., *The Golden Nightingale: Essays on Some Principles of Poetry in the Lyrics of W. B. Yeats* (New York, Macmillan, 1949)

Stock, A. G., *W. B. Yeats: His Poetry and Thought* (Cambridge University Press, 1964)

Thuente, M. H., *W. B. Yeats and Folklore*, (Dublin, Gill & Macmillan; Totowa NJ, Barnes & Noble, 1980)

Torchiana, D., *W. B. Yeats and Georgian Ireland* (Oxford, OUP, 1966)

Ure, P., *Towards a Mythology: Studies in the Poetry of W. B. Yeats* (London, Hodder & Stoughton, 1946)
Wilson, F. A. C., *W. B. Yeats and Tradition* (London, Gollancz, 1958)
Wilson, F. A. C., *Yeats's Iconography* (London, Gollancz, 1960)
Zwerdling, A., *Yeats and the Heroic Ideal* (London, Owen, 1965)

TITLE INDEX

INDEX OF FIRST LINES

GENERAL INDEX